RED STAG
HUNTERS
CLUB

FURTHER
OFF THE
BEATEN
TRACK

SOUTH
SEAS
SPEARO

FURTHER
OFF THE
BEATEN TRACK

Epic Hunting Adventures on Land and Sea
The Red Stag Timber Hunters Club & South Seas Spearo

DAVE SHAW

BATEMAN
BOOKS

Dedicated to Ava, Sadie, Eloise, Georgie, Marty, Cian, Sam, Caitlin, Grace, Ashton, Lilly, Olivia and the ones to come.

Don't walk in our footprints, carve your own path instead.

Published in 2024 by David Bateman Ltd
2/5 Workspace Drive, Hobsonville, Auckland 0618, New Zealand
www.batemanbooks.co.nz

ISBN 978-1-77689-098-9

Cover images: Dave Shaw
Internal photography: Dave Shaw
Book design: Nick Turzynski, redinc book design, www.redinc.co.nz
Printed in China by Toppan Leefung Printing Ltd

MIX
Paper | Supporting responsible forestry
FSC
www.fsc.org   FSC® C104723

Enjoying the warmth of Summer
hunting in the high country.

CONTENTS

INTRODUCTION: THE DARK SIDE

For many thousands of Kiwis, hunting provides an important release. It's a chance to vent the many pressures that build up through our modern existence and to strip things down to the fundamentals: 'back to basics' as they say. In a world that's become increasingly aware of the fragile nature of mental health, hunting's a chance for many to rebalance and centre themselves. It provides an extra degree of motivation to work hard in their chosen profession, to work hard at the gym, to work hard at being a better mate.

For me, someone who discovered hunting late in life, it's become my surrogate sport. I hung up my rugby boots a long time ago, but through hunting I still get to experience the deep joy of success, as well as the crushing lows of defeat. However, rather than putting my ageing body through an 80-minute thrashing once a week, it's now thrashed at a lesser intensity for days on end.

Like all sports, hunting also requires teamwork and provides a level of camaraderie that we all crave. It often challenges you to overcome your fears and to push yourself outside your comfort zone, but it also grants you the chance to lose yourself in the solitude of the great outdoors. As J R R Tolkien once said, 'Not all those who wander are lost', and I've found over the years that my time spent in the hills has helped provide a sense of scale to life's little problems.

It's become a crucial part of my life but, after nearly a hundred trips over the past decade, earlier this year I noticed the edges were starting to fray.

At some point during the previous twelve months, the pressure to succeed and continually improve on what we'd done before had started to creep in, and the stress it brought had made me short-tempered. I was stretched thin, in the words of Bilbo Baggins — 'like butter scraped over too much bread'.

In the fledgling days of *The Red Stag Timber Hunters Club*, I was responsible for creating just ten half-hour episodes a year, equating to

Lugging a heavy load of meat off the hill, Dre's pack was well over 50 kg.

around five hours worth of content. Now, within the same period, I'd committed to producing eighteen hours of content.

I can sum up my mood by paraphrasing a couple of famous Pink Floyd lyrics: When at last the filming was done, I couldn't sit down; it was time to film another one.

Perhaps I'd bitten off a bit too much? Had I become uncomfortably numb?

I wouldn't say I was in danger of being burnt out, but I just wasn't as able to roll with the punches like I could during the earlier days of production. Maybe it was just a natural part of getting older, but I was turning into a bit of a grumpy bastard, and I knew it.

Filming for me has always been hard on the brain, as it's a mentally taxing process trying to ensure that you capture all the pieces of the puzzle required to pull together an episode, but I figured that this period of prickliness was nothing that a decent break couldn't remedy.

And the end was now in sight; we had a hell of a series under our belt, and enough time before broadcast to ensure it was looking and sounding its best.

Mental fatigue is one thing but, physically, I was in a much worse state. For too long, I'd been lugging my heavy pack around the forests and mountains of New Zealand in pursuit of adventure, disregarding the little niggles for long enough that they had now begun to develop into genuine liabilities. However, like a sportsman well past his prime, I arrogantly believed I could get by with a cortisone injection or two. But in the space of one shoulder press too many at the gym, reality caught up with me.

The MRI was conclusive — a bone fragment floating free in the shoulder joint, a full-thickness tear and retraction of the infraspinatus muscle, a ruptured biceps tendon, inflammation of the labrum, a Hill-Sachs lesion. Surgery was my only option.

So, like the dozens of animals featured on the show over the past decade, it was now my time to go under the knife.

That was eight weeks back. To be honest, an enforced sabbatical was just what the doctor ordered, physically and mentally. It has allowed me to catch up on a few pressing tasks that I've been too busy to get stuck into such as writing this book!

For the past couple of months, I've been riding the couch, bingeing multiple TV series that have been on my watchlist for too long. But even though I'm often watching multiple episodes back-to-back, I still appreciate the little 'refresh' given before each new episode kicks off, just to ensure I haven't missed any major plot points.

So, even if you've already read my first book, here's a handy little refresher for you about how someone with practically zero background in hunting came to be in the strange position of writing their second book on the subject.

I spent my pre-teen years mucking around with my mate's family handycam, filming ridiculously bad (and often offensive) short films that we would proudly show off to friends and family. To paraphrase Pink Floyd again, I was kicking around on a piece of ground in my hometown, waiting for someone or something to show me the way.

Once at Otago uni, things got more serious (but just as offensive), as I continued making outrageous videos which would air on the student channel, COW TV.

After completing my zoology degree, I decided that I'd try to turn my silly little hobby into a career, so I left dirty Dunners for the bright lights of Auckland City, landing minor production roles on some horrific reality TV shows, before getting the chance to prove my worth on a few more rewarding projects.

After a few years, though, the bright lights of Auckland had dimmed for me, so my girlfriend and I embarked on that famous Kiwi rite of passage — an OE to Europe.

I found that in jolly old London town, my New Zealand television credits counted for very little, but I was lucky enough to blag my way into a couple of great roles, first for Discovery and then for The History Channel. Both involved a great deal of filming throughout the United States and Europe.

I even got to film an interview in the inner sanctum of the Pentagon of all places!

However, after a couple of years gallivanting around the world, Joe Strummer's 'London Calling' had been drowned out by Trinity Root's 'Home, Land and Sea', so my now wife and I returned to Aotearoa. My overseas experience enabled me to get a foot in the door with *The ITM Fishing Show*, where I worked for the next six years, developing the skills that allowed me to branch out and start a show of my own — *The Red Stag Timber Hunters Club*, having had a brief taste of what the great outdoors has to offer during a hunting-based *ITM Fishing Show* episode.

We had a merry ride producing the first few *Red Stag Timber Hunters Club* seasons on a shoestring budget, making things up as we went along, but eventually we found our legs and developed a voice of our own. I'd wholeheartedly adopted the 'fake it till you make it' approach — having pretty much zero experience in hunting when we set about pitching the idea of a series to broadcasters and sponsors, but thanks to having surrounded myself with a dedicated group of hunters who were keen to showcase their passion to the masses, the show grew in popularity year on year. It became so popular in fact that after five seasons, we were approached by a publisher about the possibility of writing a book based around our numerous hunting adventures.

Which brings us to where we left off. At the end of the previous book, I asked myself 'Where to from here?' At that point, we'd just begun production on the sister series to *The Red Stag Timber Hunters Club*, a spearfishing-based show called *South Seas Spearo*, which had yet to hit New Zealand screens. It's a rainy Tuesday right now in the Bay of Islands, and as I type this text, the show's narrator (and regular source of comic relief) Ant Niterl is recording the voiceover for the final episode of Season 3, due to air this coming Sunday night on TVNZ Duke — nothing like leaving it to the last minute!

South Seas Spearo evolved in quite a similar manner to *The Red Stag Timber Hunters Club*. We were perhaps guilty of taking ourselves a little too seriously in the early days of the show, but having now produced 22 episodes, the guys have really warmed to the task of being in front of camera, allowing their true personalities to shine through.

Over the course of this book, I'll bounce back and forth between both shows, but to kick things off, I thought I'd recount a tale from a mission that focuses on the 'unmissable' link between *South Seas Spearo* and *The Red Stag Timber Hunters Club*, the incomparable, irrepressible and inimitable Tim Barnett.

Tim glassing for game in stunning West Coast tahr country.

PART ONE

UP . . .

1 LET OFF THE LEASH

As the old proverb goes, hindsight is 20/20 and, in the decades to come, I think you can confidently state that 2020 will be remembered vividly by all those who lived through it.

As a producer of outdoors content, the lockdowns certainly created a few headaches, but they also presented us with unique opportunities. The fact that the entirety of the New Zealand backcountry hadn't been hunted for months meant that once restrictions were finally lifted, there was every opportunity for success in areas that normally receive a fair amount of hunting pressure. So, when the country finally moved down to Alert Level 2 and hunters were allowed off the leash to hunt public land, Tim and I wasted little time in making the most of our newfound freedom, beelining straight for the wild West Coast, with plans for four days chasing big bull tahr in some rugged alpine country.

We would be joined by Tim's mate Nick Barnett, whose aim was to try to nail his first-ever tahr. While not related, Nick and Tim share the same surname and the same sense of humour — both were terrific value on the hill — and not shy about doing the hard yards, which would be a requirement for this mission thanks to a slight miscalculation.

There're a couple of schools of thought when it comes to hunting tahr. The first is to base yourself relatively low, in order to open up angles into the surrounding hills, and to be able to move about more freely on the less steep terrain. It also reduces the risk of being caught out by extreme conditions in the tops, but the downside is that it requires you to climb a long way to get into your hunting zone, and to descend at the end of each day, which in the winter is often done under head torch.

The second approach is to camp up high, along the snowline, right in among the animals. This approach risks scenting the area and spooking animals, and if you get the landing site or the weather forecast wrong you could find yourself stuck hunting a very limited area, and often in testing conditions. Get it right, though, and you save yourself hours each day in climbing time.

What it really boils down to is the height at which the animals are living. In our case, given that no hunting had taken place over the previous few months, we had no reliable intel as to what altitude the tahr were living at. So, after poring over the maps at the helicopter hangar in Franz Josef, we

Even a bloke the size of Timmy looks small in this massive alpine terrain.

took an educated guess based on chopper pilots' experience, picking a flat site at around 1000 metres to drop our comfy M.I.A base camp.

It would turn out to be the wrong call. Once we'd made camp and cast an eye around the surrounding hillside, we realised the animals were all living far higher than we forecast, so it looked like Nick would need to spill some gravy in order to earn his first bull.

The next morning we set out early, sidling our way upstream towards the head of the Whymper Glacier. We'd have to climb 800 vertical metres to get into our target zone, but we also needed to play the wind right, which meant covering a massive amount of ground.

Throughout the morning, we were kept on our toes by a series of rockfalls and avalanches on the far face, including one huge vehicle-sized boulder that broke off and tumbled down a steep gut, leaving a dusty trail of destruction in its wake. These massive mountain-shaping events are certainly humbling to witness and, for me, they put into scale the relatively minimal effect that the tahr themselves have on this dynamic environment. The snow and rock falls also added a little more jeopardy to the climb, keeping us alert as we made our way up the steep jumble of huge boulders.

It was a bluebird day, with hardly a breath of wind, and with the sun now high in the sky, the heat was starting to play a role. So, after a few hours' climbing, I began to break off large slabs of ice to stuff down the front of my shirt in order to remain cool, certainly a refreshing way to keep the body temperature down on a long climb.

As I was going about installing another makeshift air-conditioning unit, Tim spied a tahr on a steep face above us. Unfortunately, the tahr had also spied him and zipped off out of sight behind a steep bluff. The sighting put renewed spring in our step, though, and after another hour or so, we'd worked our way up into the area on which we wished to focus our efforts. By now, it was nearing 2 p.m., so we had only a few hours of huntable light left in the day, but the hard work was now done, and we were determined to make the big effort worthwhile.

Thankfully, it didn't take long for another opportunity to present itself. We'd spied a decent bull on a precipice far above us, but just as we were analysing the country ahead in order to work out a viable approach, another bull materialised on a small ridgeline very close by, seemingly curious about the noises he was hearing from the three bipedal intruders below.

He was hobbling badly but seemed intent on cutting the distance to us, hopping his way down the steep face in our direction. There was no time to frame up a stable shot on the tripod, so I was forced to shoot off the shoulder with the long lens and just hope not to flinch too badly at the sound of the shot. Nick dropped down into a prone position, squeezed off a round, plugging him right in the boiler room.

After the relatively slow day spent slogging our way up the boulder-strewn mountain, the intensity of the action took us all some time to

The lads get to work behind the glass, scouring the distant hills for game.

The smile of a man who's bringing home the bacon.

recover from — it was like a marlin strike while out game fishing, where hours of boredom are broken by 30 seconds of chaos.

The tahr was by no means a showstopper, but he was a representative animal that Nick was proud to claim as his first. His reaction was one of genuine stoke, although his phrasing could probably do with a little work, delivering the memorable line: 'Always good to pull one off with you Timmy . . . hunting's all right, too!'

However, the evening's fun and games were far from over. En route to collect Nick's prize, Tim decided to first poke his nose up and over to check there wasn't a bigger bull lurking around just out of sight, and sure enough, as soon as Tim cast an eye into the new terrain, he quickly picked up a big, old puffball working its way down the hillside in our direction.

Mature bull tahr are a sight to behold, especially when there's a bit of wind around to fluff them up, and this guy looked like he'd just stepped out of a salon, with a flowing mane and luscious blond kidney stripes. But unfortunately for Tim, his horns didn't quite match the majesty of his cape, looking to be only around the 11-inch mark.

Tim quickly determined he wasn't the bull for him, and with Nick's first tahr ticked off, we were now only looking to take nannies for meat, or genuine monsters for the wall. So for the moment, we were content to hold our ground and admire the bull from afar, but pretty soon far became near, as like the hobbling tahr that had met his end moments earlier, this guy was once again making a beeline directly for us.

Maybe these animals had forgotten what hunters looked like after having the best part of four months to themselves in the hills, or maybe it was just an innate curiosity, but the bull kept on coming: 100 metres, 80 metres, 60 metres.

We remained as still as possible, the only movement being the continual focus shifting required to keep him sharp in frame on my long lens. He was so close now that I was able to pick up individual eyelashes and his rapidly flaring nostrils.

But those nostrils were in for a rude awakening.

Every hunter knows that managing wind is critical for success, but the gust that eventually alerted the tahr to our presence wasn't generated by the usual means. Instead, it came from a high-pressure system situated somewhere in Tim's lower intestine.

Now, if you've spent any amount of time in the hills existing purely on dehydrated meals, you'll know well the effect it can have on your bowels. With the tahr staring directly at us, Tim decided now would be the appropriate time to show his class, dropping his guts and unleashing a swampy barrage that sounded a lot like a duck being choked to death — THPPT, PHTPHPHHPH, BRRRRRRP!

I'm not sure if it was the auditory or olfactory cues that caused the bull to bolt, but either way, he certainly wasn't hanging around for an encore

Nick's first-ever bull tahr, one that he really had to earn.

performance. Meanwhile, we were all trying our best to hold it together, given the absurdity of the situation.

After a few minutes, and with the dust now settled, we made our way back towards Nick's bull and set about the task of breaking it down before beginning the long trek back to our campsite, which it's fair to say was quite an arduous task in the dark. We made it down unscathed but had a couple of close shaves on the loose scree. I was certainly glad to have the Garmin navigation gear on hand, as traversing this broken country after dark without it would have been incredibly risky.

We continued to hunt hard over the next two days, bagging a meat animal for Tim, before relocating downstream to the iconic Whymper Hut for our final night. Considering the lack of hill fitness leading into the hunt due to the lockdown, we did bloody well covering the amount of country we did, but there was a feeling of mild disappointment as nanny numbers weren't quite as high as we'd hoped.

On the morning before the flight into the mountains, Tim had delivered a great line to camera about not setting our sights solely on bagging trophies: 'We're not overly concerned this trip, we're just going to thump some stuff!' Two tahr from four days of hunting wasn't quite the return he had in mind, but, hey, at least we'd had a chance to finally blow off some steam!

Speaking of 'blowing off', once we were all off the hill and back at our accommodation on the coast, I had a rather interesting task to perform. Given that I was running a shotgun microphone, two radio mics on Tim and Nick, and a GoPro clamped to the tripod, I had captured four channels of audio of Tim's extreme flatulence, so I needed to evaluate each option to determine which produced the cleanest sound.

The Sennheiser shotgun mic I use is very directional, meaning it only picks up sound emanating from where it's pointed, which in this instance, wasn't towards Tim's arse. The audio fidelity on the GoPro wasn't great, but its position close to the sound source meant it captured an extra bassy element that the other three mics didn't pick up, so in the end, I mixed the GoPro audio with the feed from Nic's radio mic to create a pretty punchy blend.

If you're keen to listen to the result, here's a QR code that'll direct you to the scene in question, but be warned — once heard, it cannot be unheard . . .

Tim's two cents

Lockdown for a mad-keen outdoorsman like me felt like being a rat stuck in a cage. So, unsurprisingly, when the doors were finally open, I was straight on the phone to Dave to see if we could hatch a plan to get out and stretch the legs. The wild West Coast is one of my favourite places to hunt, and for me, there's nothing better than spending a few mint days in the hills with a couple of good mates, doing what we love.

While shooting a trophy is a bonus, most of the time it's far from the top of my priority list. There's nothing quite like a good old meat-gathering trip, putting some animals on the deck to take home for a feed for friends and family. Tahr is beautiful eating if treated properly, so they make a great target for a meat hunter.

Taking anyone on a hunt for their first of any species is always rewarding, but taking a good mate for their first is even more so. I've been incredibly fortunate with the hunting I've managed to do, and to be able to share an opportunity like this with a great mate, to score a good animal, and to share in his stoke, was something special.

Enjoying a high-altitude brew on a bluebird day.

2 SUB-ZERO CHAMOIS

With the tahr box ticked, we turned our eyes to our next alpine prize, hitting the hills in Central Otago in search of chamois. For this mission, I would be tagging along with Anto and Yuley, as well as Yuley's black Lab, Jess.

Jess had joined us on a number of trips over the past few years, and in the lead-up to this trip, I was keen to test a theory that I'd heard on a couple of occasions about how a rutting chamois buck will sometimes come racing in to investigate a dog, especially a dark-coloured one. I wanted to go a step further, painting white streaks over Jess's face and muzzle to make her better resemble a chamois, but white zinc is surprisingly hard to come by these days, so we missed the opportunity. To be honest, I'm not sure Yuley was that keen on me painting up his dog either.

The site that the fellas had selected for the hunt was a high plateau near the boundary of Mount Aspiring National Park, an absolutely stunning location that provided me with no end of incredible scenic vistas to film and photograph. Anto had hunted the area before, but that was during summer; this mission would be an entirely different kettle of fish. We were to base ourselves near a frozen river flat at about 1480 metres, nestled between two steep ridges running parallel along the length of the valley floor.

Once again, we made use of the big M.I.A base camp to ensure we could withstand the extreme weather forecast. There was a gigantic high-pressure system over the South Island, 1040 hPa for the trainspotters out there, which was expected to bring with it a plunge in temperatures to double-digit negatives in some places.

After a short flight in, with snow and sleet falling, we quickly erected a bulletproof camp, cranked up the fire and settled in to wait out the weather. Thankfully, it broke with about an hour of light left in the day, giving us the chance to get out for a quick scout.

There's something quite magical about the mountains after a bout of bad weather, especially now that it was late in the day. All around us, rays of light pierced through the gunmetal sky, lighting the giant walls which hemmed us in in an orange hue. The mountain tops around us were now covered in deep drifts of fresh snow, interspersed with ragged bands of ice, both grey and bright blue, running like scars down the rocky face.

Glassing into country of this magnitude takes patience, but we soon

Battening down the hatches
before the big blow.

found what we were after. Our elevated vantage point was next to a frozen horsetail waterfall that plunged 84 metres to a bed of rock and ice, and from here we located a small mob of cham feeding among the tussock, which clung precariously to a steep face. A strong wind made evaluation near impossible, so we weren't able to ascertain if there were any trophy bucks within the mob, but at least it provided us with a good starting point for the morning's hunt.

But before morning came the long cold night. Being the 'skipper' of the show, I often try to take it upon myself to bear the brunt of any hardships, to lead by example. There's a loose rule in the military that officers should always eat last, waiting until the soldiers under them have had their meals. This rule is in place to help create a sense of unity and loyalty, but there are certainly times where I admit I've been unable to wait until the fellas have eaten before tucking in myself!

What I do always try to do is ensure the guys get the best sleep possible, giving them first choice on tent sites and bedding arrangements. It's often a matter of convenience, as I'll be up late shooting astro timelapses or up early to film sunrises and change-of-light shots, so there's no point waking up the fellas in the process. But sometimes, as on this trip, leadership requires me taking a bullet for the boys.

With our big Tatonka Bison packs, a fireplace, a card table and a few other luxury items, not to mention a full-sized Labrador, there wasn't enough room in the M.I.A for three large camp stretchers.

So, rather than taking the plush sleeping option, I opted for the icy floor. We'd pitched the M.I.A on a flat section of snow, so while Yuley and

Anto snored comfortably away in their beds above me, every couple of hours, the chill would creep its way in through the frozen ground and wake me up. I'd then sit up and add more wood to the fireplace to kick it back into life to provide enough respite to get back to sleep, but heat rises, so pretty soon I'd be feeling the chill once again.

Thankfully, the hours of darkness in the Deep South during winter stretch on for long enough that I was able to snatch enough sleep over the course of the night, but it wasn't the ideal preparation for our first big day of hunting.

Morning eventually rolled around, so with hot coffee under our belts, we made our way back down to our vantage point from the night prior. 'Don't leave animals to find animals,' they say, and by now, the wind and weather that had plagued us the previous night had died off, leaving conditions perfectly still but bitterly cold.

That morning a few animals were spied, but nothing to get the heart racing. As the rising sun began to hit the faces, though, more chamois started moving about on the steep hillsides, and one animal looked particularly promising.

Yuley evaluated it as a good buck, potentially touching the magical 10-inch mark that we'd been seeking since the very first season of the show. Anto concurred, so he set about doing what he does best, making warm bodies turn cold, although after removing his thick gloves, his warm hands turned so cold that he struggled to feel the trigger mechanism.

Despite being based in Queenstown year-round, I'm continually surprised about how much the cold affects Anto. I'll be blunt — the man's soft. I once saw him wrestle his way into two down-filled sleeping bags, all while wearing a puffer jacket! He also had his insulated roll mat inflated and stretched out on a camp stretcher, and where was I sleeping during all this? That's right, the good old ground.

Here's another example of his thin skin. Following a recent hunt which involved the team splitting up into two groups to hunt opposite catchments, I was reviewing some footage shot by another cameraman, when I noticed something odd. After taking a screenshot and zooming in, I was able to count five individual layers of headwear on Anto's head. In his defence, he hasn't got a lot of insulation left up there these days, but five layers is still ludicrous!

While not wanting to brag, despite calling the subtropical Far North my home, I can get away with not wearing much in the way of warm gear. I guess I'm lucky to run a pretty hot motor; as soon as I start moving my body heats up rapidly, so I try to adhere to the 'be bold — start cold' mindset to save myself the hassle of needing to remove layers over the course of a morning hunt. Everyone's built differently — Anto could quite rightly argue that I thermoregulate well as I eat twice as much food as him on any given hunt.

But back to the chamois. After warming up his dainty little fingers, Anto lined up and pulled off a cracking 400-yard shot, sending the buck on a rapid descent down the snowy hillside.

Despite the cham falling a hundred metres, it was still a long, steep climb up into the zone where he lay, and with a rising sun melting the snow and ice around us, we needed to be particularly careful with our foot placement.

The cham stretched the tape to a shade under nine and a half inches, so not quite the calibre of trophy we were hoping for, but it was still a nice way to break the ice.

For the afternoon hunt, we decided to punch our way up valley, but it was quite slow going due to the heavy snow load, and not a lot was seen. Given there weren't even any animal tracks up in the higher reaches, we figured the chamois must be living in the lower reaches, so en route back to camp for the night, we made a plan to climb up and over a steep saddle in order to glass down into a new catchment the following day.

The next morning, after another broken night's sleep on the ice where, at one point I even contemplated snuggling up with Jess, we found ourselves standing at the base of a steep face, peppered with boulders and broken rock, peering up towards a snow-covered ridgeline. It looked fairly innocuous from my vantage point, but having spent a decent amount of time in the alpine environment, I now knew not to take these things at face value. Anto had ascended the same slope on his previous summer hunt so was pretty sure we wouldn't run into any nasty surprises, and with ice axes, ropes and crampons, we had the necessary safety gear to ascend with confidence. But even then, Anto managed to climb himself into a tricky spot and required a bit of assistance with the rope before finally managing to crest the saddle.

For some reason, I was feeling surprisingly confident this morning, perhaps because my pack was slightly lighter than usual, having left behind my rather bulky timelapse slider and equipment, so I was quite happy skipping around the hillside getting shots of the fellas climbing from a variety of angles.

However, as we ascended further, my confidence got me into trouble. I'd decided to take a route directly up the face rather than sidling around a rocky bluff, and I soon found myself in a bit of a pickle. It really is a horrible feeling climbing into a position where you've got no other option than to keep pressing ahead; in fact, writing about it now is making me feel a little sick with anxiety.

With Yuley and Anto well off to my right, carving steps into a tight snow chute, I had no one to help guide me back down from my precarious perch so was forced to risk serious injury or death by putting my full weight on an icy overhang, and clambering my way up and onto a thin, rocky ledge, much like a swimmer exiting the side of a pool. Complicating matters, I had to do it with a pack on my back and had an expensive camera to try to deal with.

It was a heart-in-mouth manoeuvre. If the rock wasn't entirely secure, or if my hand slipped, I was toast. Luckily for me, I made it up unscathed, with white knuckles that weren't just from the snow and ice.

It took another half an hour for Yuley and Anto to eventually make their way up to my little alpine nook. By then, I'd given myself a stern talking to and resolved to follow in their footsteps for the remainder of the day's hunting.

We were now up into some stunning country that provided amazing views down into some promising-looking chamois terrain, so we took some time to get the Jetboil cranking for a hot brew before pressing further on.

A few hours later, having seen four-fifths of f-all, we reluctantly accepted defeat. It's certainly disheartening to have risked life and limb to climb all the way up into an area, only to find it was a complete waste of time, but that's the joy of hunting.

On the descent, I picked up some classic banter on the radio mics of Yuley and Anto, most of it not fit for broadcast. We'd each had a couple of nasty slips while navigating a razorback ridge, as it was covered in a uniform layer of thick snow that concealed any holes or boulders. The only one in the team who was taking it all in her stride was our four-legged friend Jess, who seemed right in her element.

We eventually made our way right down to the valley floor, and much like the situation 48 hours earlier, we only had an hour or two up our sleeves to try to make some magic happen.

It didn't take long for Anto to pull a rabbit out of his hat, though — within a few minutes, a young buck was spied in pretty much the same position on the hillside as the first night, but he was clearly not a shooter. With the light weakening, another few animals were then spotted, and this time, without a strong wind playing havoc with their glassing, the fellas were able to identify a standout among the three.

Their behaviour, rubbing horns on vegetation and chasing each other madly around the hillside, added weight to the assumption that these were all bucks, but the fading light complicated identification of the exact animal for Yuley to take. They were all bouncing about the hillside, like a magician performing a sleight-of-hand trick with cup and ball.

It can be quite a stressful situation ensuring that the shooter is lined up on the same animal that I have framed up on camera, especially when time is of the essence. In this case, the frantic back and forth banter between all three of us captures that confusion well, as we first battled to identify the target buck among the animals moving about the face and then to confirm that both Yuley and I have the same chamois within our sights:

YULEY: Those two together?
ANTO: The one on its own is the bigger one.
YULEY: The one on its own?
ANTO: Yeah, out to the right.
YULEY: Okay, I can see two.
DAVE: The single — he's climbing up now . . .
YULEY: Oh, is that the one then, okay, the one climbing up?
DAVE: He's looking at us now.
YULEY: That's not the same animal . . . that's not the big boy?
DAVE: You don't think it's the big one?
YULEY: The middle one, it's the middle one. We need to be sure here . . .
DAVE: The one at the back.
YULEY: Is that the better one, 100 per cent sure? I reckon he's one of those front two . . .
DAVE: Okay, stop then . . .

This exchange continued for a couple more minutes, before Anto was able to make a definitive call on which animal to take, and Yuley squeezed off a perfectly placed shot, dropping the cham on the spot.

Given the late hour, there was absolutely no way we'd be recovering the chamois till the morning, especially given the precarious terrain we'd need to navigate, so we used our fancy new Garmin watch to project a waypoint of where the cham fell onto the inbuilt topographic map and made our way back to the M.I.A with a newfound spring in our step.

You should always do your best to recover a shot animal right away, but since that wasn't a possibility in this instance, we had all night to speculate on just how big a trophy it might be. It's a unique position, the anticipation

Crampon country. Jess was the only one comfortable thanks to running a full-time 4WD.

Anto's impressive winter buck where it lay following his pinpoint shot.

of what's waiting for you in the morning, so we were a bit like kids on Christmas Eve, speculating as to exactly what we'd find for us the next morning under the tree.

As day eventually dawned, we eagerly made our way back to the frozen waterfall. Looking at it in the light of day, it was going to be a quite technical descent to get across to where the chamois lay. After using the drone to survey some of the country that was hidden from view, it was time to break out the ropes, ice axes and crampons once again.

I found the descent of the icy face relatively straightforward; again, was this overconfidence perhaps? With my camera strapped to the top of my pack, it was certainly a nice change having two hands free.

After half an hour of careful navigation, Yuley and I finally laid eyes on the cham, piled up on the tussock ahead of us. These moments are important for me to capture well, as the raw emotion on seeing and evaluating a hard-earned trophy is not something you can fake. Yuley can be a hard nut to crack, but he lets his feelings shine through when he's truly stoked, so I rolled continuously as he approached the animal, hoping to see a beaming smile that you would expect from someone banging over a buck near the 10-inch mark.

The first words out of Yuley's mouth extinguished that hope, though.

'It might be a doe, bro.'

One of the peculiarities of the chamois is the lack of sexual dimorphism — meaning that there's quite a similarity in appearance between mature does and bucks. In this instance, the behaviour of the animals the night before led us to believe they were all bucks, but obviously, we'd got that assumption wrong, as Yuley had bowled over a nanny.

Emotion runs hot in both directions, and it's not just the smiles I was after; disappointment and regret also make for compelling viewing. Yuley was clearly extremely gutted about the turn of events, and it showed. It was a hard pill to swallow, but to his credit, he laid the blame squarely at his own feet.

The nanny measured 9.5, a touch more than Anto's buck from earlier in the trip, but again shy of that sought-after 10 inches. All in all, though, I was happy with this mission. Visually it was a feast for the eyes, and while the animal numbers and calibre of trophy weren't quite what we wanted, the drama of how it all played out made for quite a memorable episode.

Yuley's two cents

Chamois have always been at the top of my list for several reasons: their impeccable eyesight, their incredible agility in steep terrain and the dramatic change in coat colour from summer to winter, all contribute in my opinion to making the cham one of our finest game animals.

The subalpine country which they call home is rugged and will demand the most from any hunter willing to take it on. This country certainly gets under your skin, and any time spent here will leave you wanting more.

We had tried to get this trip off the ground two weeks prior, but a massive snowfall extinguished our hopes. This would also lead to a change in location. We confirmed our fly-in date as 11 June, and in my mind this would be too late for the bucks to be in full rut mode, but the prospect of exploring some new country was a big enough carrot.

Approaching the basin which would become our home for the next few days, it became apparent just how much snow was around, and I knew we were going to have trouble getting about the place.

The walls of the valley were steep and covered in snow and ice, and as the hum of the heli faded, only then could the true scale of this place be appreciated. We set up our big M.I.A base camp rather hastily, as the weather was deteriorating rapidly and it was bloody cold!

With Anto securing a good buck on day one, spirits were high as we sussed a plan for the following day, which involved climbing high to investigate a new catchment. But as Dave alluded to, due to the amount of snow it appeared that the animals were living lower down on the scrubby faces. We admitted defeat and made our way off the hill. Navigating the snow-covered chute without incident, we found ourselves at the bottom with an hour of daylight to spare so we beelined for the vantage point we had used on the first evening.

It didn't take long to pick up a few animals. Anto got to work assessing them as I got set up for a shot. Now, trying to assess trophy chamois on the hoof can be hard enough at the best of times, but in fading light and with the animals moving around, it added another layer of complication that we didn't need.

Deep down, I reckon we were all thinking we needed one more animal sequence for a full episode, so there was an added sense of urgency resting on my shoulders.

After a lot of back and forth, an animal was finally selected as being worthy of a shot, so once in position, I sent the 175-grain

It's always a treat having a canine
companion on a hunt.

Berger on its way and it delivered the knockout blow.

The mood in the tent that night was one of satisfaction and excitement, knowing that we would now have enough footage for an awesome episode. The bitterly cold night slowly gave way to morning, and before long Dave and I had taken turns descending the icy face with the aid of ropes, crampons and an ice axe, crossed a creek and a steep scrubby gut and were within reach of our prize.

As I approached the animal, I immediately took note of the lack of hook in the horn and felt that sinking feeling. I proceeded to flip the animal over only to confirm what my churning gut had told me only seconds before — it was a bloody doe!

I felt like an air mat that had been stabbed with a Spaniard, and in the space of 30 seconds our hopes of what we thought was a decent buck had been quashed.

There are a couple of scenarios as to how this could play out. The first option was to scrap this sequence altogether, but I knew this would leave us well short of the crucial footage we needed. I made the call on the spot to suck it up and roll with it. I think how the show played out in the end was a good way of portraying the highs and lows that come with the territory, and we all know that just like anything in life, we need the lows to appreciate the highs. Thankfully, it wouldn't be too long before the three of us would make amends on our next outing for chamois, but that story's for later in the book.

3 STEWART ISLAND EPIC

We didn't leave ourselves much time to defrost following the alpine chamois mission before the next major expedition kicked off, and this was one that I was absolutely fizzing for.

A few years back, the team and I had an absolute blast on a liveaboard mission into Dusky Sound. It was my first-ever trip into that phenomenally beautiful part of New Zealand, and the episode that resulted from our seven days aboard the MV *Flightless* with the Pure Salt team was one of the most talked about of the season, in part because we used a wide range of guys and showcased a mix of diving and hunting.

A year later, we adopted a similar approach on a mission to Chew Tobacco Bay on Rakiura Stewart Island, taking along seven keen lads and having an absolute ball chasing the elusive whitetail deer, as well as spearfishing and diving for pāua, crays and paddle crabs. Again, that episode was a ripsnorter and a fan favourite.

As they say, lightning doesn't strike twice, so even though those trips will go down as two of the most memorable of my life, I was reluctant to simply rehash either trip for the new series. The risk we faced was that the resultant episode would undoubtedly be compared to the previous ones, and like most sequels, would probably not live up to the lofty expectations.

So, in an effort to try to recapture the magic of those trips, I decided to merge the two, jumping aboard the MV *Flightless* once again, but this time for a circumnavigation of Stewart Island, with a similar ragtag mob of outdoorsmen and camera jockeys.

Returning from the first Pure Salt trip would be Anto Hall, Kieran Andrews, Larry Dougherty, Sam Wild, Marty Verry, me and stills photographer Ben Vercauteren, and from the Stewart Island mission we also had Tim Barnett, Dwane Herbert, James Jubb and *Hunters Journal* editor Cam Henderson.

The wild card along for the ride was a keen young fella by the name of Drew Avery, whom we'd selected to join us as part of a Stabicraft competition that we'd run online. Drew was selected thanks to a pretty ballsy entry vid which saw him fishing, hunting and diving from the North Island to the South Island over a 24-hour period, crossing the Cook Strait in his wee tinny.

Setting sail aboard the *Flightless* from Bluff on a warm winter's day, it's fair to say the lads were frothing! It was always going to be a risk heading into the wild Southern Ocean in mid-winter, but we'd got lucky. We had a picture-perfect forecast for the next three days, so were eager to get stuck into our week of hunting, diving and adventure in some of the most remote parts of the island, areas that are normally off limits thanks to the tumultuous Southern Ocean.

Things certainly started well. After pitching up in a sheltered bay for the night, we launched the tenders on first light, and Tim, Sam, Anto and I made our way in towards a sandy beach. Less than a minute after Sam was regaling me with how he'd popped his whitetail cherry on this beach the previous year, his eyes lit up as he spotted a brazen young deer walking on the edge of a small creek.

A rather frenzied dismount onto the rocks followed, and within 30 seconds of setting foot on Stewart Island, we had our first whitetail down, as Anto expertly dropped the deer from less than 100 metres.

After patting ourselves on the back, we removed our lifejackets and wandered on over to check out the deer, but on arrival it's fair to say we were all a little surprised by its size — it was no larger than a Labrador!

I've learned a few tricks over the years about how to make animals look bigger on camera, but in this instance, there was little I could do, despite Anto's insistence on me filming it at a low angle from a distance to make it look a little more impressive.

Anto gutted the small deer and hung it in a low branch, and after more gentle ribbing from Tim, we all set off in different directions, hoping to stalk a larger deer in the dense Stewart Island bush.

The country was pristine, with the morning light casting golden rays down through the foliage, but we all returned to the boat a few hours later empty handed. The remainder of those aboard who put the tenders to use to hunt further south along the coast also drew a blank, but at least we had Anto's 'rabbit' to keep spirits high.

The beauty of the liveaboard scenario is that it allows you to cover new ground, so for the evening hunt we relocated further south into some terrain for which Dwane had high hopes.

Being a Bluff local and commercial diver, Dwane has dived and hunted the island a great deal over the years, so he was willing to share a few of his honey holes with us. After allocating areas and boundaries on the topo map to the various hunting parties, once again we all set off to different areas of the island, either to stake out beaches and clearings, or to stalk the coastal bush country.

En route to the designated drop-off point for Tim and me, we spied a few deer out on the rocky coastline but were unable to get ashore in time to make it count. Our hunt that evening played out similarly to the morning mission, with nothing seen, but over on a sheltered beach down the coast, Anto and Sam were able to add another deer to the day's tally.

Sitting on a rocky outcrop a hundred metres from a sheltered sandy beach, they didn't have to wait too long before a whitetail materialised on the edge of the sand, fairly engrossed in eating the kelp and other seaweed

A perfect spot to try and catch out an unwary deer.

littering the shoreline. Another solid shot from Anto did the job, dropping the hind on the spot. Luckily, this animal was a much more respectable size, and it would provide more delicious venison to feed a dozen hungry mouths over the days ahead.

The following morning, rather than head back into the bush, we decided to make the most of the glassy calm seas and spend the morning session collecting a little seafood from around a remote island group to the south-west of Stewart Island. During the weeks leading into the trip, Dwane had informed us that the visibility was uncommonly good down around this part of the island, but dropping over the side into 20 metres-plus visibility took all the lads by surprise.

In a short time, the fellas had nailed a few tasty trumpeter and blue cod on spear, as well as some XXL crayfish and an octopus to boot, which was a special request from Anna the chef, who wished to prepare a deep-fried occy delicacy for the evening meal.

If there's a point of difference that sets the Pure Salt team apart from any other charter operator that I've been involved with over my years of making TV shows, it's the quality of the cuisine. The wild game served up to us each night was simply out of this world, and one of the main motivators to succeed each day was to ensure we'd be able to keep eating like kings at the end of each day's hunt.

One species that we perhaps regretted adding to the bag was the telescope fish. These school up in large numbers around Stewart Island, and a handful were shot by the lads as they were believed to be good eating. However, back aboard the boat we discovered the rather soft flesh had a nasty metallic tang to it. A quick perusal of a fish identification book from the ship's library led to the discovery that another common name for the telescope fish is real bastard trumpeter, which seemed rather apt.

However, the policy of the Pure Salt team is to never waste anything that's taken, so we resigned ourselves to eating telescope fish sandwiches

The team celebrate after a successful morning mission, with Anto's rabbit hanging off the stern.

for the next couple of lunches. To be fair, though, once smoked on the Traeger, the metallic tang was somewhat lessened.

The neoprene was switched back out for camouflage for the evening, and whereas the previous day's honours went to Anto, today it was all Drew. After nailing the best crays of the morning, he rounded out the evening with a rather dramatic sequence which saw him leaping from the Stabi 1450 onto an exposed group of rocks to nail an oblivious whitetail out feeding on the shore. The level of stoke was absolutely infectious, and we were all rapt about his success back aboard the boat later that night, although for Tim and me a bit of pressure was starting to build.

Being the most experienced at hunting and filming the tight bush of Stewart Island, we were supposed to be the ones delivering the goods, but despite maintaining a high degree of stalking discipline during our bush hunting, we were yet to even bump a deer.

With the weather forecast set to take a turn for the worse, we decided to set sail for the east of the island, where we'd shelter for the night in the protected waters of Port Pegasus, the liberation point of the original whitetail herd way back in 1905.

The next day saw more traditional winter weather roll in, with big seas and squally rain, but it didn't dampen the team's enthusiasm. Again, we split into six pairs and headed into the bush, although getting ashore certainly took more effort on this more exposed stretch of coastline.

Tim and I were determined to get on the board, but once again we drew a blank. However, at least this time we laid eyes on an animal.

We'd been stalking stealthily for a good few hours, trying to stay on top of a shifting wind, when we broke into an area of crown fern that looked

particularly promising. However, as we made our way silently along, I made the mistake of getting 10 metres behind Tim, and as luck would have it, at that very moment, a nice 6-point buck came strolling along about 20 metres below us on the face, obscured from Tim's view but right in my field of vision.

I froze, but then made a massive mistake — I tried to whistle gently to Tim to alert him that I'd seen something, but the alien noise was like a starter's pistol, setting the buck off like a rocket, and I was only able to capture a fleeting glimpse of his white flag of alarm as it boosted off into the bush.

Luckily for the team's tally, Kieran and Dwane performed better, nailing a deer each, although Kieran's superseded Anto's first in the race for the smallest deer of the trip. But that was no consolation for Tim and me. So, for the final full day of hunting, we decided that we'd pull out all the stops.

We set out in darkness along with our hunting buddies from day one, Anto and Sam, using the tender to work a fair way inland via a snaking river system. Again, the weather looked ominous, but we hoped that rain might prove advantageous given that it would help to dampen the sound of our movement.

With the light strengthening, Tim and I wished Sam and Anto luck and moved off into the wet undergrowth, with a steely determination to finally deliver the goods.

We were no more than 20 minutes into the day's stalk when a shot rang out close by. Anto, the lucky bugger, had nailed one already! While we were stoked to have another deer on the deck and an additional sequence in the can, I'll admit there was an element of frustration creeping in. We were doing everything right, so why couldn't we get lucky!

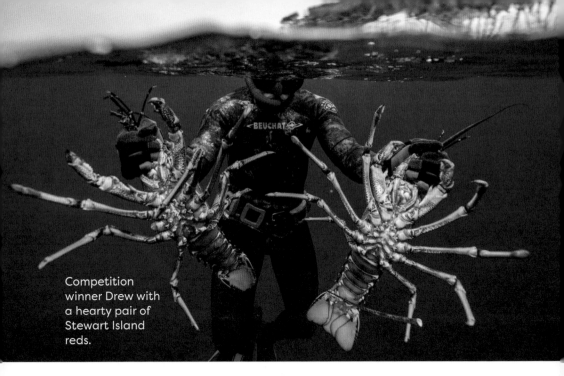

Competition winner Drew with a hearty pair of Stewart Island reds.

Another couple of hours later, and another gunshot rings out, this time a little further off. One more deer down for the dream team; however, this time it was cameraman Sam putting his name on the scorecard. Bloody hell, would we ever catch a break?

Short answer, yes. Not long after congratulating Sam on the radio, Tim and I were moving through some rather unglamourous-looking country, pretty much just covering ground, when suddenly a large shape leapt out of the bushes no more than 10 metres ahead of us and bolted off. But this time, the presence of a cameraman proved to be a benefit and not a curse. The deer stopped 30 metres from us, before turning to look back at me through a thick tangle of vegetation, completely unaware of the fact that 5 metres to my right a long-haired, pot-bellied commercial fisherman was lining him up in his crosshairs.

With a loud crack, we finally had our prize, a 4-point buck, certainly no wall hanger but definitely cause for celebration!

With three deer for the day, and a bucket filled to the brim with beers waiting for us back at the pick-up point, we decided to rest on our laurels and head back to enjoy a brew or two before our scheduled collection at high tide, which was still a good four hours away.

By the time the tender arrived, it's fair to say that we all had a good head of steam up, and why not? Marty had jokingly informed us the night prior that it was a par-3 day, so we were certainly looking forward to delivering the good news to the rest of the lads. It would make a refreshing change from constantly coming home with our tails between the legs, as had become the norm for Tim and myself.

The final day saw the team complete the circumnavigation by heading into the township of Oban, where the venison was broken down and divvied up,

While it's no wall hanger, this was without a doubt one of the most hard-earned deer in the history of the show.

before rounding out the trip in style with a raucous session at the local pub.

Now I've had a few good nights at the Oban Hotel bar, which has that real 'salty' old-school character, and there's always an old boy or two keen for a yarn. But on this occasion, we really hit the ground running, with a dozen thirsty hunters looking to cap off a great week, so we were perhaps a little guilty of 'commandeering' the place.

After introducing the team to a few classic Otago uni drinking games, things began to get a little boisterous. Pretty soon, a commercial fisherman took a dislike to our rowdy behaviour and began pushing around one of the guys in our group on his way to the bar, knocking off his hat in the process, which he then refused to return. When Tim and I heard what had happened, our protective instincts took over; what right did this clown have to pick on one of our team?

With Timmy at my back, I approached said clown, my cockiness bolstered by the knowledge that I also had Drew, a competitive MMA fighter, ready to step in and shut things down if needed.

It didn't get that far — after some tough words and a bit of push and shove, the bartender, who'd probably quashed his fair share of scuffles over the years, quickly stepped in and gave us both our marching orders. Problem was, I was staying at the hotel. I informed the barkeep of my situation.

'Well, go to your room then, I don't want to see you down here again!'

Not since leaving home had I been red carded to my room, and never with such force. Dejected, I retired upstairs, leaving the lads to themselves, although I could hear their racket through the floor for the next hour or two. It was an unceremonious way to end such a memorable mission, but in hindsight, it was certainly far better than being floored by a hard-hitting local hellraiser!

Marty's two cents

I reckon hunting whitetail on Rakiura Stewart Island is the New Zealand hunter's equivalent of the Muslim pilgrimage to the Holy City of Mecca. It's just one of those things you have to do once in your life.

Having ticked this box on the earlier Chew Tobacco trip, I was stoked to get another shot. On that previous trip, Sam Wild (on camera duties) and I had overnighted after a couple of hours bushwhacking down the coast, and we successfully ambushed a hind at dawn at the far end of the beach on which we had set up. The 200-metre shot across the water of the horseshoe-shaped bay looked awesome on camera, and the hunt played out exactly as Tim had planned for us the day before, so well done that man!

For this trip, then, the challenge was to shoot a whitetail in the bush, a far tougher proposition. Whitetail down there are small, measuring around a metre high. That would be fine if they hung out in open areas like fallow deer, but they don't. Stewart Island is covered in crown fern — also about a metre high. And it's very noisy when you brush against it, tipping the scales in the deer's favour.

On the way down the west side of Stewart Island on the first two days, we kept an eye out for surf breaks, having brought some boards in case we could pull off a rare surf-hunt combo. It was not to be, so smooth was the swell. The bonus, though, was very easy access to the coast from the little Stabicraft tender we'd dragged down to put through its paces. On my first hunt, I leapt off the tender and landed in an ankle-high rock pool — absolutely full of pāua! You hear stories of the olden days in New Zealand when you could pick crayfish and pāua off the reefs, so I couldn't believe my luck. I decided to make the most of this bonus delicacy by plucking off my quota and moving them up the reef where they would be safe from the incoming tide while I hunted. It was lucky I did, because the whitetail were a no-show.

The next two days involved fishing, diving, day stalks and setting up on beaches to try to ambush deer coming out at dusk to eat the seaweed. Again, I had no luck, although one blazing tail was seen boosting through the crown fern in the opposite direction — a sight any Stewart Island hunter would be very familiar with. Ben (aka Fez) was my patient cameraman. I really wanted to bag one for his sake too.

On the fourth day, we had come around the south tip of the island and spread out at various catchments along the coast to day hunt. The weather was forecast to cut up bad and getting onto the reef required swell timing and ultimately a leap of faith into the bull kelp.

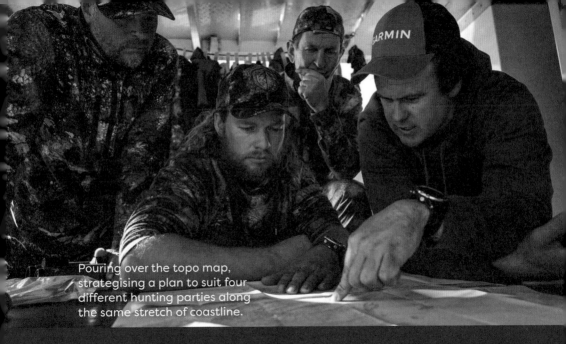
Pouring over the topo map, strategising a plan to suit four different hunting parties along the same stretch of coastline.

Fez and I hunted our way in an arc deep into the island's bush this day, covering some excellent habitat. When I say deep, I am talking maybe 2 kilometres, such is the glacial speed and regular stops that one does in hunting whitetail. The weather was coming in, and it was forecast to get pretty wet. My scope was foggy, so I decided to use my scope cover, the plan being to whip it off if need be.

After a few hours of deteriorating sea conditions someone on *Flightless* decided to call it a day. The Garmin Rino VHF radio crackled to life, and I turned it up high to get the instructions which boomed out across the forest. 'That's definitely it now,' I said to Fez as I packed the radio away and started walking towards the coast. I took a few steps and couldn't believe my eyes. Right there, less than 10 metres ahead, were the faces of two whitetail peering at us out of the fern. I couldn't believe they hadn't boosted at the sound of the VHF. Instinctively, I immediately brought the gun to my shoulder to aim and, you guessed it, the scope was black. Bugger, in the time it took me to remove the scope cover and re-aim they were gone! There was definitely a window to take one, had I not made that schoolboy error. Snap shooting in bush is so instinctive and automatically reactive, you just never think to take the extra step of removing a cover.

Waiting for our pick-up, I decided to try my luck reverting to the old beach ambush technique that had worked last trip and for Anto and Drew earlier this trip. We selected an ideal bush for cover overhanging a likely beach. As I crawled under the tree, to my shock (and his) I came face to face with a very large and now very agitated seal. After a strategic retreat on my part, I just had to have a chuckle. That about summed up the mission for me. Apart from a few pāua and cod, the island's wildlife had beaten me this time. But I'll be back, with lessons learned.

4 GO WITH THE FLOW

As I type these words, it's currently early November, a time of the year that for us traditionally involves heading out in search of meat to fill the freezer. However, with shoulder surgery ruling me out, the closest I'll be getting to a November meat hunt is reminiscing on our mission from Series 6.

Once again, for this trip I would be following Anto, Sam and Jess the black Lab. For the sake of variety, we chose to fly into an area that would provide us with solid tahr hunting opportunities, along with a good chance to bag a red deer or two.

The chopper flight in from Mount Cook Village was quite an eye-opener. Earlier in the year, strong westerly winds during the runaway wildfires in Australia had deposited a thin layer of red dust on the snow and glaciers along the spine of the Alps, with some parts of the range looking like they'd been dusted by a giant paprika shaker.

These same winds are also responsible for aiding the aerial self-introduction of a number of Australian bird species to the New Zealand mainland, such as the silvereye, spurwing plover, grey teal and the welcome swallow.

Seeing the red dust brought back memories of when I was living in London and the whole city awoke to a faint, pungent smell, which turned out to be due to French farmers fertilising their fields with manure. Thankfully, in that instance there was no visible residue present, otherwise I doubt the Underground could have coped with the number of Londoners seeking refuge from the shit-blitz coming from across the English Channel.

Along with bagging a bit of fresh protein, another aim of the trip was to try to do our part to tell a story to the public about the important role hunters play in animal control. The newly formed Tahr Foundation had recently been working with agencies, such as the New Zealand Game Animal Council and DOC to develop an app for hunters to help quantify hunter effort in controlling tahr numbers in the backcountry, so we wanted to shine a light on how it all worked to help encourage uptake.

The best way to do this would be for us to bag a few nannies, but once again, we were frustrated by the lack of nannies seen during the trip. While nannies were in short supply, there was an abundance of juvenile and mid-aged bulls, so in the end, we decided to take a couple of juveniles.

Even taking juveniles had me worried, though. 'Tahrmageddon', the rather heavy-handed government tahr-control operation at the behest of Conservation Minister Eugenie Sage, had left many hunters worried that tahr numbers could have been decimated beyond the point of recovery, so only absolute trophy bulls in their prime (we're talking 13 inches plus) should be taken.

However, I believe the fact that we were taking the animals for meat, while also educating the public about the role hunters play in terms of population control, outstripped these concerns. Seeing viral footage a fortnight later taken by a hunter in the same catchment of a mob of young bulls left to rot in the sun by aerial cullers also helped soften the unease I felt.

In the years since the tahr cull, it's become clear that the control work didn't impact the numbers to unhuntable levels. They've definitely been knocked back heavily in some areas, but tahr hunting is still viable in most wilderness areas of the alps. Only time will tell, though, if we'll continue to see the big 14-inch monsters coming out of the hills each winter.

Thankfully, it seems that hunters' voices are now being heard, and rather than basing control work on an outdated control plan, or even worse, on ideology, there's now more of a focus on science and hard data.

But back to the hunt at hand. In the three days we had up our sleeve, we would be travelling upstream from a wide, open, grassy valley to a hut perched on a steep rocky spur.

The plan for the first afternoon was to split up and cover a bit of ground, with Sam heading downstream and Anto and me heading up. As evening approached, Anto spied a hind feeding out on a grassy fan across a river on the opposite side of the valley. We weren't quick enough to get a shot away before it retreated into the cover of the thick bush, but we stayed vigilant in the hope it would reappear before dark.

Sure enough, an hour or so later, the deer re-emerged, and this time her meal was lead rather than grass. We were stoked, as it's always nice to get an action sequence on the first evening of a hunt, but what we didn't realise was that the action was only just beginning.

Making our way down from our elevated position, we soon hit an obstacle — the swollen river, discoloured grey by glacial flour from recent snow melt. There's a rule of thumb that you shouldn't attempt to cross a river that's flowing faster than walking speed. In our defence, those race walkers at the Olympics can move damn quickly, so I felt we were okay to give it a crack.

The first attempt was a bit of a shock, and not just from the icy cold temps hitting high in the thigh. We backtracked and gave it a bit of thought — we needed to take this crossing with more caution, so linked arms and put the bigger unit (myself) upriver. We made more progress on this attempt, but once the bottom of my pack started hitting the surface, we did the old *Tina Turn Around* and pulled pin once again. Talk about *River Deep — Mountain High.*

Anto and I cross the tumultuous
river — ninth time's a charm!

Anto made the correct call that rather than persisting with trying to
cross at this point, we'd be better to scout a viable spot to attempt to cross
further downstream, even if it meant having to cover a lot more ground to
retrieve the deer, so off we went, assessing the muscular river for any sign
of weakness.

We found it a fair way down, at a spot where the valley opened up
slightly and the river broke from running as one continuous stream into
two wide branches.

Carefully, we entered the water. The speed of flow combined with
the depth and lack of visibility made movement very difficult. In some
places, lifting a planted foot was like performing a squat at the gym, and
complicating matters further was my need to document the crossing as
best I could without trashing the main camera, but after exercising plenty
of caution, we eventually made it across to a rocky island in the middle of
the river.

Halfway there.

The next leg would be harder. The river was just 10 metres wide at this

point but flowing fast. We linked arms once more, holding each other's pack straps tight, with Anto taking the upstream position.

We started well, but within a few seconds, Anto was swept off his feet. Luckily, we stayed connected, and I was able to yank him back into a standing position before he became submerged, but it was a close-run thing!

Once on the opposite bank, we assessed the situation. The packs had kept our gear surprisingly dry, and Anto's rifle would soon dry out, so all in all, it was a bullet dodged.

Now it was time for us to find the critter that didn't manage to dodge a bullet but, again, that task would prove to be easier said than done.

Anto's shot didn't drop the hind on the spot, so it had managed to run out of sight, possibly into the thick native on the edge of the clearing. And since it had taken us so long to cross the raging river, by the time we began searching for the deer in earnest, it was pretty much dark, which made finding a blood trail near impossible.

Anto searched high, while I remained midway up the face, but after half an hour of fruitless search, things were getting desperate. Then an

Yuley glasses for game, hidden
way up in the higher reaches.

idea came to me. After reviewing the impact shot on the main camera, I was able to identify a dead tree in the frame, which proved we were both searching at the wrong elevation.

Once we'd worked that out, it didn't take long to find our prize. With Anto and I extremely relieved that the risky river crossing wasn't all in vain, we broke the meat down and saddled up our heavy packs, but our Tatonkas weren't the only thing weighing heavily on us. To get back to our campsite, we still had to return across the river, and the thought of doing so in the dark and under an even heavier load was looming large on our minds.

Anto seemed confident, though.

'We'll just work our way down the river until it widens out and cross there.'

Seemed like a solid plan. So, rather than returning the way we had come, we started walking the river edge hoping to identify a better option. Problem was, every few hundred metres, another tributary would join the main flow, adding more water into the mix. We made quite a few genuine efforts, before deciding that it wasn't worth the risk and, instead, we'd rough it for the night.

Anto and I were fortunately carrying enough basic supplies between us to make life relatively comfortable. We managed to get a fire going without too much trouble and did our best to dry ourselves off before tucking into a hot Back Country Cuisine meal.

When the sequence aired, I had a few people suggest that we'd staged the scene, given the gear that we were carrying, but the reality is that I try to ensure the guys always have a Jetboil on them at all times, mainly for a caffeine pick-me-up. I also always carry a freeze-dried meal on me too, because as I may have hinted at earlier, my mental state and the quality of the footage I film is directly related to the level of 'hungriness' I am experiencing.

So, with some warm grub in the gut, we donned our wet weathers to keep the dew off and bedded down next to the crackling fire on our makeshift fern mattresses to get a little shut-eye before dawn, when we'd have another crack at the river.

Early the next morning I put the drone to use, and after scouting the river from the air, Anto and I believed we'd identified a suitable crossing point just a few hundred metres downstream.

We made our attempt but, again, were forced back.

ANTO: I'm sort of stuck.
DAVE: I gotcha, climb up.
ANTO: You got me?
DAVE: Veer off to the right if we can.
ANTO: This is bad, bro.
DAVE: Nah, this is all right, we can power through it.

ANTO: I don't think we can.
DAVE: Yeah, we can, we can, go to the right.
ANTO: It's just too deep.
DAVE: Okay, let's go back.

The river seemed to have risen from the day before, the water now getting up to waist height in places. Over the course of the morning, we made a few more attempts but each time were rebuffed.

Better the devil you know as they say, so with most of our options now exhausted, we made the decision to trek all the way back upriver to the point where we'd crossed the previous night, for our seventh attempt.

By this stage, fatigue was setting in, and things were getting serious, so I decided this attempt would be make or break. I still needed to document the crossing for the scene to make sense within the show, but holding the main camera was proving too big a hindrance, so I stowed it away in the top of my pack, and instead sent the drone up 15 metres above us and set it to follow our movement as we made the crossing.

After a solid pep talk, we committed to the river. Although the flow was still fast and the water quite deep, it was a hell of a lot easier up at this point than the failed attempts earlier in the morning, and we made it across without incident, the eye in the sky capturing the action from above.

It was a relief to be back on the right side of things, but the crossing had me nervous in another sense. This whole sequence was another that we were cagey about including in the episode, as the last thing we wanted to do was encourage viewers to make similar dangerous crossings.

We were between a rock and a hard place — if we'd left the animal to rot on the opposite side of the river, we'd have been seen as callous and wasteful, but, conversely, risking your life for a bit of meat is ludicrous. Drowning in backcountry rivers in the nineteenth century used to be so common it was dubbed 'The New Zealand Death', and to this day, it's the second-highest cause of tramper fatalities in the country.

So, much like the crossing itself, we needed to tread carefully — not glossing over the dangers involved and ensuring we didn't come across as being cavalier about our own safety. In the end, I think we struck the right tone and am proud of the way the scenario played out in the show, but we've definitely learned a lesson for future hunts about scouting out rivers and other obstacles well before any trigger is pulled.

If I thought that the water-related dramas for the trip were over, however, I had a surprise coming. After bagging a brace of tahr on day two, where Anto mirrored the river-crossing failures by taking seven attempts to correctly pronounce the word 'anonymous' during an explanation of the new Game Animal Council app, the final full day greeted us with steady rainfall.

We tried our best to find a decent bull, but with the intensity of rain

Chef Yuley prepping some gourmet backcountry protein.

increasing, we soon had to focus on just making it to the hut. By this stage, my main camera was seriously on the blink — it's very hard to keep electronics dry in high rainfall, and most of my gear by now was quite damp, so my spirits certainly weren't high on the long hike upriver.

It was only four hours' hike, but my God, it was a tough old slog. Any semblance of a track had been washed away by the raging river, so we were forced to clamber up and around rocky bluffs and outcrops. With the rain now pelting down, we were also racing against time before the rising river completely cut off access to the hut.

Even Jess the Labrador was having a tough time of things, losing her footing and ending up in the river, but luckily, I was able to do a decent David Hasselhoff impression by reaching down and grabbing her by the collar before she was swept past. However, I wasn't lucky enough to prevent my camera from completely giving up the ghost, meaning the remaining sequences at the hut had to be filmed via GoPro and DSLR.

One of the final frames taken by my trusty FS700, before the torrential rain killed it for good.

But at least we were now warm and dry, and we had a mountain of fresh venison and tahr meat for dinner, along with a pretty entertaining episode.

I've just got one final piece of drama related to this trip to recount. Within the episode, we set aside time to explain to viewers what was happening with the government-led tahr cull, including some strongly worded language at the very end over some graphic shots of the destruction left in the wake of recent control work. After the episode aired, I had a message from our broadcast partners at Prime, who had concerns raised with them about us using the show as a tool to convey overt political messaging.

I completely understood the position they were in, so we agreed that in the future we'd let them know well in advance of broadcast about anything that could be considered controversial within the series. From that point on, though, we'd be under the microscope, and it wouldn't be the last time that someone, possibly from the government and possibly with an anti-hunting agenda, would be running interference.

Anto's two cents

After this episode aired, I received a massive amount of feedback.
Usually when people reach out to me online, it's about the animal that
got away, or the epic flight path of a bullet flying 500 yards before
hitting its target. This time, however, it was mainly about the dodgy
river crossing and Dave and I having to sleep rough for the night.

Thankfully, the messaging was super positive, with most saying
it was good to demonstrate how dangerous rivers can be, and to
always be prepared for an unexpected night out. One question I
had, though, was: 'Did you not know the river was going to be hard
to cross before taking the deer?'

It may seem like a bad error to overlook something as important
as this. However, we flew into this spot, and I vividly remember looking
down at the river and thinking that the flow looked good and should
be simple to cross. When looking at the river from a few hundred
metres back, it still looked good, and it was not until we stepped into
the river that the reality of its speed become obvious to us!

The one rule I failed to follow was to follow your path back. Things
went a little off track due to the feeling I had that the river would
get easier downstream from our initial crossing point, when the
reality was it got bigger and more dangerous.

While this whole process was a challenging one, it's times like
this that you look back on and consider what decisions went well
and what ones didn't, but it is also these situations that make you
mentally stronger and in a better position next time you're faced
with adversity. These challenges are what makes an adventure and
strengthens the bond between mates, creating stories to be told
around the campfire for years to come.

PART TWO
. . . AND UNDER

5 ROBBING THE BANKS

It's always exciting launching each new series of *The Red Stag Timber Hunters Club*, but it's doubly exciting to bring an entirely new show to local screens, so for me, the highlight of 2020 was undoubtedly the debut of *South Seas Spearo*.

With the series being an unproven entity, we really needed to grab people's attention right off the bat, so we chose to kick off with an episode that would do just that — a spearfishing trip to the legendary Wanganella Banks, a sea rise located a third of the way between New Zealand and Australia, which was known to be home to gigantic schools of fired-up striped marlin.

To get all the way out there, we would be making use of a commercial fishing vessel named *Florence Nightingale IV* that belonged to *South Seas Spearo* team member Nat Davey, a world-class spearo who loves nothing better than putting pins into massive fish. Alongside Nat for this massive undertaking was his wife Rochele, an equally accomplished spearfisher with many New Zealand and world records to her name, Tim Barnett, whose gassy exploits I elaborated on earlier, underwater camera op and qualified marine biologist Sam Wild, and a salty sea dog by the name of Bill, who we were relying on to do the bulk of the skipper's duties while Nat was in the drink chasing trophy fish.

The crew would share driving and diving duties over the course of the trip, so we needed a good contingent given that the steam out would take us 40 long hours, with every team member expected to take their turn at the helm for a 90-minute overnight stint, as once we pushed off from Mangōnui wharf, we wouldn't be stopping till we reached our destination. For me, that 90-minute stint meant alternating between driving and vomiting out the port-side window, which is poor form really — green is supposed to designate the starboard side of a boat.

The nausea wasn't limited to just me, though, as even commercial diver Tim, who's far more at home at sea than I am, struggled to keep his dinner down on the steam out. I think this was due mainly to the nature of the *Florence*. Commercial boats like her are designed to perform when their holds are laden down with many tonnes of ice and fish, so the stripped-back *Florence* bobbed around like a toy boat in a bath en route to the Banks.

But, eventually, we made it.

With the dawn light strengthening, the level of fizz was sky high.

We'd been waiting in line for two days and here we were, at the gates of Disneyland, with a full-day pass to go on all the wild rides we've heard about from those who'd gone before.

At the risk of stretching the metaphor, the next twelve hours were an absolute rollercoaster of emotion. We began the day by dragging lures to try to work out where the fish were holding, and while we did have a couple of strikes early on, the marlin seemed to be spread far and wide.

There's absolutely no point floating around the big blue hoping for the fish to simply show up; what we really needed to run across before suiting up was a concentration of marlin, preferably working a bait ball on the surface.

By 3 p.m., things were looking grim. No bait balls, no birds, nothing to get our hopes up.

As Sam sunbathed on the bow, I retreated to the rear of the boat, sulking under a dark cloud of frustration. I flashed back to experiencing the same emotions during filming for the pilot episode of *The Red Stag Timber Hunters Club*, immediately after giving my notice on *The ITM Fishing Show*. In fact, my mental state was so similar that it's worth providing a cut and paste of that moment from the first book:

> *I remember at one stage during an arduous climb back up to base camp on the final night, having once again fallen well behind, thinking to myself, 'What the hell am I doing? I could be sitting on the back of a boat with a beer in hand waiting on a marlin to appear in the lure spread! Instead, I'm cold, hungry, knackered and sleeping in a tent tonight.'*

The very same questions were running through my head. What the hell were we doing coming all this way and pinning so much on something as inherently fickle as game fishing? With the amount of fuel we were burning, I may as well have been tossing 20-dollar notes over the side of the boat, depositing my money in the Bank of Wanganella. At least with hunting you had some kind of control over the situation, but this fishing caper seemed to be pure luck . . .

Birds! Birds up ahead!

The rollercoaster began its upwards trajectory.

Ahead of us, a bunch of birds were circling, while on the surface below we could see the odd splash of white, but rather than the target species, it was just dolphins, teasing us with their playful antics.

Still, it woke us all up and shook me out of my lethargic state. We were back in the game, and sure enough, it wasn't long before we spied what we'd laboured two full days to find — a work-up of marlin, feeding on a ball of bait right on the surface.

Now, I've filmed some crazy stuff over my time making TV, but nothing quite as chaotic as this next five minutes; it was pure pandemonium. We were all frantically yelling about the marlin we were seeing, pointing this way and that, screaming at each other to get into the drink.

Throwing additional fuel on the fire was the presence of Timmy, whose infectious enthusiasm is enough to raise your spirits at the worst of times, so you can imagine what a firecracker he was with a bunch of lit-up marlin busting up all around us!

Within 30 seconds of spying the marlin around the boat, Sam and Nat had dropped over the transom in hot pursuit. Rather than the traditional speargun set-up, Nat was targeting a fish with a pole spear, hoping to land a world-record stripey. Pole spears certainly up the degree of difficulty; to pull off an effective holding shot you need to be much closer to the fish than you would when using a high-powered speargun. But luckily for Nat, just as the prop wash behind the boat cleared, one of the marlin that was busy feeding on the bait ball broke off and angled directly towards him, presenting a perfect side-on profile, and Nat didn't waste the opportunity.

The spear punched through the side of the large fish, and the marlin powered away with Nat hanging on for the ride. Back aboard the boat, we were doing our best to steer clear of the chaos in the water, trying to prevent getting tangled with any float lines, but we needed to stay close enough for me to capture the unfolding mayhem on camera. While Nat focused on trying to get the big fish under control, between breaths underwater cameraman Sam tried valiantly to commentate on what was happening in the water.

He had to swim hard to keep up with Nat and the rampaging fish, and the bulky underwater camera didn't help his cause either, but his years as a competitive swimmer helped him keep within range. Given the fish Nat was connected to was in all likelihood a potential world record, Sam had to be particularly careful that he didn't touch anything that was connected to either Nat or the marlin, including the trailing float lines, or else it would immediately disqualify the fish.

Once things settled down a touch, Tim tossed another pole spear into the drink, to allow Nat to put a second shot into the marlin, as it appeared that his first shot hadn't punched all the way through, only just holding within the flank of the fish.

For the next ten minutes, the fight was delicately poised. While he was being towed, Nat had to work his way gently towards the marlin, reducing the gap enough to allow him to make a second shot. However, Nat's a big unit, well over 100 kg, so had to be careful not to apply too much pressure or he risked the slip tip pulling free. The longer these fights go on, the more risk there is of this occurring, so he couldn't afford to simply wait for the fish to exhaust itself like a big-game fisherman would.

But Nat's a pro. He has landed dozens of big tuna and marlin over his years of spearfishing, and he managed to pull off an effective second shot without any complications.

The shot gave the tiring marlin a new lease of life, though, and it lit up

Nat wrestles with a world record.

once again, making another powerful charge, dragging Nat along. This time, the exhausted Sam was left behind in their wake, so we quickly hauled him up onto the transom of the *Florence* and raced ahead to try to drop him into a position where he could capture the final stages of the fight on camera.

By the time Sam caught up, Nat was right at the pointy end of things, wrestling the marlin beneath the surface and trying to grab a hold of its bill which, in Nat's own words, is the most critical point in the battle: 'When I've got it by the bill, it's game over for the fish, because I'm not letting it go. Once you've got it, you've fought hard to get to that stage. It's grabbing hold of the bill that is the dodgy bit because it's thrashing around. At the end of the day, we're just fighting for a feed; he's fighting for his life.'

The footage of Nat doing battle with the big marlin is without a doubt some of the most gripping vision we've ever captured on the show, with its vivid colours flashing and its tail whipping the water white. Somehow, Nat and Sam manage to avoid the tangle of ropes and floats on the surface and, eventually, Nat was able to deliver the *coup de grâce* with his dive knife, and the celebrations could then start in earnest.

But that was only half the story. Once we'd all calmed down and had the fish on the boat, it was Rochele's turn to try to break another record. Despite the earlier chaos, the marlin were still intently working the bait ball, so she had a terrific opportunity to double the team's tally.

Dropping over the side, she and Sam swam carefully towards the work-up, as multiple marlin cruised nearby. Unlike Nat's situation, where he only needed to surpass 40 kg to take the record, meaning any fish would likely do the job, Rochele needed a fish over 100 kg, so she needed to seek out one of the largest in the pack.

There were certainly a few options. Most of the fish circling the bait ball looked to be in the 100 kg-plus bracket, but one fish stood out, peeling away from the bait and swinging in close to Rochele, who lined up on it and let rip.

A miss!

Normally, a missed shot on a potential world-record fish would be the absolute worst-case scenario on the show, especially since it now required Rochele to return to the boat to reload her specialised high-powered speargun. But in this instance, it provided us with the most silver of silver linings.

With Sam freed from his main role of capturing any *Spearo*-related action, he was free to get right in among the bait ball, and now untethered from a diver, over the next five minutes he captured some truly jaw-dropping footage of marlin crashing through the bait. Sam was in heaven, and the noises coming out of the man were borderline pornographic!

But being totally immersed in the swirling mass, he got a hell of a wake-up call when one particularly boisterous marlin breached through the bait school and came crashing down just inches from him, bill first. Looking back at the footage, he was very lucky not to be skewered by the big fish, which would have been disastrous way the hell out here at the Wanganellas.

After a few minutes, Rochele had reloaded her gun and had slipped quietly back into the drink, but Sam was unaware, still totally mesmerised by the marlin meatball, so it came as quite a surprise to him when she suddenly materialised on the opposite side of the bait. Literally a second after entering frame, she squeezed off on one of the fish that Sam had been filming, and this time the shot found its target, with the fish powering off and leaving a trail of blood in its wake.

I mentioned earlier that Nat's a big fella, and that he had to be careful not to apply too much pressure to his shot marlin. Well, that wasn't the case now — Rochele's only half the size of Nat, and the fish she was connected to was substantially bigger than his, so the size differential meant that she had to do all she could to try to slow the fish's powerful run.

A second gun was soon called for to allow Rochele to better secure the fish. Nat entered the fray to assist as best he could, aiming to swim the gun over to her. However, Nat and Sam found themselves battling to keep up, as Rochele was being towed behind the strong-swimming fish at a rate of knots, so a new approach was needed.

Rather than the time-consuming task of hauling both lads back aboard, which would require them to remove their fins, we decided to simply tow them behind the boat with ropes. Tim joked to me that I should keep rolling on Nat and Sam as we dragged them along like human livebaits, but behind

Multiple lit-up marlin working
a tightly packed bait ball — the
stuff dreams are made of!

the humour, there was some genuine risk in this tactic.

By now, the shot marlin had been putting out distress signals for close to half an hour and pumping a lot of blood into the water. The Wanganellas are known to be home to large numbers of big mako and great white sharks, who rise from the depths to feed around dusk, so while we were having a laugh at the lads' expense as we dragged them along the surface, it was a little unnerving to film.

Thankfully, we had no strikes on either 'lure', and managed to get Sam and Nat back up alongside Rochele, and soon, they were able to swim the second gun across to her.

For a world record to stand, Rochele had to load the gun herself, but by this stage of the fight, her arm muscles were cramping and nearly exhausted, and it took her a few attempts before she was able to stretch the powerful rubbers all the way back. Likewise, on her first attempt to squeeze off a second shot, she discovered that her hand didn't even have the strength to pull the trigger, thanks to it having been cinched in the shooting line for so long.

After taking the time to stretch out her fingers and forearm on the surface, she dropped down for a second attempt to close out the fight, and this time, she managed to get an effective shot away. Much like Rochele, by this stage of the battle, the marlin was also pretty worn out, and unlike Nat's fish which really came to life once he grabbed a hold of it, from here on out it gave her little trouble, and she was able to shut it down with her dive knife without too much drama.

What a turn of events: we'd gone from zero to hero in no time at all. When the rub of the green isn't going our way on shoots, I often thought

Nat and Rochele's two prized fish, and
one seriously satisfied Sammy.

back to this two-hour period to give me hope, as it's a great example of how your luck can change in the blink of an eye.

After getting the fish aboard, it was now Tim's turn to try to add another to the team's tally, but unfortunately, a miscommunication in manoeuvring the boat meant that we scattered the bait ball, and while Tim did have a couple of half chances, he wasn't able to get a shot away before the final buzzer blew, as the light was now at the point where underwater filming became problematic.

Once back aboard the boat, an updated weather forecast meant a decision needed to be made. We had planned on having another half day up our sleeve to get some more action the following morning, but a fast-moving front was approaching from the west, which meant that staying out for another night risked us getting caught out in some nasty conditions for our long run back to the mainland. Nat explained that he'd been in a similar situation a few years before when fishing commercially in the area, and having chosen to stay out, the onerous 38-hour run had become an arduous 90-hour ordeal — youch!

The only voice of dissent about an early withdrawal from the banks was from Tim, who had yet to pin a fish, but I think even he knew it was the right call. The Wanganellas is certainly no place to go rolling the dice with weather, and with a couple of potential world records aboard, we had to be happy with how things had played out.

A couple of days later, as we finally tied up back in Mangōnui, I was close to kissing the dock, I was just that over being on the boat. But the job wasn't over — we still needed to go through the complicated process of weighing and measuring both fish. As expected, they blew the previous world records out of the water, which was a relief, as given how washed out I was feeling at that stage in the trip, I made a vow to never ever do another Wanganellas mission again.

A couple of days later, once I'd recovered my composure, I had my first decent look at some of the underwater footage that Sam had captured. It was mind-bogglingly good. So good in fact, that it immediately erased the memory of my earlier vow, and we began planning a return mission.

At the risk of potentially alienating half the audience, there's an analogy to be made here about giving birth: putting yourself through an incredibly painful and traumatic experience that's quickly forgotten once you witness the fruits of your efforts. Plus, it's often a lot of fun planning the trip with enthusiastic team members nine months out.

Unfortunately, since that first episode, we've yet to return to the Wangies. A mission we had lined up needed to be canned due to poor weather, but we have an even more monumental trip planned in just a few months' time. By the time this book hits shelves, we'll likely be at sea on the way to Minerva Reef, twice as far at the Wanganella Banks, but rather than the commercial boat the *Florence*, the plan is to do it in a little more comfort this time around!

Sammy's two cents

The Wanganella Banks. What. A. Place! What. A. FISH! We have been fortunate enough to see some incredible things and visit some amazing places, but that first trip for *South Seas Spearo* is one that has not been topped in my eyes. It was my second trip to the Banks, but it was my first trip targeting the marlin that make those waters famous, and I had no idea what to expect. The initial expected excitement after seeing those first couple of fish early added weight to how down we were feeling as the day dragged on with no action. However, that in turn *really* cranked up the excitement when the fish finally did show face!

For me, I was fast asleep on the floor in my gear after being bashed around for hours and staring at the horizon with hopes dwindling by the hour and the slow realisation that we may have one of those days that result in nothing (which we all know is a part of what we do, even in a place like the Wanganellas). The excitement started in my dream and carried through to waking up to the deck yelling and running around and Nat seconds away from jumping in. Mask up, camera in hand, fins on and BANG — over the side and looking for Nat through the bubbles, but it was the feeling when I first laid eyes on the marlin that I won't forget. In the rushed madness I wasn't even processing what we were doing until I was looking at this amazing fish and watching Nat do what we had gone there to do.

One of the most incredible things I have seen in my life came an hour or so later when Rochele missed her first shot on a fish and I was left with nothing but the tightly packed bait ball, the big blue and a dozen hungry marlin. If I could bottle that feeling and put it in a pill, I would make millions! The fear, excitement and adrenalin were one hell of a cocktail.

Being in the water with something that makes you feel so small is pretty awe-inspiring, and having dozens and dozens of marlin milling around at all different depths and taking turns to light up and feed as if you weren't there was beyond anything I could have ever dreamed! Now, my biggest dream is to get in the water with those fish again for a day or two, not just the fifteen minutes I was lucky enough to get. *South Seas Spearo* Season 4? All fingers crossed!

6 FRENCH CONNECTIONS

With a pilot episode under my belt, it was time to see what the international appetite was like for spearfishing, and there's no better place to test the water than at the annual MIPCOM event in Cannes, France. This four-day convention draws well over 10,000 attendees from all corners of the world, with buyers and sellers mingling and doing deals at the world-famous Palais des Festivals, situated right on the Cannes beachfront. My aim in attending was to try to gauge the interest of potential international distributors about a spearfishing-based series, and to help refine the future vision for the show.

It was also a chance to rub shoulders with a few heavy hitters in the global TV game. Being an MIP virgin, I'd arranged to crash at a rather ritzy house on the hill along with a few Kiwi TV industry stalwarts who'd all been before, including the prodigious Bailey Mackey, *Once Were Warriors* author Alan Duff, and actor/producer Julian 'Sonny' Arahanga. At one stage, there was even talk that Cliff and Taika might possibly be staying with us. I later found out that the year prior, a similar crew had been joined at MIPCOM by Clarke Gayford, who was there on behalf of his show *Fish of the Day*, and that for this iteration of the event, I had inherited his title of 'token Pākehā', a mantle I wore with pride.

It was a surreal few days in France. There was no time to deal with jet lag, as once I dotted down in Cannes, Bailey insisted we needed to get straight into our work — so we headed out for a boozy dinner on the waterfront. In attendance was Dame Julie Christie DNZM, my former boss at Touchdown TV who gave me my first real start in the industry, TVNZ Commissioner Kathryn Graham, and All Black hardman Liam Messam, a good mate of Bailey who at the time was playing professional footy in the south of France. As I recall, I ended the night in the wee hours at the dining table back at our pad discussing New Zealand gang hierarchies over red wine with Alan Duff. It was certainly an eclectic mix of Kiwis!

A few hours later, I was tagging along with Bailey and Sonny to a couple of the meetings they had scheduled with broadcasters and producers, to try to pick up a few pitching tips from the pros. The main takeaway for me was to leverage the Kiwi factor as much as possible, as Europeans seem to love anything to do with New Zealand and New Zealanders.

The author, schmoozing with industry folk in the South of France.

The other lesson I learned was that it's not the scheduled meetings at the Palais that count the most, it's the chance encounters at the plush hotel bars along the esplanade in the wee hours, usually over expensive whisky, that often lead to the most productive talks.

In hindsight, most of the connections I made over that time didn't amount to anything, but despite a distinct lack of sleep it was an eye-opening experience, especially watching Bailey absolutely owning the room during meetings with foreign producers. And while I came away from those few days feeling invigorated to make the best possible series I could, I also better understood my own weaknesses — I'm definitely no salesman, preferring to let the footage do the talking for me. But, hey, if a picture tells a thousand words, then I'm rattling off 25,000 words a second, surely that's sufficient?

7 MANAWATĀWHI

After returning from my brief French sojourn, we cracked straight back into production.

The next shoot for *South Seas Spearo* was a return mission to Manawatāwhi, the Three Kings Island group, located 55 km off the tip of North Cape.

Once again, the Kings fired for us, but it was certainly not without incident.

Compared to most shows, we produce ours on a shoestring budget. So, to try to get the best bang for buck on this major mission, we also intended to film an episode of *Pure Fly NZ*, a fly-fishing series that I had a hand in getting off the ground. We had three different Stabicraft boats lined up for the trip, and I'd arranged for an old mate of mine to do the camera work aboard the designated *Pure Fly NZ* vessel. He'd just returned from a stint filming a series aboard salmon boats in Alaska so had the maritime pedigree for the job, but it seems he must have left his sea legs behind for this trip.

After a sloppy steam out to the Kings, the poor bugger was in no state to film, losing his lunch over the side multiple times, before collapsing in a nauseous mess on a squab at the front of the boat.

Meanwhile, we were getting stuck into the early stages of filming. Things were going 'swimmingly', but then a call came over the VHF from Brendon, the skipper aboard the fly-fishing boat: 'Hey Dave, old mate's not looking too flash. He's asked if we can run him back to the mainland, over . . .'

My answer was a straightforward 'Nope'. Returning all the way to the beach at Tapotupotu would be a major headache, requiring the boat to be refuelled and then relaunched, and would pretty much rule out any chance of getting a *Pure Fly* episode filmed. It was also a big risk, without any support vessel around, because if they got into trouble in the swell, things could get deadly.

Instead, Nat suggested that the fly-fishers drop our old mate off on his commercial boat that was working in the area nearby. Over the course of the afternoon, we were fed regular updates as to how he was getting on in his battle with the green monster, which involved taking some heavy-duty anti-nausea medication, including one administered 'via the stern' shall we say.

His extreme seasickness certainly put me in a bit of a quandary.

Being down a cameraman, I was now required to bounce between three boats to film two different shows. Luckily, the fly-fishermen were able to capture the basics needed on phone, DSLR and GoPro, and the 'bite' didn't really come on until I joined them late in the day, just after the spearo team had called it quits due to low light.

All three crews overnighted aboard the commercial boat, sleeping rough on the deck, and made an early start the next morning, aiming to nail a few more sequences to ensure we had plenty of material with which to build a couple of solid episodes. Old mate was still a write off, so I had another big day ahead of me.

But despite the pressure, there's always time for a cheeky in-joke, although this one was perhaps a little borderline. Being full-time commercial divers, Tim and Dwane know what an inconvenience it is to need to evacuate your bowels when fully suited and booted, so before donning the neoprene for the day, they needed to fulfil their regular morning routines.

While doing just that, with both hanging off the swim steps at the back of the boat, I decided to get a little update from each of them on the weather situation and sea conditions. Both provided succinct answers, maintaining eye contact with the camera lens, and as a result I'm fairly certain that we are the only series in the history of New Zealand television that's had two presenters delivering piece to cameras right down the barrel, while pinching off a loaf.

After a solid day of diving, where Dwane and Nat both managed to bag themselves 40 kg-plus kingfish, we finally made it back to the mainland a little before dusk. Old mate's face when he finally touched dry land again looked a bit like mine following our return from the Wanganellas, and as expected, once off the water he quickly rebounded to full health.

What wasn't expected, though, was that despite all the obstacles, the

Nat's big kingi nears the surface

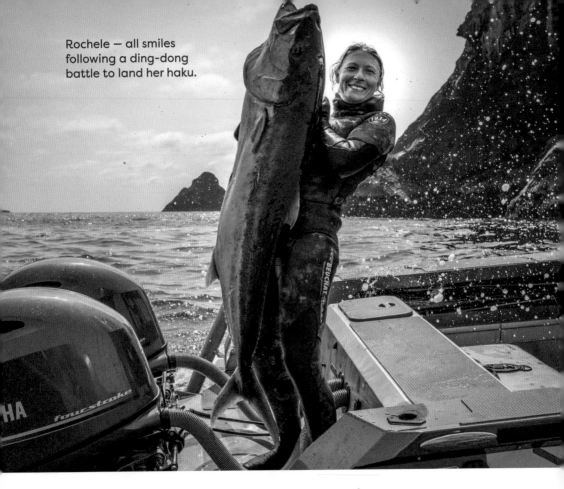

Rochele — all smiles following a ding-dong battle to land her haku.

team and I had managed to capture enough material to create a pretty sharp episode of *Pure Fly NZ*, as well as not one but two bloody entertaining *South Seas Spearo* shows — now that's good bang for buck!

At that early stage of the production, getting bang for buck was crucial. We have quite a few budgetary constraints on the show, but most of these are actually self-imposed. In the show's infancy, we didn't want to follow the well-trodden path of most other outdoor shows by taking on a dozen sponsors which we'd need to shoehorn into each episode.

The feedback I had from Cannes was that if I wanted the show to sell internationally, we had to minimise the amount of overt branding within it. So, we made the decision early on to try to scale back the in-your-face sponsorship elements, and simply allow product placement where and when it naturally occurred, purchasing a number of products (at a sharp discount it must be said) rather than accepting them as freebies — as they say, there's no such thing as a free lunch. Exclusivity with certain partners has worked well on *The Red Stag Timber Hunters Club*, but this approach would hopefully result in more lucrative overseas sales.

That being said, the pandemic curtailed those plans somewhat, preventing us from being able to put much time and effort into our international sales, so in recent seasons we have taken on a few more partners, in order to keep the wolf from the door.

8 PORT FAIRY TALES

With the purse strings tight, we also decided to produce just six episodes for the first season: the Wanganellas marlin episode, a dogtooth tuna mission to Tonga (which was discussed in the previous book), chasing boarfish and snapper in the Coromandel, and a brace of shows from our trip to the Kings, so there was only one more episode needed to complete the season. For that ep we decided to venture across the ditch to the historic seaside town of Port Fairy, Victoria, to try our luck in spearing a highly sought-after southern bluefin tuna.

While a few bluefin tuna were starting to be caught in New Zealand waters, there hadn't been one shot by a spearo in local waters for over 45 years, but that's not through lack of trying. Dwane had set aside a couple of days each year for the past seven years to try to finally pin one of these elusive trophies, but without any success.

However, in Port Fairy, the southerns had been showing up regularly for a decade or so, with some absolute barrels regularly caught on rod and reel, and a few nice fish getting shot by spearos every year, so we had high hopes.

The team for the trip would be Dwane, Jools, Kieran, Sam and myself, as well as a couple of mates from Garmin Australia, but what's most notable was who wouldn't be joining us.

This would be the first *South Seas Spearo* shoot without Tim Barnett front and centre. Up until that point, Tim had been heavily involved in every episode and was responsible for the bulk of the presenting duties, so it would be interesting to see how the remaining lads would step up and fill his rather hefty boots.

The other variable was the weather. Overseas filming has an inherent lack of flexibility. Normally, we make a call a week out from any shoot about the weather, sea conditions, visibility, fish numbers and the like to determine if we pull trigger on the trip or not. In this instance, the flights and logistics were all booked and paid for, so we were going no matter the conditions.

Standing on the rocky shoreline at Port Fairy on the first evening, staring out at the pumping waves and rollers crashing 100 metres offshore, I wondered if perhaps we should have scrapped the whole shebang, but the enthusiasm among the lads was infectious.

And we still had an ace up our sleeve, our man on the ground in Port

Fairy — Pete Riddell, an experienced spearo with his finger on the pulse.

Thankfully, the 2-metre swell died down overnight, so our first morning on the so-called 'shipwreck coast' was a lot nicer than forecast. The visibility certainly wasn't ideal, but we were confident that if we found the fish, we'd make it count.

Once out wide, we soon located birds working in the distance, and the drone confirmed the presence of small bluefin tuna picking off baitfish on the surface beneath them. However, by the time the lads were suited up and ready to roll, the fish had sunk away out of sight.

That process continued for the next few hours — finding birds on the radar, racing over in the boat, and tossing a handful of pilchards over the side while the divers eased themselves gently into the water without making a splash. Then it was just a case of keeping the gun pointed at a sinking pilchard and hoping a tuna would swing in and snaffle it, providing enough time to pull the trigger and connect with the zippy little buggers.

A few fish were seen underwater, but it was certainly a frustrating process. Over three hours, the fellas made a couple dozen drops, but each time came up empty handed.

But the team's patience and discipline paid off, as Kieran finally connected with a fish, pulling off a great snapshot in the pea-green soup.

Kieran's fish opened the floodgates, with three more fish shot in quick succession, one each to Jools, Sam and Dwane. On the steam back into Port Fairy, we were all feeling damn chuffed with ourselves, as it really took the pressure off with two more days of diving ahead.

The next morning, though, conditions had returned to the volatile state from earlier in the trip, with a 20-knot onshore breeze. So, rather than busting a gut chasing tuna out wide in the slop, we decided to take the opportunity to explore the shallows with pole spears and 'prangers'. The main target of this undertaking was the tasty King George whiting, and after a few misses and close calls, the fellas managed to bag enough for a decent feed, and it played out as a solid sequence in the episode.

However, ending the episode with a dozen whiting being speared in 5 metres of water isn't exactly what I had in mind with this mission, so we were pinning our hopes on being able to get back out the following day to end the trip with a bang.

Morning rolled around, and we eagerly made our way down to the beach once more to see what the weather had in store for us. But before the light had even got up, we knew we were screwed. The wind hadn't let up from the previous day, it was still blowing hard from the south, and the seas were now looking even less inviting.

It was a kick in the guts. We clambered back aboard our 'soccer mum' rental van and tossed about a few ideas on what we could do to salvage the day. Perhaps another shore dive, or maybe we could drive a few hours up the coast to see if conditions were better elsewhere? None of the options

The second fish of the day welcomed aboard.

sounded all that exciting, but as we debated to determine the best of a bad bunch, Dwane stepped up and made a bold call.

'Little bit of wind out there, little bit of chop, but we've all picked up our balls and decided it's time to get out there and stop pussyfooting around and get it done . . .'

Thus began the epic final sequence for the episode.

To get a better idea of the sea state, Sam and I joined the Garmin lads in their much bigger boat on a quick recce out past the bar to see what we'd be getting ourselves into, and straight away we took a large wave right over the bow, momentarily turning us into a submarine, soaking everyone aboard. Returning to the ramp, we made the call that we'd be better off basing ourselves in the little boat, to stay fast and nimble. It would be wet, that's for sure, but we'd hopefully be able to keep the main camera dry until it was needed, filming primarily on GoPro and underwater camera.

With five guys jammed into a small open-top boat, we set off, punching our way into the heavy seas, but despite my best efforts to remain dry,

I was soon soaked to the bone. It was going to be a battle to keep the camera alive over the course of the day, as salt water is absolute poison to electronic equipment.

We didn't need to travel far, though, before catching sight of birds, and once again, they were accompanied by large packs of small southern bluefin. The morning followed the same script as two days earlier: the lads spotting work-ups and then dropping over the side, only to find they were too late and that the fish had moved on. After a half-dozen attempts, however, Julian was presented with an opportunity.

Tracking a shiny pilchard as it sank down in the green gloom, a flash of colour indicated a tuna close by, so he let his spear fly, and it connected with the fish, which immediately raced off, tearing line from his reel gun.

Back aboard the boat, despite the strong wind, we clearly heard Jools' call of 'Fish on!', and a massive cheer went up. We didn't care if it was big or small; we had our fish! But less than ten seconds later, the bubble was burst. The fish had pulled off. Talk about going from hero to zero. Jools was lambasted by all those aboard, but to be fair, considering the conditions and the visibility, he'd done bloody well to even hit the thing in the first place.

Following the close call, we continued our hunt with renewed vigour, encouraged by the number of fish now being seen, but every chance we had on a fish ended up in failure.

Kieran's gun went off early when a tuna was close by, and while reloading, he managed to snap the wishbone. On his next attempt, as he was lining up on a nice-sized fish, he noticed that his slip tip had fallen off his spear, ruining a plum opportunity. Every time we dropped the fellas into the drink on the starboard side, the fish would reappear on the port side; it was driving us bonkers!

Somewhere around the third or fourth hour of being bounced violently about the angry ocean, a song lyric crept its way into my head. I'm not sure how or why, maybe someone had suggested that perhaps we 'turn around', and that was enough to sow the seed.

Whatever it was, with sea-madness now having set in, Dwane and I inexplicably found ourselves belting out a heartfelt rendition of the timeless classic *Total Eclipse of the Heart*: 'Every now and then I fall apart!'

We battled on into the wind, blasted by the saltwater spray, our eyes scanning the skies for birds and the surrounding sea for any sign of tuna . . .

We needed tuna tonight. We needed tuna more than ever.

Kieran spied a few fish breaking the surface close by, so Dwane swung the boat in for a closer look.

Dwane killed the motor, and Kieran moved to drop over the side, but a rogue wave hit and he fell backwards into the cockpit with a heavy thump.

It was madness, and getting a pin into a fish was starting to look futile. Kieran decided enough was enough, and that he'd call it quits for the day, passing the torch to Dwane for the final hour.

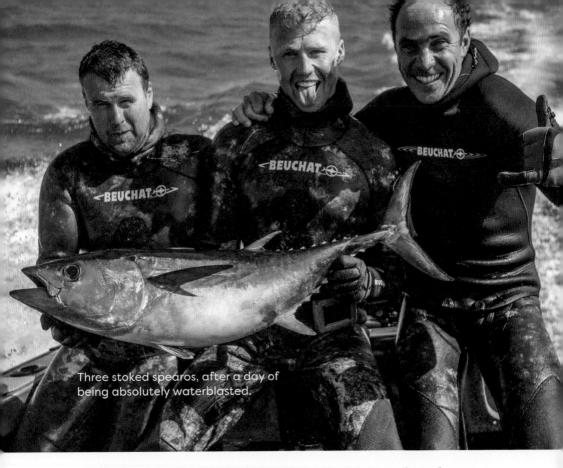

Three stoked spearos, after a day of being absolutely waterblasted.

By now, I'd given up on the impossible task of trying to keep the camera from being caught by spray and splash, and it was taking a beating, but, thankfully, it was still operational.

With a diver of Dwane's quality in the water, though, anything can happen. There's a reason the bloke's won nine national titles; he just seems to have a sixth sense for shooting fish. And after six frustrating hours of being waterblasted, finally, Dwane proved his class.

A tuna came rocketing in, snaffling a pilchard, but Dwane was up to the task, pulling off a shot from the hip like an underwater gunslinger. But the speed at which it all happened meant that old Quickdraw McGraw wasn't quite too sure on the holding strength of the shot.

JOOLS: Where did you hit it?
DWANE: Don't know man, I just shot at something!

Unlike Julian's fish, this time round there was no premature celebration. You could detect a note of exhaustion in our voices, as we were all pretty much spent, but once Dwane had a second shot in the tuna, the relief and elation was palpable. Dwane had a hell of a messy end to the fight, with the tuna tying him up in knots near the surface, but the job was now done.

With this stretch of coast being a notorious hotspot for great white sharks, the combination of 5-metre visibility, a resident seal colony, and fresh tuna blood in the water meant there wasn't any appetite for hanging around taking underwater photos. We needed to get the fish back aboard the boat, get the hell off the water, and get into a few celebratory frothies, but we did have one more task to complete, and that very nearly ended in disaster as well.

I wanted to capture a couple of topside photos of the hard-earned tuna and was keen to get a shot that showcased the rough-as-guts conditions we put ourselves through to get it. It's a hard task making seas look as angry as they feel, so I asked Kieran to chuck the boat into reverse and back into an oncoming wave in order to get a decent amount of sea spray and wash in the photo, to give it a more dynamic look that was reflective of the conditions we'd been battling.

Kieran started reversing, but I couldn't quite get the timing of the photos right, continually missing the key moment, so I encouraged him to just keep at it. He seemed reluctant, but duly kept backing into the oncoming waves at my command. It wasn't until a real beauty hit the back of the boat that we cottoned on to exactly how much water we'd taken on. Another decent wave would put us in danger of going under, so we immediately scrapped the photo session and punched our way back for the safety of dry land. We'd had more than enough drama for one day!

But the stories from this memorable mission weren't limited to our activities on the water. Unbeknown to us when planning the shoot, the annual Port Fairy Folk Festival would be taking place over the time that we were there, a four-day music event that draws many thousands to the small seaside town. This ensured there was no shortages of revellers out and about to help us celebrate our hard-fought victory, and celebrate we did.

I'm reluctant to go into too many details about the level of tomfoolery that evening, so let's just say the fellas had plenty of hilarious tales to recount on the long drive back to Melbourne the next day, including Sammy Wild receiving his marching orders after a minor scuffle with a local lout that Julian had thrown a beer at, VB Longnecks at quarter to eight at the Cowdownie, a memorabilia heist gone wrong, and a dislocated shoulder for me after being tackled by 'Dwangerous' Dwane Herbert.

We're mapping out a return to Aussie in the coming years, with Tasmania the likely next destination, so you can expect some more 'devilish' behaviour off the back of that trip!

Dwane's two cents

Kieran and I had previously visited Port Fairy for the Australian spearfishing champs about a year earlier and had been accommodated by a local legend, Pete, who also took us out for an arvo chasing bluefin.

On that trip, the conditions were near on perfect, 5 to 8 knots variable and cleanish 10- to 15-metre vis. Oh, and big schools of tuna milling around on the surface, so it's understandable that we were fizzing for a return mission.

However, when we arrived to film our episode a year later, I was definitely a little disappointed in seeing the dirty water and sloppy sea conditions. It was certainly going to be quite a challenge to get any tuna on the deck.

Pete also informed us that tuna in dirty water are a lot more cagey than normal, and will not want a bar of any diver they see. This would mean we'd be targeting fast-swimming shadows darting in and out of visibility, creating quite a few headaches when it comes to trying to film underwater action to produce a viable sequence for the show.

But persistence paid off, and we came away with a great story and had an absolute blast while doing it, especially considering how new to the whole filming gig we were.

The antics Dave mentioned at the end are a part of what makes us enjoy each other's company when we get together to make these episodes exciting, as you always arrive expecting to leave with another story that'll be told for years to come.

Happy divers celebrating a few hard-fought fish.

After a busy winter spent in the editing room, both Season 6 of *The Red Stag Timber Hunters Club* and Season 1 of *South Seas Spearo* began airing in the spring, but on different channels. This made promotion on social media a slightly tricky task. Facebook and Instagram are important tools to help grow the reach of a show, but I see them as necessary evils. It's a time-consuming part of the business on which I'm certainly no expert, and to use both effectively requires constant attention. The fact we had our accounts hacked and spammed repeatedly over this period also tainted my appetite for managing our social media promotion.

I preferred instead to focus on the real meat of the business, the broadcast episodes, and thankfully the debut series of *South Seas Spearo* was very well received. On the day after my fortieth birthday, I received an email from TVNZ giving us the green light to produce a second season. It was a validation that the show was as good as we all thought it was, and the fellas had no shortage of grand ideas of the adventures we should embark upon for the follow-up season.

However, it soon became obvious that our aspirations to film throughout the South Pacific and even further afield would need to be put on ice for the time being, as pandemic restrictions began to take hold and New Zealand's borders were slammed shut.

Meanwhile, off the back of continued steady ratings on Prime, we had also been given the go-ahead for another season of *The Red Stag Timber Hunters Club*.

PART THREE
PAY DIRT

Dre surveys the Central
Otago high country in
the morning light.

9 HIGH-COUNTRY COOKING LESSONS

The first hunt of the year saw Yuley and Andre heading into some stunning Central Otago tussock country in early February, in search of trophy red stags. We hoped that by this time in late summer, the stags would have stripped their velvet and hopefully be mobbed up in large groups living in the higher-altitude tussock country. Stags tend to do this before splitting up and dropping down into the lower catchments when the days shorten in the lead-up to the roar.

But at this time of year, the days were still long, and they were baking hot. To minimise the physical duress, we decided to make our way in under head torch, and after a couple of hours of uphill slog with heavy packs, we dropped our first camp just after midnight.

We managed to sneak in a few hours' kip before the light was strong enough to glass, and soon we were able to make out a few animals on the opposite face, including a couple of decent-looking solitary chamois, both living surprisingly low. One buck must have detected some movement on our side of the hill, possibly a glint of light as we packed up our gear, and bolted off up-valley, but the other seemed quite content with life, bedding down in the morning sun a little over a kilometre from us.

As the sun slowly rose over the next hour, a fair few deer were located as well, but nothing that jumped out as being a potential trophy. As we expected, they were all living very high, so we knew that we'd have a big day of climbing ahead of us to get within the range required to properly assess them. However, before saddling up and making our way uphill, we decided that the chamois buck that hadn't bolted was worthy of a closer look.

But for the very first time in the history of the show, Dre's hill fitness became more of a liability than a strength.

I'd had a relaxing summer up to this point, filming a couple of *SSS* Season 2 episodes, but with my kids now older and more independent, I still found enough time to work on maintaining my base fitness, so the climb wasn't such a shock to the body. The same can be said for Yuley. His kids were of a similar age, and his day job as a builder seemed to keep him lean and mean, hill fit all year round.

But Dre had only recently had his second child, and as any new parent

There's never any shortage of beautiful things to point a camera at when you wake up in the tops.

Yuley's respectable chamois buck, resplendent in his summer coat.

will attest, spare time to work on getting fit was in short supply. That, combined with a less hands-on approach at the CrossFit gym he managed, and more time spent riding a desk, meant he was quite undercooked heading into this mission, so rather than leading the way, he was more often than not bringing up the rear.

After working up a good sweat, we'd soon climbed into a position to lay eyes on the buck, and unlike the last time when Yuley lined up on a cham, there was absolutely no rush to evaluate the animal. Once Yuley was quite sure it wasn't a nanny ('If this chamois is a doe, I'll eat my pack'), he stepped up to the plate and delivered the goods, dropping the buck with a perfectly placed round.

The buck wasn't a world beater and seemed to suffer from a unique phenomenon known by hunters as 'ground shrinkage' — what was pushing 10 inches before the shot rang out had shrunk by close to an inch by the time we arrived, but we were still happy to have tasted success early in the trip.

After filming the requisite material for the show, we took the time to refill our water bladders in a small stream close by, before beginning the steep slog up to camp 2, at 1400 metres elevation, which would take us the best part of three hours.

But slow and steady wins the race, and the long days meant we were certainly in no rush. After a big grunt up into the rocky tops, we eventually located a pristine campsite punctuated with huge schist boulders and slabs, looking a bit like the monoliths of Stonehenge, one of which provided Dre with a nice little rock biv to recoup out of the sun.

We killed time until 7 p.m., doing our best to stay out of the direct sun. Hydration at this time of year is key, especially when you're reliant on freeze-dried food for sustenance which often requires half a litre of water per meal, so we really needed to locate a reliable water source up here in the tops to save us the rigmarole and discomfort of having to conserve water.

Yuley and I had found ourselves in that very position about a year earlier, on a mission that preceded this hunt within the broadcast episode. Off the back of some information from a reliable source, we set out to hunt an entirely new area of Southland that neither of us had ever been into. From the topo maps, it looked like promising country, steep and rocky, but great-looking terrain for all manner of big game to be holed up in.

The slog in was testing to say the least. Naively, I'd loaded up my pack to breaking strain, so with camera and tripod I was pushing 40 kg. After finally arriving on a steep ridgeline on which we planned to base ourselves, we quickly realised that water would be an issue — the streams and creeks up here in the tops were all bone dry, and it would require an arduous descent to get into any accessible water.

Compounding the discomfort, my air mattress split open as I was inflating it on the first evening, meaning a good night's sleep on this rocky terrain was out of the question. I accumulated as much moss and bracken as I could to cobble together a makeshift bed and tried to make the best out of the situation. The upside of being physically shattered from the day's climb was that I was able to nod off without too much trouble.

Throughout the remainder of the hunt, thirst was never far from my mind. It's hard to push aside the craving for water when you know you can't quench it. While it never evolved into the all-encompassing lust for moisture you read about that drives those lost at sea mad, it certainly made life miserable.

There was one moment on that trip, though, that pushed the water situation to the side. From our elevated perch, Yuley spied some movement way, way off in the distance, but the heat haze made identification hard. There was speculation it might have been the paddles of a large fallow buck, and because it was in the direction we planned to hunt, we decided to drop down for a closer look.

Sure enough, once we'd cut the distance to within 1500 metres, it was clear that the antlers belonged to a fallow buck, and what a buck he was. This thing was a damn moose! While we weren't targeting fallow, there was no way we were going to turn down this opportunity, but the prevailing wind and his position on the steep tussock face left us no viable options to get into a shooting position.

Instead, we chose to take shelter from the sun and wait for the winds to shift on evening, hoping the buck wouldn't travel far from his secure bolthole. A few hours later, after I treated myself to a few more sips of my dwindling water supply, we set out to try to relocate the big beast.

Unfortunately, the winds weren't playing ball, so we were forced to bite the bullet and attempt to stalk right down on top of his position from above. An hour later, we found ourselves standing in pretty much the same spot that we'd seen him in earlier that morning, but despite our best efforts to flush him out, making noise and even rolling some large rocks down the face, it seemed he must have wandered off at some point earlier in the day.

Having admitted defeat, I put the little Mavic Air drone up to get some aerial shots to help me better explain the situation within the episode in order to salvage some kind of sequence from the failed hunt.

Three days later, I found myself at Queenstown Airport awaiting a flight home following what had been a disappointing and ultimately unsuccessful trip, but happy to once again have H_2O on tap, when I decided to cast an eye over some of the drone footage from the trip.

It hit me like a sledgehammer. On the 4K screen of my laptop, there he was, the big fallow buck, as plain as day, bedded down among some thick scrub. And there we were, standing maybe 50 metres directly uphill from him! Despite all our efforts, the cunning bugger had the wherewithal to just sit tight and wait us out, so hats off to him. Given the nature of the country in which he was holed up and the lack of hunting pressure the area gets, there's every chance that he's still roaming around up there.

But that was all a year earlier. Back up on the hill with Yuley and Dre, with the sun now having lost its sting, we ventured out for our evening hunt. We were lucky to stumble over a healthy soak not far from camp, providing us the chance to fully rehydrate. It's incredible the difference to your mental state having an abundant supply of water brings, and like a camel in the Sahara, I made the most of the situation by drinking my fill, replacing the fluids lost throughout the afternoon climb.

That was the highlight of the evening, though. We located a mob of

While it was a shame not to claim him with the stick and string, Dre's still pretty satisfied after pulling off a good shot to nail his stag.

young stags, but there was nothing to get excited about among them. Arriving back at camp after dark, we made plans for an early start. As always with summer hunting, mornings seem to roll around way too soon, but at least we were greeted by a beautiful painter's sky, shot through with stunning shades of red and orange.

We didn't stick around to enjoy the serenity, saddling up to head out in search of bigger and better things. It wasn't until early afternoon, though, that we laid eyes on any stags worth pursuing. There was one standout among them, but the heat haze and the fact he had recently stripped velvet hanging from his ample rack made evaluating the calibre of trophy a tricky task.

Our plan alternated at least four times between going after him with bow or rifle, but after deciding the country didn't offer enough cover to make a viable stalk to within 50 metres, the call was made to play it safe and put the bang stick to use. This was one of those times when the extra pressure to deliver an action sequence for the show outweighed the potential prestige of taking an animal on bow, so rather than risk spooking one of the many stags lounging around just 170 metres from us, Dre lined up on his target, and after waiting a good ten minutes for it to present a shot, he squeezed off.

Much like the chamois that had suffered from 'ground shrinkage' earlier in the hunt, by the time we arrived at the stag, we'd gone from being a pretty even 12 points to a rather lopsided 11, with a dried-up piece of velvet tricking us into believing he had more points than he actually possessed.

Our disappointment from the realisation of the true calibre of the trophy was softened by the amazing condition the stag was in: he was fat as mud and had obviously been making the most of his time in the tops.

After finishing the dirty work of breaking the stag down, we began the big haul back to camp, but by the time he'd hauled his heavy load of meat and bone all the way back up the steep tussock face, Dre was completely shot.

To be fair, I wasn't in great shape either, having stupidly experimented with some new insoles in my boots that weren't working too well for me. So, rather than continue with the planned evening hunt, Dre and I decided to just put our feet up for the night. And while Dre and his hard-earned meat set about chilling in the shade of the rocky cave, Yuley headed out solo to see what he could find.

Hours later, he returned into camp with some good news. Right on dark, he'd found a group of three stags, including one absolute thumper. For Yuley to get excited about a stag, we knew it must be an impressive animal, so there was no mucking around the next morning — alarms went off at half four and we were soon punching our way up the steep face in the direction Yuley had spied the big boy eight hours prior.

It didn't take us too long to locate him. He and his offsiders had fed their way slightly lower in the catchment, and in the morning light we all agreed that this was a proper stag, one that we'd all be proud as punch to add to the collection.

From our vantage point, the stags were a bit over 600 metres away, putting them within range for a sharpshooter like Yuley, but beyond *The Red Stag Timber Hunters Club* protocol of 500 metres. We had agreed upon this as a max distance in the early days of the show for a couple of reasons. The first is that it minimises the chance of an outright miss or, much worse, the chance of injuring an animal, and the second is that it just looks a lot better on camera the closer you get.

With an entire day up our sleeves, there was certainly no need to take a rushed shot, so we backtracked and looped around a large rocky outcrop, working our way higher up the hillside in the hope of opening up a view down on top of the stags.

After half an hour, we'd made our way into the spot we had in mind, putting us within 400 metres of where the stags were last seen, but they were now obscured from view. We assumed they'd bedded down for the morning, so followed their lead — withdrawing from the edge of the outcrop to refresh with a cuppa and a quick bite of brekie.

The next twelve hours were a real test of patience. The stags refused to show themselves, so with boredom setting in, we made a couple of incursions around the face to try to lay eyes on them once more, but the steepness of the country and a swirling wind made this a tad risky, so we backed out and returned to playing the waiting game.

The troglodyte emerges from his cave in the pre-dawn light.

I theorised that we'd stumbled across the world's only population of subterranean stags, convinced they must be living in burrows underground, considering the way they were able to seemingly vanish from sight.

By 6 p.m., after taking regular stints on sentry duty from our elevated lookout but with no luck, we decided it was time to move back around the face to open up our original angle. By this stage of the day, we were starting to rue the decision not to have a crack at 600 metres, but we still had plenty of minutes on the clock and were confident we'd relocate the big bopper before dark.

But it wasn't to be. We picked up a few other promising animals, but the big fella had managed to give us the slip. It was bloody frustrating, but that's hunting for you.

After a pow-wow on the long trudge back down to camp, we made the call once more to allow Yuley to go solo and boost all the way back up the hill in the morning for a final crack at him. By this point in the trip, Dre and I were quite footsore and completely washed out, and would have really slowed Yuley down, especially with my need to film and document everything as it happened. Dre and I also needed to conserve our strength to ensure we didn't break down on the long hike back to the truck, a genuine risk with the weight of meat and bone we were now carrying.

In the end, Yuley's morning skirmish proved fruitless, and a little over two hours after setting off, we found ourselves back at the vehicles, a bit disappointed but, on the whole, content with the way the hunt had played out.

Dre's two cents

Over the years of doing the show with the crew, it has become a little more challenging balancing life, work, kids and a business, all while trying to remain an active hunter and outdoorsman.

The peak of this juggling act comes around during the roar and rut periods between late March through to May/June each year. With that in mind, and another year of filming ahead of us, Sam and I had thought that while everyone is getting geared up for stags in the mainstream season, we'd quench our thirst in late summer and put some bone on the deck early, especially with the threat of Covid still lingering in New Zealand at the time. There was an element of uncertainty whether we may potentially have another season foiled due to the dreaded virus.

From late March to May, it's usually some varying degree of organised chaos for the team. Back-to-back hunts at a time when the changing seasons provide highly variable weather conditions to contend with inevitably throws up complex logistical issues. Then there's the constant curse of animals not playing ball; and the fact that the team are stretched across both North and South islands — often all at the same time. I sometimes forget that Davo is the poor bastard caught in the middle of this shit-storm, wielding nothing else other than that battle axe of a camera of his, probably regretting that he ever got involved with this motley crew of hunters and spearos.

So, in my eyes, an early-summer stag hunt was a good way to get some content in the can early to buy ourselves some breathing space on the red stag front ahead of the roar. It also provided an opportunity to dust off some summertime cobwebs to get some much-needed kilometres under the boots, while hedging our bets against Covid spoiling another season.

In most cases leading up to any hunt, I don't often think about the physical component of the mission. I'm usually focused on the planning, execution and sometimes gear for the trip, mostly because I've banked the hard work in the off season and usually maintain an active agenda on and off the hills. In other words, I've never had to worry about my hill fitness or not being in top condition to hit the ground running on a hunt no matter what time of year and no matter what the terrain, species or climate. In fact, I pride myself on having that 'ready for anything' capability. Well, this time round I was chewing on those words the whole trip — especially when teamed up with a guy like Sam, who on a bad day has a clean set of heels on him to rival anyone I've ever graced a mountainside with.

This was pretty much the first time in my memory as a backcountry hunter that I felt beaten by the mountain, and this mission was by no means anywhere as challenging as some of the arduous multi-day trips over the years. A lot was going on in my life in the lead-up to this hunt, and I'm sure a lot of others all around the world were in a similar boat between 2020 and 2022 due to the disruptions of the pandemic. Many are still living with some of those impacts now. The virus affected my professional career overseas, which required an abrupt pivot; among a string of lockdowns, it made trying to operate a domestic business remotely through the pandemic challenging, while also trying to move across country to a new town and fostering a new job. Also, having only just welcomed our youngest daughter into the world all meant there was not a lot of time for hunting or training.

I'm somewhat of an 'all-in' or 'not-at-all' kind of guy. Only twelve months previously, I had just returned from competing at the world CrossFit Games and was in peak condition, and having qualified again for the 2020 season, I had real reason to stay in full training mode, training twice a day, eating right and doing everything to keep my close to 40-year-old carcass in fighting-fit condition almost obsessively. This is my 'all-in' state. However, with the onset of Covid and the ensuing lockdowns basically stopping me in my tracks, and as many international sporting events were either postponed or cancelled, I found myself having no real reason or drive to train aggressively any more (my 'not-at-all' state). Moreover, like every other hunter in New Zealand, I wasn't able to hit the hills other than some fleeting windows where we filmed in between lockdowns.

Covid for my household did have one silver lining — it allowed me to stop the frantic life I was living to really just focus on our newborn child and family. The downside was that fast forward nearly a year later to this summer hunt in early 2021 and I was one very undercooked goose . . .

But there is no better way to find that motivation to get back on the horse by bleeding some serious gravy on a hunt with the lads and have it all recorded on camera to relive into perpetuity to remind you that it takes a level of preparedness to wander in these wild places. I found myself making all manner of excuses not to be in my 'all-in' state during lockdowns and in the months leading up to this hunt, but I was certainly reminded on this trip that the ancient act of the hunt itself is more than enough motivation and reason to stay sharp and mountain ready.

10 VENI, VIDI, VICI

After a physically demanding trip like this, I really enjoy getting stuck straight into the editing process. Sitting in a dark room, with unlimited coffee and snacks, it's a stark contrast to the more frugal lifestyle that's required on the hill. After a week or so of hardcore cutting, I'd massaged the footage into a viewable clip, which as per usual I then sent out to the hunters involved to critique and provide feedback.

It might have been the excess caffeine consumption, but Sam's email back gave me the jitters.

Having had the time to study the footage of the stag that gave us the slip, Sam had decided he wasn't content to simply call it a day. He needed to head back in after him again before the chance was lost, as the stag would no doubt drop down out of the catchment for the roar. His plan was to go after him solo, using a GoPro to document the hunt himself, but I couldn't handle the thought of dealing with substandard headcam footage of such a prize animal, so bit the bullet and made the call to join him in a week's time on a return mission. After informing Dre of Sam's decision, he too agreed to tag along for another crack, and rounding out the team would be one of Sam's hunting mates Brayden, aka Langers.

So, a fortnight later, I once again found myself at the base of the mountain, this time with Sam and Langers, saddling up a heavy pack for another gut-busting climb. However, this time, rather than humping in a heavy load under moonlight, we'd be battling away under a hot sun, but at least we didn't have to each cart in 5 litres of water.

With work commitments delaying his departure, Dre's plan was to fly in later that afternoon, and then walk in under head torch, but as things played out, he left his run to the airport a bit late, and after getting caught up in roadworks he missed his flight. So it would be just the three of us.

Despite the heat, the knowledge of the terrain ahead made the climb more bearable this time around, and the added strength and endurance gained from the previous hunt no doubt helped as well. After a good old-fashioned slog, we pitched camp in the exact same spot next to Stonehenge and set out in search of our old mate.

Sam seemed positive about our chances, but I thought the idea of stumbling over the exact same stag was a bit fanciful. Two weeks had passed since we saw him last, and by now he could be many miles from this catchment, or given this was all readily accessible public land, he may well be adorning another hunter's mantelpiece.

As I explained earlier, we deem anything over 500 metres as too risky for the show, but this undertaking could be deemed far more of a long shot. We'd been confident a week back in our online communications, talking up a big game about how we'd be able to get back in and finish what we'd started, but now that I was out on the hill, the situation seemed more reminiscent of that famous Jim Carrey scene in *Dumb and Dumber*:

What are my chances?
Not good.
You mean, not good like, 1 out of 100?
I'd say more like 1 out of a million.
. . . So you're telling me there's a chance!

But in my mind, just rolling the dice on making a return effort was a strong enough storyline to justify filming, so as we climbed, I set about the task of capturing the footage required to tell the story of our against-the-odds attempt at glory.

We'd only gone half an hour before Sam spotted something that stopped him in his tracks.

Over the years of filming the show, I've become much more aware of the guys' body language on the hill, as verbal cues are often impossible when in proximity to big-game targets. In this instance, up ahead of me I saw Sam and Langers freeze, which said to me that the animals they'd spotted were really close to us.

We sank down slowly into the tussock, trying to hide from sight, and snuck our way towards a large boulder that would provide us with some semblance of camouflage. There was a mob of stags 400 metres from us, and standing proud as punch in the very middle of them was our big bopper from a fortnight back, identifiable thanks to the same 'poxy little bez tine on his right' that Sam had pointed out on the previous mission.

The stags had definitely seen us, though, so we needed to make a decision fast — we could try to get a shot away before they bolted or sit tight and wait for them to go back to eating. Sam felt they were alert but not spooked, so we just slowed things down, waiting for the adrenalin to flush through our systems and for the stags to bed down again.

Finding a shooting rest was the next obstacle, as the steep terrain didn't lend itself to taking a shot from a prone position, so after trying to open up an angle from a number of spots, Sam decided the best plan would be to drop a hundred metres to a flat bench, reducing elevation but not distance. He and I slid our way down the tussock, trying to stay as low as possible,

If you keep rolling the dice, you'll eventually end up with double sixes.

but eager to avoid hitting any Spaniards, a particularly nasty speargrass capable of penetrating through the thickest of canvas. It would have been hard to stifle a scream if either of us took a Spaniard to the backside at the speed we were sliding, but we managed to make it to the flat bench undetected and unpunctured.

The stag had already put on a disappearing act by vanishing into thin air before reappearing two weeks later, so it was apt that one of the last things Sam said to me before lining up on him was: 'Righto Dave, let's make some magic happen, boy.'

Abracadabra. The bullet hit hard, right in the shoulder crease, and hey presto, we'd managed to pull a rabbit out of a hat and had secured the trophy we'd worked so hard for!

Sam was absolutely pumped, and the glint in his eye as he delivered the piece to camera immediately after the shot was pure gold. He can come across as a little aloof at times our man Yuley, but when he lets his guard down in moments like this, his enthusiasm and genuine stoke really does shine through. It was a hell of a moment, and without a doubt one of my favourite memories of the past eight seasons.

The stag was a cracker: a 12-pointer measuring 39 inches long by 37 inches wide, but during the fall after the shot, he'd managed to snap a tine clean off, which we were unable to locate despite a thorough search. But thanks to an abundance of imagery, the taxidermist responsible for the mount was able to recreate it after the fact without much trouble.

With the job now done, rather than spend another couple of days hunting, we decided to make an early exit off the hill the following morning. Having waved goodbye to Sam and Langers in Cromwell, I made my way back to Queenstown with a couple of days up my sleeve, which I intended to use for a bit of R&R before my next southern sojourn.

But if I considered this summer stag mission to be a bit of a long shot, our chance of success for this next undertaking would be like winning the lottery. Pulling it off would require a us to break a 49-year drought, but in the words of Lloyd Christmas — *you're telling me there's a chance . . .*

Yuley's two cents

While the first trip with Dre was an eventful one, the disappointment of not securing the big stag was a tough pill for me to swallow; in fact it would prove to be too tough, so a plan was hatched to head back in for another crack.

Personally, I felt like we had a better than average chance of finding him again, but being public land, a lot can happen in the space of two weeks. I always put a lot of pressure on myself to succeed and make episodes to be proud of, and I knew if we could pull this off it would make for some epic television.

With camp set up we headed off in search of the stag that I had been thinking about for the past fortnight. He wasn't the classic Otago 12, but had good length, even tops and some of the longest brow tines I had ever seen.

As we climbed, I remember thinking that we needed to locate him that night to give us the best chance of success. Even if he was found at a distance, at least we could hatch a plan that night rather than blindly setting off for our morning hunt with the pressure building.

We started our sidle at around 1500 metres, as this would give us a straightforward approach while still offering enough height to remain above any animals encountered along the way.

I must have been guilty of watching my feet and not paying attention to what was ahead of me, because we were being watched. My heart sank. I turned to the boys and signalled to get down, and they hit the deck with military precision. There was a mob of stags not 600 metres away, and the one animal sky lining himself gave up their gender. As we nestled into what limited cover was on offer, we set about getting the spotter dialled in for an assessment.

As our wind was good, I was confident the mob would relax so long as they caught no further movement from our direction. Looking through the spotter, one stag stood out straight away, but I would need him to turn his head for me to assess his antlers. He did this almost instantly and I indicated to the boys it was the stag we were looking for!

With the stags still edgy, I was battling to find a suitable rest, so I made the call to Dave that we would need to slide through the tussock with the hope of finding a more suitable shooting platform.

A small swampy bench revealed itself after 50 metres or so, and with the stags now in clear view I knew even more than ever we were on borrowed time. Dave is pretty good now at keeping a low profile, but I gave him a friendly reminder to keep his head down as we had come too far to cock this up now.

I set up, ranged, checked my drop chart, and dialled the 6.2 MOA into the Leupold VX-6, gave one final check to make sure Dave was happy, and I settled in behind the rifle.

The shot was a good one, and in a matter of seconds, the stag had crashed headfirst into the tussock, and we had our prize.

The sense of elation and achievement was huge, a hard feeling to beat, and at this point I felt a massive load lifted from my shoulders. I could now soak up the moment knowing that what we had just achieved would make some epic television!

11 WET DREAMS ARE MADE OF THESE

There's an old cliché that says records are made to be broken.

American long jumper Bob Beamon's record leap at the Mexico City Olympics stood for almost 23 years. Garfield Sobers' tally of 365 not out was the test-cricket benchmark for 36 years, until Brian Lara came along. And in February of 2021, a 49-year-old New Zealand spearfishing record was rewritten. Here's how it all unfolded . . .

For those who haven't had the pleasure of driving the Milford Road, it is without a doubt one of the most picturesque stretches of tarseal on planet Earth. Just three days after the epic stag encounter with Sam, I found myself emerging from the Homer Tunnel right on daybreak, just as the sun began to pierce through a wispy layer of fog. My job is not always as glamourous as it may seem, but on mornings like this, the feeling was hard to beat.

Alongside me for this undertaking were Dwane Herbert, Julian Hansford and Sam Wild, and our excitement levels were all sky high as we wound our way down the steep and snaking State Highway 94 to its point of termination at the head of magnificent Milford Sound.

Our plan was to roll the dice and head out in the hope of encountering a southern bluefin tuna for the second season of *South Seas Spearo*. That was the stated goal, but in reality the main ambition was to get enough material to make up a short, 10- to 15-minute sequence that would eventually go into a future episode that would perhaps encompass action from three or four trips around different locations in search of the prized fish. We all knew it was a long shot to think we'd succeed on our first attempt, especially when it had been almost half a century since the last southern bluefin tuna was shot and landed, which was also the reigning New Zealand spearfishing record.

We were rank outsiders, but like a horse favouring a heavy track in a storm, conditions were on our side. In the build-up to the mission, we'd heard a few rumours being spread online of fishermen out targeting albacore tuna on the West Coast hooking up on bluefin, and given that I was already down in the South Island filming the summer stag mission, we figured it was a worthwhile punt.

Luckily for us, the team at Stabicraft had loaned us a brand-new 2250 Walkthrough for the trip, and as we backed the green machine into the drink, we set out in the knowledge that the day's sloppy seas were forecast to settle down overnight. But upon exiting the mouth of Milford Sound, the predicted calm weather to come provided us with little consolation, as a nasty 2-metre chop and gusty winds made filming rather uncomfortable.

Despite the testing conditions, we stuck to our guns and continued with our plan, which was to tow lures on our way offshore towards a large seamount in the hope of encountering albacore tuna schools, which we predicted could also hold congregations of their much larger southern bluefin cousins.

The first few hours saw a handful of albies hit the lures, but nothing to suggest it was time for the fellas to get suited and booted. We were seeking a more consistent patch of fish, and a double hook-up on the lures, so we just kept plugging along into the swell. Sam and I soon nodded off, leaving Dwane and Jools at the helm, as there wasn't a hell of a lot worth filming.

When that double strike finally did come at around 2 p.m., I think all aboard had well and truly foregone the possibility of nailing a bluefin, and we would have been content to head home with a couple of albacore in the bin. But, as has become a bit of a cliché for us now, the regular refrain 'We're not a fishing show, we're a spearfishing show' was once again raised, so Dwane and Sam reluctantly began getting changed into their neoprene 'business' suits, in the hope of being able to nail an albacore or two on spear.

The new model Stabicraft 2250 Walkthrough was the perfect vessel for this undertaking.

We made the call to leave one of the tuna hooked up below the boat, in the hope that it might entice a few friends to join it, a tactic that was equally as likely to attract a fish with a much more elaborate dental configuration than a tuna but, unfortunately, the hard-fighting fish soon broke free.

By then, Dwane and Sam had slipped over the side and were now floating 50 metres off the stern, and all while Julian kept himself busy with the glamorous task of getting a chum trail going, chopping up a box of pilchards and regularly tossing the chunks over the side.

After fifteen minutes, it became clear that the local albatross population were more interested in the chum than the local albacore population were. Drifting out in the current behind the boat, Dwane and Sam's thoughts were no doubt starting to head towards climbing back aboard, following my lead and cracking an ice-cold beer, when out of absolutely nowhere, something truly special happened.

I heard Sam's screaming first. The frantic pitch of his snorkel shriek suggested something serious, and I think both Jools and I jumped to the conclusion that a shark must have shown up. However, when I saw Dwane's fin disappearing below him as he dropped down on a dive, I began to relax, figuring that possibly a school of albacore may have swung in close.

As Dwane surfaced, the intensity of the screaming remained, but there was also an edge of exhilaration to it. It wasn't the sound I'd expect him to make if he'd just shot a lowly albacore. With a gusty wind blowing, it was hard to make out what he was saying, but my highly directional shotgun mic with its heavy-duty windjammer caught it all clearly:

DWANE: There's about 200 massive tuna right here!
JULIAN: Have you shot one yet?
DWANE: YEAHHHHH!!

It was pure elation! Hearing those words come out of Dwane's mouth, the reaction was like hearing the full-time whistle when the All Blacks won the 2011 Rugby World Cup at Eden Park; we all momentarily lost our minds.

However, anyone who's shot a large fish on spear knows that the job is far from finished when the trigger is pulled. Bluefin tuna are an incredibly hard fighting fish, so there was a lot of work that still needed to be done before we could get our hands on this trophy.

Complicating matters tenfold was the fact that the powerful spearguns we intended to use for shooting a 50 kg-plus bluefin were all lying in the cockpit of the boat — the lightweight gun Dwane had in his hand that was attached to the rampaging tuna was only suited to spearing albacore!

After Jools informed me that the shooting line on it was worn and frayed from a summer of hard use spearing kingfish and snapper in the Coromandel, my jubilant mood developed a hard edge of anxiety. But if

The incredible sight of a school
of bluefin tuna that vortexed
both Dwane and Sam.

there was anyone in New Zealand capable of getting the fish to the boat, it
was nine-times national spearfishing champion Dwane Herbert.

Dwane was well aware of the precarious state of the gear and knew
not to put too much pressure on the fish or he'd risk a catastrophic
failure. However, this wasn't Dwane's first rodeo. He fully understood the
importance of the occasion, and once we'd all managed to get our emotions
back in check, he began the slow task of raising the large fish, where he
would need to quickly secure it with a second shot before it went on a
second powerful run, which tuna are apt to do once near the surface.

With it easily being a record fish, just as with the marlin at the
Wanganella Banks, we needed to be careful to ensure that we adhered to all
regulations — so underwater cameraman Sam couldn't offer any assistance
to Dwane, having to remain clear of any trailing lines in the water, or we'd
forfeit the record. After 20 minutes of gentle persuasion, the fight was
finally out of the fish, and once Dwane had it up near the surface, he was

able to regain a grip of the small gun and release the float line. Julian then tossed a second gun to him, and he managed to deftly drop down a couple of metres and place a perfect shot into the side of its head, flicking the tuna's off switch and killing it immediately.

It had been all business since the initial explosion of emotion. There had been no hooting or hollering, but as Sam and Dwane hit the surface following the kill shot, the pent-up adrenalin boiled over and the celebrations could start in earnest.

The remainder of the afternoon was a euphoric blur. After spending just 20 minutes in the water, Dwane had achieved something he had been attempting for the previous eight years. We celebrated, hard! A rather nice bottle of rum was dispatched dangerously fast on the long run back into Milford, which also involved a short detour to a waterfall for a nude team pic — something I'd joked about doing earlier that morning on the steam out if we managed to pull off the unthinkable.

The fish that propelled us
into a momentary state
of madness.

At the time, there was no cellphone reception in Milford, but we were eager to share the news of our success with the rest of the *South Seas Spearo* team. So, once the off-water filming formalities were completed, the Milky Bars were on me. I pulled the gorse out of my pockets and shouted the fellas to a fancy dinner and all they could drink up the road at the luxurious Milford Sound Lodge, where we could also hook into their Wi-Fi to let the team know of our epic achievement.

We certainly took centre stage at the hotel restaurant that night, at one point encouraging all the other diners to gather around the laptop to check out the amazing footage we'd captured. While not everyone was eager to bathe in the reflected glory of what we had achieved, I'm pretty sure our enthusiasm at the bar that evening won the show a few new fans.

We eventually wandered our way back down to the boat, continuing our celebrations into the wee hours. But after taking the time to run through the footage in my head, I realised that the job wasn't quite complete. The tuna-spearing sequence was undeniably epic, but there wasn't enough to sustain an entire episode; we still needed around fifteen more minutes of action.

So, after a sluggish start, we gingerly ventured back out in search of more fish. We were all feeling bloody rusty, and it was certainly one of those days when I was happy to be the topside cameraman, but credit to Dwane and Jools, they stepped up and managed to slot a few more good fish to provide enough material to round out the episode. With the weather greatly improved from the day before, we even bandied about the idea of heading back out wide to try to get Jools a bluefin of his own, but in the end decided not to. The one fish we had was enough to feed all our families and more.

The tuna pulled the scales down to 54 kg, destroying the previous New Zealand record, which was just 12 kg. However, it should be pointed out that the fish Dwane decided to shoot was one of the smallest of those on offer, as there were some much larger specimens in the school, likely upwards of 80 kg. The knowledge that he was undergunned meant he passed up the opportunity of bagging a much bigger model, so there are certainly plenty more monster fish kicking about for any budding record breakers out there.

The New York Yacht Club successfully defended the America's Cup for 132 years until a bunch of Aussies snatched it away from them, so there's every possibility that with the increasing number of southern bluefin being caught in New Zealand waters our benchmark will be surpassed by the time you're reading this.

Along with providing an absolute career highlight, the bluefin trip also gave me my first real look at the mouth of Hāwea Bligh Sound, a spot where I'd be returning to in a month's time for a week-long *Red Stag Timber Hunters Club* shoot, as we'd drawn Mt Longsight, Period 2, in the annual wapiti ballot. But between now and then, we had three more *South Seas Spearo* episodes to film and well over 2000 km of State Highway 1 to cover.

Dwane's two cents

Spearing a southern bluefin tuna in New Zealand waters was something that kept me awake at night.

I had thought and dreamed about achieving this feat for the eight years that I'd lived in Southland. I'd approached the task from a few different angles, trialling a handful of techniques to see if I could crack the elusive tuna formula, but despite my best efforts, I had been unable to seal the deal. So with a rather loose game plan in place, we set out in the hope of going one step further, but knowing that success would require plenty of luck to be on our side this time.

When you've made a game plan, I've found that it's important knowing when to stick to it and knowing when to try something new. By mid-afternoon, we began contemplating whether it was time to change tack and head in to try something a little more 'high percentage' for the sake of filming but, luckily, the stubbornness came out and we stuck to our initial plan.

The whole crazy scenario when the tuna school swam in to us was something I never imagined I'd witness in my lifetime. It truly was a moment I'll never forget, and one that we're so lucky to have had the cameras rolling for. As for spearing and fighting the fish, it once again went to plan, and we were celebrating enthusiastically not long after. Despite feeling a little under the weather, the diving the next day was actually good, with plenty of respectable fish around, but I think by this stage in the trip, we were all eager to get back on the road to share the news of what we'd achieved with the rest of the *Spearo* team, who were all just as stoked as we were when they heard the news. Just for the record, spearing this tuna wasn't about breaking any record. While I appreciate records, it is a good level or benchmark to base fish that have previously been speared, but this was about achieving a goal set years ago and eventually coming away with the win.

How good!

12 THE *SOUTH SEAS SPEARO* SOUTHERN SUPER SPREADER

With the border situation preventing any international travel, we had to make the best of things by exploring our own backyard for Series 2, but rather than simply hitting the usual North Island spearfishing hotspots, we wanted to showcase the opportunities on offer in the South Island by embarking on a week-long road trip. I dubbed it the 'Southern Super Spreader', as we intended to spread the good word about the sport of spearfishing among our South Island brethren.

We set out from my home in Kerikeri, with a plan to tow our big new Stabicraft 2500 Ultracab XL, named *The Orca*, all the way to Dwane's hometown of Bluff, picking up and dropping off various team members en route. An undertaking of this scale presents many logistical challenges, so we needed to work to a well-laid road map, but it almost all came unstuck on the second morning.

For the drive south to Wellington, I would be joined by Nat Davey and Beuchat's Ants Broadhead. Leaving the Far North, we made good progress on the first afternoon, stopping briefly at The Bull Ring between Tokoroa and Taupō to catch the final race of Team New Zealand's successful defence of the 36th America's Cup, before continuing south to overnight at the home of Brock Terry in Acacia Bay. Despite being based 60 km from the nearest ocean, Brock and his old man Trev had been staunch supporters of *South Seas Spearo* in the early days of the show. Without the assistance of the Trev Terry Marine team, we would have struggled to even put fuel in the boat!

But I'd received a warning from *SSS* team member Kieran Andrews about staying at Brock's place. He advised me to be wary if Brock broke out the Appleton Rum at any stage in the evening, so as we pulled the big boat up his steep driveway, it was clear we would be in for a big night — my first sight of the big man was him waving to us from the deck, an unopened bottle of Appleton in his free hand.

As things played out, we didn't push the boat out too far that evening, draining just a couple of bottles between the team, as Trev and Brock were heading into the hills the next morning in search of sika deer. Likewise, I also needed to ensure that I maintained a semblance of fitness given what lay in store for me immediately off the back of the roady — our second-period wapiti hunt, which was just ten days away.

So, eager to shake off the cobwebs from the previous evening, early the next morning I laced up my runners and headed out to stretch the lungs and get a few kilometres under the belt before we hit the road again. However, within ten minutes of leaving Acacia Bay, my plan to kick the trip off on the right foot backfired, with emphasis on the words kick, trip and right foot.

Hearing some schoolkids on bikes coming up behind me, I politely gave them space to pass by veering off the edge of the footpath and onto a grass verge, without realising the long grass hid a decent drop. I took a heavy fall and ended up badly rolling my right ankle. Turns out Kieran was slightly mistaken; the rum was less of a danger than the run.

It wasn't a serious sprain, but it hurt like buggery and meant that I'd need to take things carefully over the coming week. Sprained ankles and sloppy seas aren't a great mix, but there wasn't much else to do except strap it up and hope it had calmed down in time for my Fiordland expedition.

Having collected me from the side of the road, we pressed on south, with Nat and Ants sharing driving duties for the day. There was little else to report other than a speeding ticket on the Desert Road, where from the back seat I captured a classic slice of old-school police banter:

COP: You know why I pulled you over, right?
NAT: Yeah.
COP: I saw the size of your rig and I thought, holy shit!

Once we'd battled our way through the Wellington rush-hour traffic, we boarded the Bluebridge ferry for our overnight sailing to Picton, where early the next morning we rendezvoused with Tim, Kieran, Sam and local expert Bryan from the Blenheim Dive Centre, who was tagging along to show us a few of his hotspots.

And man, those spots were hot! The top of the South Island fired for us big time, with the lads nailing a few nice kingfish at a rock not far from the entrance. With some good fish on board, the next challenge for the lads was something a little different to the norm.

The team were eager to free dive the *Mikhail Lermontov* wreck, a 20,000-tonne, 175-metre ocean liner that went down in Port Gore back in 1986. The saga of the *Lermontov* is a very interesting piece of New Zealand maritime history and one that's also shrouded in controversy. I could chew up a half-dozen pages explaining what makes the wreck special, but instead I suggest you seek out the story for yourself.

The team taking an enforced pitstop on the Central Plateau.

The wreck now lies on its side in close to 40 metres of water but comes up to 12 metres at its shallowest. At the time, being confined to the boat, I was quite jealous of the lads. Conditions on the surface were perfect, and after breathing up, they each dropped into the depths to explore the ghostly wreck. However, after seeing the footage later, I changed my tune. I'm not one to get claustrophobic, but snaking your way through portholes and along tight corridors 20 metres down isn't my idea of fun!

A thin layer of silt now encapsulates the entire wreck, and it's especially thick in the main lounge. It certainly made for some eerie footage, with tennis racquets, glass bottles and other assorted cruise-ship paraphernalia still in place after 35 years. On top of that, the knowledge that there're still possibly a few bodies trapped inside adds an extra level of creepiness.

Over eight deep dives, the fellas explored all around the boat, including into the bridge, but Tim took the honours of deepest dive, cracking the 30-metre mark. However, he didn't stay there for long:

'I went to the window and it was 31.7, so I went in, I looked in and I looked up at the light, and I looked at my watch and I thought yeah, nah, f**k that!'

The dive was undoubtedly the highlight of the day. We made the most of our remaining time in this stunning part of the country, snaffling a few crays and a couple of gurnard before parking up at a property belonging to a friend of Tim's for the evening.

Following a relaxed evening, where we were entertained by a display of bioluminescence on the jetty, we continued our way further south the next morning, with Kaikōura the next stop on the roady. After giving the first of our scheduled talks at Hunting & Fishing Kaikōura, we were eager to get back into the diving and, again, it didn't disappoint.

There were some highlights on this leg of the trip — a sperm whale encounter on the way out, Māui dolphins, a number of slender tuna being

Diving some rather tumultuous Southern waters around the Otago Peninsula.

shot, and witnessing a huge school of Peruvian mackerel. We managed to pin another kingfish and a few other good table fish, so all in all a bloody good result considering that Kaikōura's not really regarded as a spearfishing hotspot.

Once back on dry land, we had a final task to complete before we could put our feet up. We wanted to get a weight on Kieran's slender tuna, and we were stoked to learn that it surpassed the previous record, quite considerably in fact. In order to get an exact weight for the record books, we needed to use a certified set of scales, so made use of the butchery department at the local New World supermarket. If you've watched any of my shows over the past few years, you may know that I love a good pun. Dad jokes are an underappreciated artform, and the masterpiece of our second season had to be Kieran's New World record gag.

With the weigh-in completed, we waved goodbye to Kieran and Tim, who needed to tag out for the next leg to get back to their real jobs. Sam meanwhile was getting itchy feet. He had a new girlfriend living in Christchurch whom he seemed quite besotted with, and given there was still an hour or two of light left in the day, rather than joining the lads in cracking a few well-earned beers, he wanted to try his luck in hitchhiking south in order to spend the night with her.

As you'd expect, we gave him a bit of grief for not being a team player but ended up dropping him off on the edge of town to try his luck thumbing a lift, along with a cardboard box of crays to impress his new lady.

Back at the house, we were busy cleaning gear, charging batteries,

We promised the Stoney Creek team an awesome pic of a world-record tuna in one of their new insulated kill bags.

backing up footage and clearing memory cards, when a notification came through on Broady's phone. It was a social media post from Sam, smugly explaining to his many thousands of followers what he was up to. An hour later, another alert, this time not quite so smug. I can't recall exactly what was said, but it was along the lines of: 'It's getting late, my phone's nearly flat, this might not have been such a good idea.'

A lightbulb went off in my head. Here was a chance to get one back on young Sammy for leaving his brothers in arms in search of a little loving. We asked Anton from Hunting & Fishing Kaikōura if he knew of anyone who would be willing to help us play a wee prank on him.

'I've got just the man for the job!'

Cue the incredible Bob Rochford, a rather unassuming Kaikōura local and horse-racing aficionado, who played the role we assigned him to perfection.

The plan was for Bob to drive down and collect Sam, agreeing to take him all the way to Christchurch, but then things would really go south!

I set up a couple of hidden cameras in the cab of Bob's truck, while Broady and I jumped in the back under the tray.

We'd initially told Bob to start stroking Sam's leg when he got in the truck, but he took a different approach. After collecting the much-relieved Sam right on dark, who was beginning to really worry, Bob started heading in the wrong direction, directly inland. Sam politely pointed out his error, but Bob was adamant this was the right way. A minute or two later, things got weird for poor Sam, as Bob pulled over and began berating him for not shutting up.

BOB: You've been going on ever since we left Kaikōura, and that was an hour ago.
SAM: That was about ten minutes ago, I was just being polite . . .
BOB: Yeah, I've been on some shit tonight, Sam.

And so it went on.

SAM: You sure you're all right to drive there, Bob?
BOB: Yeah, nah, I'm good thanks, Sam. I'm all right.
SAM: You taken an acid tab or something?

From our hiding spot in the tray, Broady and I were none the wiser as to what was unfolding, but eventually Bob dumped Sam on the side of the road, miles from where he needed to be, and then drove off at pace.

After driving out of sight, Bob pulled over and let us out, filling us in on what had gone down. We then spun the truck around and headed back to Sam to put him out of his misery.

Sam later told me that hearing the vehicle pulling up behind him was perhaps the scariest part of the whole affair, and he even contemplated whether he should drop his box of crayfish and run. The bemused look of confusion on his face upon hearing Broady's voice from the front seat was absolutely priceless, and it was hard for me to hold the camera steady as I jumped out to film, given I was shaking with laughter.

The whole 'stitch-hiking' sequence is up online and is far and away the most popular clip we've ever shared to social, so I suggest checking it out if you haven't already.

To try to soften the blow for Sam, we ended up carving out a couple of hours in Christchurch the next day for him to get a little quality time with his new lady. We eventually made it to our final destination, Dunedin, right on dusk, and I must say it was a satisfying feeling driving through my old stomping ground with such a badass boat on the back.

For the Otago/Southland portion of the roady, we had an injection of fresh blood with Rochele and Dwane joining the team. We'd be based on the beautiful Portobello Peninsula for the duration, and after a rather tricky night's sleep in a boatshed among a raucous mob of blue penguins, we launched *The Orca* and punched our way out through the heads, alongside another boat helmed by a few members of the notorious Dunedin Spearo Crew.

Once we were out past the albatross colony, it became obvious that conditions for the day would be challenging. Rochele, Sam and I all quickly lost our eggs bennies over the side, and other than the ferocious seas, there wasn't a lot to get too excited about over the course of the morning.

After relocating to a more sheltered part of the coast, some playful sea lions provided some light entertainment, sneakily pilfering a couple of butterfish from the team's float lines. These playful beasts have been known to inflict a nasty bite on the odd occasion, so the team wisely decided to extricate themselves from the water rather than tempt fate.

We then chanced our arm out wide, encountering another giant school of Peruvian mackerel, and unlike the sighting in Kaikōura, this time Nat and Dwane were able to pin a couple of large specimens. Once off the water, we felt Nat's fish warranted another supermarket visit, and — just like that — we had our second world record in three days.

Following another well-attended team talk, this time at the local dive centre, I took the evening off to catch up with a few of my university friends at a bar in the Octagon. As tends to be the case when catching up with old mates, a few quiets quickly turned into a few louds, especially when the remaining *South Seas Spearo* team plus the Dunedin Spearo Crew lads arrived to add fuel to the fire.

With quite a head of steam up, I forgot about the tight budget the show was on and ended up playing 'big shot' — splashing out and shouting half the bar. It was certainly a far cry from my time as a broke student in North Dunedin, searching behind the couch to scrape together enough coins to go halves in a cask of Country medium red, but I felt I needed to step up and be the person that I wanted others to be when I was a scarfie, living on the bones of my arse.

By the time the Uber dropped us back at our rental in Portobello, though, things had got a bit silly. What began as a rough-and-tumble playfight in the back of the vehicle spilled out into slightly more serious shenanigans, and like a pack of aggressive dogs, I was forced to separate the lads from one another, tossing one into the shrubbery. Luckily for all our sakes, Nat and Rochele had retired much earlier in the night and were able to keep the train on the tracks for a pre-dawn departure the next morning. So, after a tough old start to the day, we hit Bluff just as the sun was rising.

It had been exactly one week since we rolled off the ferry in Picton, and since then we'd covered all 918 km of South Island State Highway 1. A southern roady would never be complete without making the trek all the way to Bluff, but it wasn't the end of the line for us — we still had a long way to go, as our final destination was stunning Rakiura Stewart Island.

Heading to Stewy made sense for a couple of reasons. First, it's a spot that Dwane knows very well, diving the area regularly as part of his commercial work. It's also known to be home to very large trumpeter, a delicious South Island table fish that had proven elusive up to this point.

But it was also home to a large great white shark population, and at this time of the year, in late March, it was the tail end of mating season in Stewart Island. I'll admit that the chance of a run in with the king of all sharks was a motivating factor for us, as there's nothing like a drive-by from the taxman to ramp up the excitement levels, but we didn't envisage that things would play out anywhere near as dramatically as they did.

After an hour-long steam across a fairly benign Foveaux Strait, we

The islands near the entrance to Halfmoon Bay, a notoriously sharky stretch of water.

arrived at our selected destination, the islands north of the entrance to Halfmoon Bay. After the perfunctory pieces to cam explaining the day's plan, the team set about getting suited up, while I focused on getting a few shots of a large albatross circling close by. But while readying themselves for the first dive of the day, a sudden arrival took everyone's breath away.

I heard Sam's 'Oh, my God' first, so I swung the camera in the direction of whatever he was looking at. As best as I could tell, it just looked like a patch of dark water. I couldn't make out anything specific underneath the boat.

'There! THERE!'

Like a magic-eye painting, my brain eventually filled in the blanks. I had been staring at the back of a gigantic great white shark, slowly cruising beneath the boat; it's just that it was too wide for my brain to properly gauge what it was. The shark, which Nat suspected was a big female between 4.5 and 5 metres in length, made a quick drive-by, briefly checking out the boat, before carrying on its way, not giving us much time to get anything other than an off-centred underwater GoPro shot to go with my speculative topside footage, which was ruined by the harsh glare on the water's surface. Still, it was one of the most heart-stopping moments of my entire life. This thing was absolutely gigantic.

A topic of discussion on the steam across the strait was whether any of us would have the balls to swim with a whitey if one turned up. Sam, Nat and Rochele were keen, I was decidedly unkeen, but Broady seemed to be on the fence. However, the second that he and I laid eyes on the shark, the question was instantaneously put beyond any doubt. It was an emphatic NO from both of us. But it seems Sam must be made of sterner stuff:

Heart-in-the-mouth stuff as Sam ventures away from the safety of the boat.

Getting uncomfortably close to the business end.

SAM: That is just the most insane thing I have ever seen!
DAVE: Are you going to have a swim?
SAM: F**king oath!

Much later, Broady and I talked about how the first thing that we thought of when seeing the shark was our kids, and that it wasn't worth the risk of them growing up fatherless if we were to jump in with it. On the other hand, neither Sam, Nat nor Rochele are parents, so perhaps that had something to do with their willingness to risk life and limb with the whitey. However, being a dad twice over didn't stop Dwane from suiting up and jumping over the side. By the time he was in, though, the shark seemed to have vacated the area. I put the drone in the air to see if I could relocate it but had no luck.

Over the morning dive, the team bravely went about their work, slotting a few big blue cod, and gathering some hefty pāua from the shallows, but there were no big trumpeter to be found. By midday, with little to crow about, we decided to relocate to a new area on the opposite side of the island.

Dwane was confident about the weedline along this stretch of coast but, again, it wasn't particularly fishy, holding only small trumpeter. So, rather than chew up the clock here, Rochele plugged a couple of tarakihi and made her way back to the boat. It was shaping up as a bit of an underwhelming end to the road trip. Don't get me wrong, tarakihi are a delicious table fish, but they're not exactly a scintillating species to spear.

This time round, it was Nat who first spotted the shark, coming in hot to pilfer the fish attached to Rochele's float. It was another white pointer, though it was much smaller than the big girl we'd seen earlier, and likely a juvenile male, around 3 to 3.5 metres long.

We yanked the float back to the boat, but by now the shark had gotten a taste and was keen for more, continuing to circle behind us. This provided me with a chance to improve on the rather poor footage I captured earlier that morning, and it allowed Sam to get some real gravy underwater shots from his position sitting on the transom.

After filling my boots, I passed the main camera over to Broady and deployed the drone to get a new angle on the action. The aerial shot was a ripper, showing the dark shark clearly delineated against the green water. After at least 20 minutes with the shark behind the boat, its behaviour had definitely changed since its aggressive arrival — it was much more relaxed, swimming with smooth, languid movements, with its pec fins extended wide, so Sam decided he was comfortable entering the water to get some better-quality footage. A month or two later, I found myself in a bit of a moral quandary. The sequence we captured was certainly engrossing, with Sam and later Nat and Rochele all free swimming alongside the apex predator without a cage in sight, but would we be sending the wrong message by putting it out for the world to see?

There was a lot of chin scratching as to whether its inclusion in the episode would come across as irresponsible, as we certainly didn't want to encourage copycats. I reached out to a couple of renowned shark experts to get their thoughts; both encouraged me not to put it to air.

But it was so damn good and such an amazing way to end the trip!

In the end, I met them in the middle, toning down the sequence for the New Zealand broadcast version, including plenty of narration to discourage viewers from replicating Sam's antics, and axing the footage of Nat and Rochele's swim. However, I had fewer reservations for the international version, which includes some really dynamite interactions with the shark, including one particularly heart-in-the-mouth moment right before we called it quits, when Nat and Sam drifted well away from the safety of the boat, getting to within metres of the white, which then adopted an erratic and aggressive posture. With a flick of its tail, it powered away down deep, leaving Nat and Sam to race frantically back for *The Orca*, certainly not a position you ever want to find yourself in.

Much like filming with Nat at the Wanganellas, Sam had the handicap of needing to push his big underwater camera through the water, so Nat naturally made the mad dash back to the swim step first, but rather than clambering aboard and pulling his offsider up out of danger, I thrust a camera straight in his face to get his initial reaction, leaving Sam to float anxiously about for a few extra seconds, like a human burley bomb at the back of the boat.

We later heard from a team that had been filming for Discovery's *Shark Week* in the same location a couple of weeks prior. Turns out they had some of the most aggressive shark encounters they've ever witnessed, with fierce males competing with one another for mating rights, so we can count ourselves lucky that no one in the team lost a limb!

With the roady now having reached a suitably climactic finale, we were keen to get back to Bluff and for a bit of R&R. We had one more presentation to give, this time at the Invercargill Hunting & Fishing New Zealand store, where following our talk I was given a custom-made rug bearing the name 'Orca' on it, a hell of a gift!

And it turns out the great white shark encounter wasn't our last run in with some sketchy local wildlife. Looking back, we probably put ourselves in just as much danger by mixing it with the bouncers at Waxy's Irish pub, the dancers at Divaz Revue Bar and the local boy racers at the Burt Munro memorial in Queens Park.

With the local bars closing early midweek, Sam, Broady and I decided to clamber back aboard *The Orca*, which was now parked up next to Invercargill's landmark water tower, where we carried on into the wee hours, toasting the fact that we'd made it through the whole ordeal unscathed.

But in the back of my mind was a nagging thought. These late nights and exuberant celebrations weren't exactly ideal preparation for a Fiordland wapiti mission — how the hell was I going to handle that physical challenge?

A brief stop on the southern roady to enjoy the view.

Broady's two cents

As team manger (self-appointed), my job on the roady was to make sure everything ran smoothly, to ensure the team maintained the professionalism they are known for, and that we all arrived at our required destinations safely.

But after the first day, Nat kicked me out of the driver's seat, so all I had to do was sit back and enjoy the experience. Happy days!

And boy were there some experiences! New World records, great white sharks, 3-metre swells, 3 a.m. starts, 3 a.m. finishes, sea lions, bioluminescent phytoplankton, sprained ankles, bruised faces (maybe a bit of Sammy's ego too), bedding down among a raucous blue penguin colony, and of course — the infamous Acid Bob prank!

You could hardly pick a better spot for a roady than the east coast of the South Island; the diversity of marine life, topography, visibility and people made this a special trip. The Marlborough Sounds, Kaikōura, Dunedin coastline and Stewart Island, on their day, are world-class destinations, and with the weather gods for the most part on our side, we enjoyed some epic diving conditions.

Everyone in the team (except Jules) made an appearance at one stage or another, but poor old Sammy had to endure the pain of putting up with Shawsy and me for the entire trip. Looking back, I think Sammy will agree that this roady was some of the best days of his life; it probably made him a better person and he made some lifelong friends. I know he still is penpals with Acid Bob!

There has been chatter about a follow-up North Island-based roady, but this one will be hard to beat, and for all of the stitch-ups that Shawsy came up with, I'm pretty sure there's a number on his back next time around.

13 FIORDLAND WAPITI LIVEABOARD

Luckily, by the time that I arrived at Anto's place in Queenstown the next day, the ankle sprain from my ill-advised morning run in Taupō had settled down, allowing me to boot up and spend an hour walking around the Shotover River with a heavy pack on my back, just to try to 'shock' the body and get used to having a bit of weight on the shoulders, before the real deal kicked off in 24 hours' time.

But it was a token gesture really. Fiordland has a well-earned reputation as a breaker of men. It's a place that takes no prisoners, and I was kidding myself if I thought an hour-long pack march would make much of a difference. In the build-up to both previous Fiordland trips, I'd committed to a month-long training regime, laying off the beers and dropping a couple of kgs to reduce the load on the knees.

I knew I was undercooked for this one, but I had one ace up my sleeve. Unlike the 'use it or lose it' nature of physical fitness, one thing that doesn't fade when ignored for long periods is mental strength. By now, I had come through a couple of full-on Fiordland wapiti hunts, plus I had the rather arduous summer stag mission from a month before under my belt. I'd just have to suck it up and give it my best.

Another thing on my side was the fact that the block we'd won in the ballot wasn't known for being one of the tougher blocks to hunt. Unlike some of the core areas which can require days of climbing to reach the main hunting zones, ours was a coastal block, Mt Longsight, with only limited options for tops hunting.

Being coastal, we were also able to make use of what had been my surrogate home for the past week, *The Orca*, and our basic plan was to spend the first four to five days in the hills before dropping back down to the boat, ending the mission with some fishing and diving.

Joining Anto and me would be Brad and Morgan, the same foursome from our eventful mission into the Mid Burn block the year prior. On that trip, the hunt was cut short due to the sudden Covid lockdown, but there were no such issues for this iteration of the ballot.

After attending the compulsory safety briefing in Te Anau, we towed the boat all the way to Milford under cover of darkness. We awoke to find

Enjoying our first night on Longsight.

a thick mist lying heavy on the sound, so we wasted little time in backing *The Orca* into the drink, in the very same place that we'd had such amazing success targeting southern bluefin tuna the previous month.

We also had a couple of young hunters from Auckland with us, McGuinness and Ash, the other ballot winners who we were sharing the block with. Both guys were Fiordland first timers, and we planned to drop them off into an area of the block nearer the entrance of the sound, where they would base themselves for the duration of the trip.

A lot of planning and preparation goes into major missions like these, and in the process of ensuring everything was squared away, my wife Amber had reached out to Anto, Brad and Morgs to gauge whether any of the team had enough experience and confidence to take the helm of *The Orca* while I was tied up with filming commitments. Brad put up his hand, explaining he'd been around boats most of his life and felt up to the task.

Although I'm not a qualified skipper, I do consider myself quite well versed in boating rules and regulations, having spent six years filming with Matt Watson on the *ITM Fishing Show* and two years with all manner of commercial fishermen producing *South Seas Spearo*. With Anto having a great deal of experience in Milford Sound and a fine forecast for our steam down the coast to Hāwea Bligh Sound, I was feeling relaxed and confident in the team's combined ability.

That confidence was dented within two minutes of *The Orca* hitting the water.

The Orca looks like a toy against the majesty of Fiordland.

I was busy filming some scenic pretties of fog-laden mountain tops from the back of the boat when I heard Brad pipe up:

BRAD: Dave, where are we supposed to go? Where's the lane?

I put the camera down and approached the helm. Looking through the window ahead, I noticed we were well off to the right of the channel markers.

ME: Keep port on your right on the way out, so you want to keep the red on your right, so you've got to go over here, through that gap. In fact, hang on . . .

As I was speaking, I'd noticed the sounder reading half a metre, and the dotted trail of the boat's track moving into clearly marked foul ground. A second later, the boat shook as we rumbled directly over a shallow bar.

ME: F**k, trim up, trim up!

Thankfully, with the engine trimmed up, we had just enough water beneath us for the wind to blow us off the foul ground and into deeper water.

ME: You bloody lake fisherman!
BRAD: Mate, I've never driven out of here before . . .
ME: I'm going to drive the boat for the rest of the day, okay?

Turns out that while he'd spent a bit of time at sea, the bulk of Brad's boating experience had come from time spent on lakes and rivers, rather than out in the open ocean. I actually captured the sequence of us running aground on two cameras but didn't have the heart to throw him under the bus within the episode (although I guess I have now!).

Compounding the embarrassment was the fact that a small crowd had assembled on the wharf to see the big boat off, so all in all a rather ignominious start to the trip, but it's good to get the mistakes out of the way early on.

After a drama-free steam south, we dropped off McGuinness and Ash and continued towards a reliable mooring site that Anto had arranged in advance. Having ferried our packs ashore in the inflatable tender, the hard slog then began.

It had been raining off and on throughout the morning, and the bush was now hot and humid. Conditions were certainly testing, and we battled to locate any viable game trails for the first hour, so we just bashed our way directly uphill. We stopped regularly to roar but heard no replies.

It was another one of those tough days at the office, with the swampy country and snakelike tree roots seeing each of us take a tumble or two, but we reached our destination in under four hours, less than half the time it took to reach our first camp the previous year in Mid Burn.

After making camp, we ventured out to get a feel for what was kicking about on the clearings further up-valley. It wasn't long before we caught sight of the first animal of the trip, an inquisitive young stag, but he didn't stick around for long. We had another encounter at dusk, as having worked our way up an elevated ridge, a vocal stag appeared on the edge of a distant clearing, but being just 7 points, it was an easy decision to let him walk.

It was reassuring to hear plenty of roars but, unfortunately, the vocal stags we encountered over the coming days were all fairly average, and nowhere near trophy calibre. Which brings me to the one downside of Fiordland. It's a tricky enough place to hunt (and film) even without the complications that the extra level of scrutiny involved inevitably brings.

It's hammered home to every hunter at the FWF safety briefings that any animal that's taken out should be at its absolute prime, which means eight years plus, 12 points plus and 45 inches plus. Finding that one special bull that's worthy of putting on the wall takes a lifetime for most, and it is an especially tough task in the fringe blocks that don't have as strong genetics, but that's just the way it is. Beggars can't be choosers, and we were just happy to have won a block!

I've never had a problem with any of our team taking an animal for meat, but in Fiordland, knocking over a 'cull' stag can open yourself up to a great deal of criticism. I've now filmed in Fiordland on three ballots, each time following a group of three hunters, which equates to around

Any chance to soak up the Fiordland sun should be taken, especially when your electronics are in dire need of drying out.

60 individual days of hunting for just one animal shot — and that was the last-minute stag which was taken just an hour before our mandatory Covid evacuation the previous year.

But getting back to the hunt at hand, after four days of playing cat and mouse, capturing some fun encounters with stags up close in some classic Fiordland jungle country, we felt we'd done our dash in the catchment, having laid eyes on most of the vocal stags in the area.

By this stage also, my main camera was almost toast. It had begun playing up on the second morning and deteriorated further when some nasty weather rolled in and kept us tent bound for the best part of day four. I was only keeping it alive through regular blasting with hot air from the Jetboil cooker. The forecast on the Garmin inReach also told us we had some horrific weather heading our way, so we saddled up our packs and made our way out of the valley and down towards the comfort of *The Orca*.

It was quite a luxury being back aboard the boat, and we wasted little time in changing out of our filthy wet clothing and tucking into a few tasty treats. After a quick dive to load up on crayfish and pāua, we pretty much picked up where we'd left off on the roady the week before, enjoying a few rums along with a delicious fresh fish dinner.

We had a barrel of laughs over the next couple of days. As forecast, the weather absolutely shat itself, so we all felt a touch smug thinking about the other second-period hunters being subjected to the very worst of Fiordland weather while we were warm and dry aboard the boat.

After a morning spent hauling in our limit of monster blue cod, we chewed up the remainder of our second day preparing gourmet pāua and coriander dumplings, and my God did they go down a treat.

But we each learned a valuable lesson after it got dark. After targeting puka on a deep pin, the strong winds that were funnelling up the sound meant we weren't able to just slowly tick our way back to the mooring site, as *The Orca*'s bow was continually being swung around in the opposite direction by the powerful gusts. The leaden skies hid any stars from view, and without a single light source to use as a point of reference, we were forced to give it a bit of gas and put our trust in the radar and electronics for navigation. It was a little unnerving, steaming along at 15 knots in the pitch black with just a screen as a guide, but thankfully we made it back without incident.

On the final day, having heard rumours of Bligh Sound having a population of puka that inhabited the shallows, I committed an hour to doing a bit of spearfishing, but it was quite a creepy feeling diving the dark depths solo, so I didn't want to push my luck. I didn't know it at the time, but I'd be back in the same area chasing puka on spear on two more occasions over the next year, but more about that later.

After packing the speargun away, Anto and Morgan eventually managed to catch a few pup puka on the electric reels, providing a great conclusion to the episode, although having cast an eye over the scene just now, it's clear that Morgs was three sheets to the wind by that time of the night.

I can hardly point the finger, though. With the weather still baring its teeth, I put on my best Lieutenant Dan impression by clambering onto the roof of *The Orca*, screaming challenges and abuse to the Fiordland weather gods. It must have worked, as we hooked up on the puka a short time later.

While we were certainly having a jolly old time of it, there was one nagging thought I was slightly anxious about.

I'd been in touch with Nat Davey through the inReach about the sea state for our run home. He'd said we needed to punch for Milford no later than the following afternoon, as a massive swell was building from the south which could make the passage difficult.

We arranged to collect the two young Aucklanders the next morning, with the aim of being back in Milford before the weather deteriorated any further. Upon exiting Bligh, though, I got my first good look at what we were in for. Compared to conditions the week prior, the ocean was an entirely different beast, with massive rollers that threatened to make for quite a white-knuckle ride.

On top of that, I was also wary of the fuel situation. We'd burned a fair bit of the boat's 380-litre tank, and as I began picking my way between the huge waves, I realised that I'd need to be on and off the gas regularly to keep from being dragged down the face of the large waves and digging the nose in. With six people aboard and a huge amount of hunting, fishing and diving gear, we were a pretty heavy boat, but I needed to keep a brave face on. The lads were all looking to me to make the call on whether it was safe, so I reassured them that these seas were nothing to be worried about. Behind the bravado, though, I knew this was our one chance, as it certainly wasn't going to get any better in the coming days.

With lifejackets on, I told the lads to close the door to the cabin and hunker down, while I cranked up some hard-hitting Tool tracks on the stereo and concentrated on picking the best line. I remember regularly looking out the window towards the coast to try to identify potential safe havens for the tender to run the fellas ashore should we experience any major issues with fuel or the outboard, but two and a half hours later we were all able to breathe a sigh of relief, as we passed through the entrance to Milford Sound — with a quarter of a tank to spare.

We may have been almost out of fuel, but the 'phew' gauge was overflowing.

We didn't find a pot of gold on this journey,
but it was still a trip to remember.

Anto's two cents

**I have reflected on this adventure many times, and always find
myself smiling. What a cool place and what a trip! Combining my
passions of hunting, fishing and diving using our own epic Stabi, in
my mind life doesn't get much better.**

The hunting opportunities were good, but not what I would look
for if after the true New Zealand wapiti experience. While never
expecting big wapiti, we were hopeful of an encounter with a big
mature red stag, but never saw anything with significant age to get
too excited about.

We were also hopeful of some roaring around the fiord when
aboard the Stabi, but we never heard any roars or saw a single deer.

One of my favourite memories was just being warm and dry on *The Orca* when all around us it was absolutely hosing down. I was sitting inside with the heater on, having a beer, while watching Dave and Brad in their wet-weather gear catching us a feed of blue cod. At one point, Dave asked me for a hand to get a fish off. Well, that was certainly never going to happen! I lay back with a grin on my face very content to be in what really is a wonderland.

Turning a feisty barracuda into a sought-after puka was also extremely satisfying and one on the list of things we wanted to achieve while filming.

Will I be back to this block? Likely one day, but more likely when my boys are of age. Overall, it was a handy block that I can boat to and have a true wilderness adventure, and that is what it really is all about.

PART FOUR
OVER AND ABOVE

14 LIKE FATHER, LIKE SON

One thing I've found throughout my time in TV that always seems to work well is a father–son story, but among *The Red Stag Timber Hunters Club* team, all our kids were still a bit too young to throw in the deep end on a major backcountry shoot.

However, Anto's mate Gordy Watson, who guides up the beautiful Rees Valley and around Central Otago, was keen to allow us to follow along on a hunting trip with him and his son Dart, who was just fifteen at the time. We also made the decision that given the fact that we'd be following Dart, we could also justify hunting on private land for once.

Over the course of two years, we made a couple of separate multi-day trips up into the Rees, a stunningly beautiful example of New Zealand backcountry. The first trip in mid-winter saw Dart nail a decent chamois buck, but we weren't able to find the big stags that we hoped to encounter. We had the use of our new Polaris side by side to get around on the flats, but still put a fair few kms on the boots, and I was certainly impressed by Dart's endurance.

Along with chamois and reds, the Rees is probably most famous as the mainland stronghold for whitetail deer, and in recent years, Gordy had been working hard on improving the health of the herd. He had a number of anti-poaching mechanisms in place, hidden cameras and the like, aimed to combat the explosion in availability of high-end thermal technology and night-vision gear, which has seen a rise in poaching in many areas. He also knew the country like the back of his hand, so upon seeing a picture of a hunter on social media with a whitetail buck, he could tell straight away whether it was shot on land he was responsible for managing or not.

He certainly had some great stories to share about surprising poachers on the hill and picking holes in their hollow excuses. You can't bullshit a bullshitter as they say.

Anyway, over the course of this first hunt, we saw a fair few of these charismatic deer trotting about freely among the tussock. Given the effort we'd gone to on the Pure Salt expedition into Stewart Island a fortnight before (which was documented earlier), it was a strange feeling seeing these elusive creatures, which we'd worked so damn hard to lay eyes on,

nonchalantly strutting around in the open without a care.

Nine months after the first Rees trip, we returned for a couple of days' hunting during the roar. Over late summer, Gordy had captured some images on his trail cams of a really impressive 14-pointer roaming around in the higher reaches, and he felt it would make a hell of a trophy for young Dart, so once again we set out on a mission with one specific stag in mind.

The first night was a fizzer, with nothing heard or seen.

It's easy to get ahead of yourselves when planning these kinds of missions. While we were hunting private, there certainly weren't any fences separating us from the surrounding public land. The station stretched over 18,000 hectares and was hemmed in by snow-laden mountain passes, so it was by no means a given that we'd be able to relocate the big stag that had been caught on camera earlier in the year.

But Gordy knew these hills. He knew where the best feed faces were, and the areas the animals favoured in any given weather, so we were relatively confident that if we were willing to put in the work and beat the feet, we had a good chance of tracking him down.

That's exactly what happened. On the second morning, once the light had strengthened enough to glass, Anto cast an eye up-valley and located a stag on the spotting scope a bit over 2 km from our location, flashing a hefty set of antlers around.

We began making our way up the hill in his direction, catching sight of a few more smaller stags en route. Once up through the beech forest and into the tops, we took things nice and slow, getting into position just back from a slight rise that provided us with a bit of cover. Anto snuck ahead to try to lay eyes on the big boy, and soon found him bedded down on the edge of a distant gut.

These moments are always hard for me, as there's so much whispering going on between the guys that often I'm left in the dark as to what they're saying or seeing. I gestured Anto back to explain the situation. The stag was now up and moving about, probably tracking a few hinds, but at over 400 metres it was going to be a tough shot. We needed to get Dart into a shooting position before we lost our chance, but just as we had him settled and ready to squeeze off, the stag dropped over a ridge and wandered off out of sight.

We pulled back from our vantage point and got comfortable, settling in for what we knew could be a very long wait. I had flashbacks to the first summer stag hunt earlier in the year, waiting out the day with Sam and Dre, but with daylight saving now over, our wait for dusk wasn't quite as arduous.

Eight hours later, there was still no sign of the big boy. By now, the sun had long ago sunk behind the distant hills, and things were looking bleak. Finally, though, with half an hour of shooting light left in the day, a couple of hinds materialised on the bush edge, which galvanised us back into action. It's fanciful thinking you can wish an animal into fruition, but after an afternoon of crossed fingers and toes, the big stag made his belated encore. It seems that good things do come to those who wait.

But spotting the stag was just the first step, we still had to hope he'd move closer to provide Dart with a viable shot. We also had the complications of filming to contend with — I've seen adult men crack under the added pressure of a cameraman on their shoulder. There's no way around it, filming disrupts a shooter's normal routine. It takes a cool head to wait till the moment the cameraman is ready, and then pull off a perfect shot on command.

The stag did us a massive favour, though, cutting the distance by meandering directly towards us, moving from beyond 500 metres to under 400. Having possibly caught sight or scent of the hinds below him, the stag then stopped and looked downhill, presenting Dart with a perfect side on profile.

ANTO: Now . . .

Dart squeezed the trigger . . . 'Click.'

Now here's where the situation differed from what unfolded within the episode. At the time, we had been taking some stills and creating a bit of video content for a high-end firearms manufacturer that had provided Anto with one of their customised rifles. Anto was a big fan of it, and the rifle had performed flawlessly up to this point, but the metallic 'tink' of the firing pin incorrectly hitting the bullet was like a resounding thud to our ears.

Shit! Anto quickly ejected the round and reloaded for Dart.

ANTO: He still there?

ME: Yep, calm it down, we've got him, take your time.

The stag hadn't moved, and it was still perfectly in frame, so I was trying to keep the mood relaxed and confident, to not let any panic creep in. Dart quickly found the stag in his crosshairs once again.

ANTO: You ready, Dave?
ME: Yep.
ANTO: Take him when you're ready, Dart.
'Click.'
ANTO: F**k, Gordy — grab your gun, grab your gun!
DAVE: Just calm it down, boys.

Two misfires, what a shitshow! We'd waiting all day for this opportunity, and it seemed that a dodgy firing pin was going to be our downfall.

As Gordy frantically made his way down to us with his rifle, Anto decided to give Dart one more crack with his before switching over.

Dart lined up a third time and squeezed off.

This time the pin hit the mark, and Dart hit a bullseye, the bullet slamming into the shoulder crease and sacking the big stag right where he stood. It was a hell of a shot considering the pressure and circumstances.

The big donk on the deck, the team are quite rightly stoked after it came very close to giving us the slip.

In Gordy's words it was 'pressure cooker stuff', but Dart was absolutely ice cold throughout. I was just stoked to have an excellent 'proud dad moment' on camera.

Even though the misfires would have made for great TV, we didn't feel like throwing the manufacturer under the bus by showing all the drama leading up to the kill shot. It's just one of those things that happens sometimes — the fact it occurred right in the heat of the moment rather than down at the firing range was just bad luck.

The stag was the ripper we knew he'd be, a nice even 14, perhaps a bit shorter than we'd hoped, but certainly a hell of a rack. With the 12 taken earlier in the year, the adventure into Fiordland aboard *The Orca*, and a couple of other quite strong episodes in the can, we were now sitting pretty for Series 7, but my personal highlight of the season was still to come.

Anto's two cents

I spend a fair bit of time with Gordy and Dart outside of the show, generally on hunting and fishing adventures around Central Otago. Now that I have two young boys of my own, I realise how lucky I've been to watch Gordy and Dart's relationship on our adventures over the years, and I really look forward to heading out on future adventures of my own with my boys once they're a little older.

Dart has experiences that most grown men would dream of, and this not only comes from spending more time out in the hills than most but being mentored by a calm and knowledgeable father.

I have seen more grown men miss animals than I care to think about. Any miss haunts me, but watching a mate get excited, panic and miss a trophy of a lifetime really puts a dampener on what would have been a trip to cherish.

However, I've found that Dart is extremely cool under pressure, and Gordy does well to allow him the space and time to go through the motions as they have done many times before.

As the old saying goes, the time to be excited is after the job is done. You've first got to focus on the process, working through your mental checklist and keeping on top of your emotions.

Accurate shooting requires calmness, efficiency and safety, and Dart certainly showed this during the 'moments of truth', taking two great animals in tough situations with cameras rolling.

Gordy and Dart working together to break down the big boy.

15 SNOW PLACE LIKE HOME

Over April, we also landed a couple more punches — a roar hunt with Yuley and bowhunter Kadin Willis, and then a sika roar hunt with Tim and Khan, both beautifully shot by our good mate Cam Henderson from the *Hunters Journal*. The build-up to the sika hunt was slightly farcical, though, and is worth a mention to give you an idea of the challenges involved in production.

Wanting to do our part to educate hunters as well as entertain them, we had been working closely with the Sika Foundation about key messages to convey in the episode, and the overall conservation theme of the hunt. We purposely chose a remote area that we knew contained too many deer, and therefore required more hunting pressure to improve the animal quality (less competition for food results in better quality animals, both in terms of meat and trophy) and to help reduce the risk of canopy collapse from over-browsing.

Despite having been aware of our plans for months, DOC suddenly rescinded our permission to film less than 48 hours before Tim and Kahn's scheduled chopper departure. We had to call in some frantic favours from people higher up the ladder to speak on our behalf and, eventually, those in charge saw sense in what we were trying to achieve.

I was with Anto up the Rees when these dramas were unfolding, though, so it was left to my wife Amber, Tim and Khan to encourage the department to see the light. Dealing with red tape's a part of running any business, so we just needed to roll with the punches.

Notwithstanding these minor frustrations, we were having an epic run, but one box remained unticked. At the start of the season, I really wanted to nail an action-packed pig-hunting episode. Our last pig hunt had been back in Series 5, where we'd nailed some big boars in the Kaikōura high country. That episode had been a fan favourite, and without a doubt the best pig-hunting footage we'd ever filmed, thanks mainly to us getting lucky with some incredible dog-cam footage.

So it would be a hard ask to top. My aim with every shoot is to try to continually raise the bar on what we'd done before, or to pave new ground with something entirely different. So, to reduce the risk of being

measured against the earlier Kaikōura Boar War trip, rather than have this
season's episode entirely focused on pig hunting, I decided to split it over
two winter trips. And to keep things fresh, we'd throw something a little
oddball into the mix up front.

The Polaris that we'd put to use a couple of months earlier when up
the Rees would be getting a new set of shoes, snowshoes in fact. It was
now mid-winter, and it had recently been snowing heavily in the hills
around Central Otago. Our plan was to hunt the tops country between Lake
Wānaka and Lake Hāwea, utilising access granted by our good friends at
Glen Dene station. On presenting duties for the hunt would be Anto, Dre
and Marty Verry from *Red Stag Timber*.

We dropped the machine off early to the team at Wānaka Powersports,
and within a couple of hours, they'd whipped the wheels off and replaced
them with a caterpillar tank-like track system, so it now resembled some
kind of snowmobile you'd expect to see rumbling around Antarctica.

We had an absolute blast smashing around the deep snow in our
souped-up snow piercer, and at times the hunting became secondary to
seeing exactly how far through the deep snow drifts we could get.

I made the mistake early on of trying to get a low-angle drive-by shot,
with the lads ripping around the corner at pace and absolutely covering me
and the camera in powdery snow.

Despite the caterpillar tracks, we still weren't immune to getting stuck,
and were forced to deploy the winch a couple of times to get ourselves out
of trouble. It was clear from the lack of animal tracks that there weren't

many animals living high in the tops country, so we worked our way along the ridgeline before descending via the popular Isthmus Peak Track.

After blasting along the tops, we took it slow on the descent, as the shaded sections of the zigzag track were rather icy in places, and because there were still a few trampers around. We certainly got some interesting looks as we rounded corners in our madcap machine to find daywalkers battling their way through the deep snow, and I was quite surprised to see how underprepared a few of them were for the winter conditions — wearing basic running shoes, shorts and shirts. No wonder people get into trouble so often, but we were nice and snug in our fully enclosed cab with the heater running.

As we trundled our way carefully down the hill, a sense of déjà vu hit me. I was in the exact same spot that I'd almost lost the show's Amarok 'Rokky' seven years prior. In that instance, I had set out with the aim of impressing our new partner Volkswagen by getting some epic still photos of the truck overlooking Lake Hāwea. On my way in, I'd been warned by a farm worker that the track up to where we filmed our pilot episode six months earlier was now impassable, and that I'd need chains to get through a section covered in snow and ice, but being a naive Northlander, I thought the aggressive tread on the new offroad tyres would suffice.

The team surveys the snowy terrain, hoping to spot a mobbed-up group of stags.

I soon reached the snowy chute near the top of the track. Rather than trying to creep my way up, I decided to floor it. To the truck's credit, I very nearly made it, but once three-quarters of the way up I started losing traction. I applied the handbrake and put it in park, but immediately found myself sliding slowly backwards down the track.

I opened the door and leapt out, impotently watching my prized possession gain speed as it slid down the icy track towards oblivion. Luckily for me, though, before it was able to go sailing over the falls at the corner of a sharp zigzag, a couple of large rocks wedged themselves like chocks behind the back wheels and slowed the vehicle's progress, and it eventually came to a stop near a steep precipice, where after regathering my composure, I was able to get some pretty punch still shots.

It was a bullet dodged, and I learned a valuable lesson — always listen to the farmer's advice.

There were no such problems with the tracked Polaris, though, and once we'd worked our way down into lower country, we started picking up a few stags, but there was nothing worth pursuing. We eventually lowered our standards a touch, taking a couple of meat animals to ensure we had something to show for our efforts.

But all of this was just a precursor to the main event — the pig hunt.

Dre's two cents

In the early days of the show, we were all adamant that it was the hardcore, purest way or not at all. I was definitely in that camp, a staunch believer that we needed to do the hard yards, replicating the backpack hunts on foot we'd all done and relished in our younger years, and were compelled to showcase that style of trip on camera, making minimal use of helicopters or other modes of transport that could aid the hunt.

Well, times have certainly changed! We came to realise that time wasn't an endless commodity for everyone, and that getting right into the heart of the backcountry with a little vehicular or aerial assistance meant that we could spend a lot more of our precious time actually hunting and filming rather than simply hauling packs.

Although a tough journey is one of the things I love about backpack hunting, the use of various modes of transport has been an effective tactic for us, especially as we've all become slightly shorter on time with families, work and other commitments that come with age (in addition to our ageing bodies breaking down somewhat!).

Our partnership with Polaris was an obvious progression for the show, as it offered another angle to hunts and provided a practical (and let's be honest, fun) way to carve up the kilometres on some of our hunts that, say, your average ute or wagon can't do.

But throwing snowshoes on one, well, that was certainly new territory for me! It was met with some apprehension, but also as an engineer, some genuine interest in how far this thing would go and how effective it could be in the heavy snow and ice of New Zealand's backcountry. So, aside from the winter stag hunting that Anto had organised, it was a chance to put this track-based Polaris through its paces. I don't know how, but I'd been assigned driving duties for the week. And as Dave mentions, we had a blast ripping this thing around in the snow drifts to the point that the hunting almost became secondary to the whole outing.

Tucked up in our heated cab, puffer jackets on, sipping piping-hot Yeti mugs of Dog & Gun coffee, all while wearing rather garish, bright white, 'eggshell' crash helmets — we looked like right piss-takers rather than serious hunting enthusiasts! Furthermore, we were up so high and in deep snow that lack of animal sign really meant we were just touring around having a blast with no real big game in our sights. So we had to get back on track. And when I mean get back on track, I literally mean we had to find a track to get off the damn mountain!

Dave kind of glosses over the descent of the 'snowmobile' Polaris down the Isthmus Peak Track. I've done some aggressive off-roading

The tracked Polaris took a few trampers by surprise during our descent.

in some of the less travelled parts of the world, but I can comfortably say that taking a tracked four-door Polaris Ranger down a steep, narrow, snow-and-ice-clad track on the side of a mountain was right up there in terms of pushing a machine (and my gonads) to the limits. The looks on faces of day-walkers and passers-by as I navigated this bloody snowshoed Ranger down the side of a mountain is quite funny to reflect on. Who knows what they must have been thinking? It surely must have been the last bloody thing they were expecting to see at that altitude and on that track, especially at that time of year.

My sphincter was genuinely puckering up in places where the boys had to get out and spot or walk, leaving me to traverse the machine solo when it got a little sketchy or the track got too narrow. I remember constantly running a checklist in my head that if the machine was to start sliding towards the sheer nothingness, the steps I had to take to get myself out of the driver's seat: 'unbuckle — door handle — out'. I was silently running those three words through my head almost the entire time in hope that if I said them enough it would become more a reflex when called upon. Fortunately, we made it down safe and sound.

I'm sure we'll keep exploring different modes of transport to aid our hunts in the upcoming missions we've got planned. Who knows, you may see us piloting self-driven drones up into the tops, or driving one of Elon Musk's cyber trucks into the back of beyond, or the spearo boys riding hydrogen-propelled Stabicrafts on foils out into the Pacific Ocean.

16 ST BATHANS GOLD

For once, it was Anto rather than Tim who was responsible for selecting the pig-hunting location. Anto and *The Red Stag Hunters Club* founding member Dan Curley had been asked to be guest judges at a hunting competition in the Maniototo a few years earlier, and had hit it off with the organiser, a hardcase bloke named Brett. Anto suggested we take Brett up on his invite to film a pig hunt around the historic gold-mining town of St Bathans, a tiny slice of New Zealand's pioneer history tucked away off the beaten track between Alexandra and Ranfurly.

Initially, filming was delayed due to a short, sharp Covid lockdown, when the Delta strain first made its way into the country, but by mid-September we were once again back into production mode, determined to nail the final episode needed to round out Series 7.

So, after collecting me from Christchurch airport, Tim, his dog Pepper and I carried on south to St Bathans, arriving early the following morning.

Being Maniototo novices, we'd be relying heavily on the expertise of the local lads for this trip, and one man who knew the area better than any was farm manager Tom. He and his bailing dogs hunted the catchment regularly, and he was confident that there would be a few big bruisers kicking about the hills for us to chase down.

The recent lockdown had also meant that the pigs had grown in confidence and were acting more brazenly than usual, having had a few weeks without any hunting pressure. On top of this, it was now lambing season, and the last thing the farms bordering the area wanted were voracious boars dropping down from the mountains in search of fresh meat. These porky pirates love nothing better than hoovering up fresh spring lambs, so we were on a seek and destroy mission.

The hunt soon got under way. After ditching the Polaris (now back to its traditional four-wheeled configuration), we started making our way up-valley on foot, coming across a fair bit of pig rooting, as well a couple of good-sized boar prints, but after an hour the dogs had yet to get wind of any pigs. We changed tack and started climbing, gaining some height to get above any hogs that might have bedded down in the thick bands of scrub punctuating the hillside. The hot midday sun carried the winds up the face, and sure enough, once up on a ridge, the dogs began tracking

Beautiful country for big boars to hide in.

away along the hillside following a scent and were soon lost from view.

A couple of distant barks confirmed they were onto a mob of pigs. The timing was good, as I had the drone in the air, and was able to capture some great bailing footage down in the creek bed, before we followed the dogs' lead and charged off downhill in pursuit. As per usual, the pigs beelined for the thickest, nastiest piece of scrub they could find.

Pig dog Shadow's on-board camera captured a high-speed downhill chase, showing the pig really put on the afterburners, leaving her in the dust. Pigs are renowned downhill sprinters, but they don't have the same straight-out speed over long distances as dogs do, so once on the flats, Shadow was soon able to cut the distance and put the brakes on the rampaging hog.

Tim and I caught up to the first pig, a sow, and dispatched it without too much fuss, before carrying on down to the creek to where Anto was keeping a close eye on the bail-up. Tim bravely committed to the thick scrub, but the boar broke away and charged off up-valley, with Shadow right on its heels.

It didn't manage to make it far, though, and Tim eventually caught up and shut it down with his knife, and just like that, we had a fairly decent first-up sequence under the belt.

But it wasn't in any danger of outshining the Kaikōura action sequence, so we still needed something special. Luckily, Tom had an ace up his sleeve. For the evening hunt, we relocated to a new location to start afresh. Tom had high hopes for this area, having spied a big boar lurking around in the tops on a couple of occasions, so for the third time this season we found ourselves in the rare position of heading out with a specific target animal in mind.

With the hot sun on our backs and the two dogs, Rosie and Pepper, patrolling up ahead, Tim, Tom and I began our climb. Tim's always been a big fella, but he's been adding a few kgs to his frame for each new season of the show, and now pulls the scales down to a fighting weight of 115 kg. The extra heft doesn't slow him down much, though; he's got a freediver's lungs and the heart of a racehorse, but even so we were soon both blowing hard as we made our way up the hillside.

We eventually caught sight of a dark shape in the distance, moving across the tussock face. We couldn't be sure if it was the big boar that we were after, but before we could get the dogs onto it, a mob of small pigs broke from a couple of hundred metres in front of us, confusing the situation for the dogs as they now had a dozen scent trails to follow.

Leaving Tim and me behind to glass, Tom continued climbing in the hope of being able to call the dogs back to him, but from his new vantage point he spied a much bigger chocolate-coloured boar sidling through the tussock high above. His task now was to get Rosie onto its scent before the boar climbed out of the catchment and over the ridgeline.

By the time we had Rosie working the area, however, it seemed the boar had given us the slip. I flew the drone around the area, hoping to catch sight of the pig, or to perhaps spook it from its hiding spot, but had no joy.

With less than a quarter of a battery left, I began bringing the drone back. Pepper was now back with Tim, so I decided to get a few aerial shots of the pair of them looking uphill towards the sun line, when we heard a bark high above us. Immediately, the VHF blared into life.

TOM: It's the boar, it almost knocked me over.

Turns out that the big boar had been playing possum all along, and as Tom was making his way back down the spur, it had leapt out in front of him and was now barrelling off downhill in our general direction.

At times like these, it's hard to know what to film. I really needed the audio of Tim and Tom's radio dialogue, so I hit record on the main camera resting at my feet and fizzed the nearly flat drone back uphill in the hope of capturing a snippet of the unfolding action from the air, tossing Tim the spare GoPro I kept in my pocket specifically for moments like this.

Using Tom's description, I was quickly able to locate both the boar making its escape, and then Rosie, who was much further up the face. As in the earlier hunt, the boar was increasing the gap on the steep downhill stretch, but Rosie was in hot pursuit, following the trail of the boar.

The keen-eared among you may be able to pinpoint the drone controller beeping in the background throughout all of Tim's audio in this sequence, incessant in its demand for me to land before the battery died and it came crashing out of the air. I needed to override the auto landing function a couple of times, but before it bit the dust, I managed to get a terrific tracking shot of the big boar bounding its way downhill. You've got to risk it for the biscuit, and when it comes to high-risk drone shots, you can call me Cookie Monster.

Here's a useful tip for beginners — pig dogs also make great hand warmers.

I was surprised not to see Rosie in shot, but with the low-power alarms going off, I couldn't afford to go looking for her, or else the eye in the sky would become spare parts in the grass. By the time I had the drone back in hand, the boar had gone all the way down the spur to within a hundred metres of us, and Tim was imploring me to hurry the f**k up so he could unleash Pepper onto its trail.

It was all a little frantic. As I was rushing to pack the drone away, and with the boar now in plain sight, Tim released Pepper, who shot off in pursuit, and Tim followed suit. By the time I caught up to him, Pepper was well gone, so there wasn't a lot for me to film other than two black shapes cresting a distant ridge. Suddenly, Rosie came racing past from our left, following in the footsteps of the big boar.

We didn't realise it at the time, but it turns out the reason for her delay was that her camera harness had become caught up in some dense scrub further up the hill. That's the big risk with using any dog-cam system; it greatly increases the danger of the dog becoming trapped in fences, vines and scrub, and that's certainly not a situation you want to be in when there's an angry boar about.

Luckily, after a minute of fighting her way through the thick bramble, Rosie had managed to break free and continue her pursuit. Tim and I were thankful to have left Anto back down on the flats with the machine, as he was able to keep us abreast of what was unfolding well ahead of us.

Pepper and the boar were hightailing it for the river, and they were now a couple of kilometres away. At the rate they were moving we'd never be able to catch them, so we punched our way through the scrub back down towards the machine to try to cut the distance. As we raced our way towards the action, we kept one eye on the Garmin tracking gear, which showed that the dogs were now together and bailing the boar on the river's edge up ahead. After rapidly carving off a couple of kilometres in the machine, Tim and I now had our breath back and were eager to bring the chase to a close, but the boar had other plans. Upon hearing the machine, it set off upriver, and over the next 20 minutes, it led us on a merry old chase.

After committing to the thigh-deep river (and consequently committing to wet boots for the remainder of the hunt), we found ourselves having to zigzag back and forth as the wily boar continued to break away from the two bailing dogs. I was lucky to have Tim acting like an 'icebreaker' ship in the Arctic, clearing a path for me through the thick bracken, but it was still tough going. We were forced to scramble along on hands and knees in many places.

Up ahead of us, we heard a couple of sharp yelps, which spurred us into action. It meant one of the dogs had likely had a poke from the boar's tusks, but no matter how hard we tried, we couldn't get close enough for Tim to take a shot with his trusty Bergara .44 magnum.

We had a couple of close calls, but each time the dogs circling nearby prevented Tim from being able to take a safe shot. It was starting to get frustrating, not to mention dangerous. The adrenalin that we were running on earlier was now pretty much rinsed out of our systems, and we were starting to worry about the dogs' health — the yelp heard earlier could be something serious, so we needed to bring the pursuit to a close.

As Tim and I battled our way through river and bush, Anto had his drone up in the air, capturing the chaos from above, which provided a handy angle to demonstrate the difficulty in getting a clear shot. Grabbing the boar by the back leg and sticking it was still a feasible option, but that can be a tricky task on a big pig without a holding dog, so we pressed on in the hope of getting an opportunity to take a shot.

While we were definitely feeling the pinch, the pig at this stage must have also decided that enough was enough. Its balance between fight and flight was tilting towards the former, and he began making more aggressive charges towards the dogs, determined to put a few more holes in his pesky pursuers.

With the dogs barking loudly close by, Tim and I snuck our way in closer, using some thick foliage as cover in the hope of taking the boar by surprise, when all of a sudden there he was, charging full tilt straight at Timmy with jaws agape! In a split second, Tim had swung the barrel down and squeezed off, the shot deafeningly loud in such close proximity.

I initially thought he'd just pulled the trigger in reaction to the unexpected charge, but the smoking hole in the boar's skull confirmed that he had pulled off an expertly placed shot at point blank.

The boar landed not at Tim's feet, but on his feet, it was that damn close! He was quite lucky to have a brand-new pair of heavy-duty canvas chaps on, as they protected him from the sharp tusks which would have torn a ragged gash in his lower leg had he just been wearing regular pants.

The shot even took the dogs by surprise, with Pepper standing over the carcass for a second, seemingly confused by its sudden lack of movement, before lunging in and grabbing an ear to ensure the pig couldn't miraculously make another break.

Everything happened so fast that I wasn't sure whether I'd managed to capture the action on the main camera, but luckily for us, the moment the boar made his charge and the flash of the Bergara were sharply in frame, and we had a suitably dramatic ending to a monumental pursuit.

As I explained earlier, the dog cam can be a liability at times. It's also incredibly frustrating when the internal battery runs flat, or the memory card fills up, or the camera orientation gets knocked, or it gets covered with mud, or it isn't rolling during the heat of the action. You certainly need a little luck on your side, and in most instances, you don't know if you've got anything usable until the hunt's over.

In this case, seeing the little red dot blinking away on the camera mounted to Rosie's back after the boar was dispatched was a huge relief, but if I was stoked by the knowledge that I had a viable dog-cam file, it was nothing compared to the level of stoke we had upon first viewing it over a beer later that evening.

The footage was jaw-droppingly good and told a much better story of the hunt than I could have hoped for. We could clearly see the behaviour of the boar change as we approached in the Polaris, but the highlight for me was seeing the exact moment that Rosie arrived at the bail-up with Pepper. Both dogs worked together like well-choreographed dancers to hold the pig in position, at times swinging in and nipping its heels or grabbing it by the ears and hanging on tight. It's incredible to witness.

It also answered a few questions, such as why Rosie was late on the scene after the first downhill chase and the sequence of events that led to her being caught by the boar's tusk. It turns out that her camera had again become briefly entangled in some thick jungle scrub, providing the aggressive boar with an open target. However, before it could do too much damage, Pepper selflessly charged in and hit the hog hard, buying time for Rosie to retreat, an impressive feat for such a small dog.

The boar wasn't the biggest in the history of the show, weighing just 115 lbs, but it was certainly the angriest we'd ever encountered. That may well have something to do with a rumour we'd heard about some Russian blood being introduced in the area a decade or so earlier.

Whatever the case, we'd struck St Bathans gold and had our final episode nailed, but the trip was far from over — we still had two full days of pig hunting ahead. My plan was to use the material from the final days in the next season of the show, but we must have used up our allocation of good luck, as like the two boars we'd nailed on day one, things rapidly went downhill from here, but that's another story for a little later in the book.

The precise moment
that Tim's new chaps
paid for themselves.

Tim's two cents

To be honest, at the moment the boar turned and charged, there wasn't really time for anything to go through my head; I was on absolute autopilot by that stage. Instinct simply kicked in, and thankfully my shot was true. It was only once the boar was on the deck that I could comprehend how close I was to copping a tusk to the groin. I've already had a vasectomy, so I certainly wasn't keen on the boar having a second crack!

For a bush bashing, gorse and blackberry hunter from the top of the south, the open country of Otago is like chalk and cheese. The highlight of this expansive country for me is getting to watch the dogs work out in the open, and the thrill of seeing the animal for more than a split second.

It blows me away where pigs will live — parked up in a tiny piece of scrub, hidden under a tussock bush, or even way up in the deep snow — but that's one of the joys of pig hunting, as you get to experience a little of everything.

17 MAINLAND HĀPUKU MISSIⱭN

**With our seventh season of *The Red Stag Timber Hunters Club*
now done and dusted, we just had a couple more *South Seas Spearo*
episodes left to produce.**

We had two quite specific fish on our spearo wish list. The first was the
hāpuku, a relatively easy catch for a fisherman but incredibly hard task for a
spearo, and the second was a snapper over 20 lbs, where the opposite is true.

The mainland hāpuku hunt would be quite a test, both for the divers
and for me. Telling a compelling story about days spent diving into the
dark depths in the hope of a miracle fish appearing could be a difficult task,
so I made a few calls to ensure we had a little extra colour and variety off
the water.

Location would be critical, so my first call was to our mates at Pure Salt
charters, who welcomed us back aboard for a four-day window diving
in stunning Dusky Sound, which would provide a stunning backdrop no
matter how little action we encountered.

The next was to Brock and the team at Trev Terry Marine. Brock was
keen to take a few spots on the charter, helping us cover the costs involved,
and would also be able to assist with the plan we had to try to raise the fish
on rod and reel.

The final call was to the show's narrator, Ant Niterl, who I was keen to
have aboard to provide the bulk of the topside commentary when the team
were going about their work in the deep. Ant had been the voice of *South
Seas Spearo* from the get-go, and his silky tone, tongue-in-cheek delivery
and incredible turn of phrase had really raised the show's quality. A good
narration and insightful voice-over can really lift an average show, but
there's one thing I'd like to quickly point out.

In both of our shows, the narrators haven't been your run-of-the-mill
voice-over artists. Ant was born in South Africa before his family relocated
to New Zealand, but while his accent isn't detectable, his te reo Māori
pronunciation requires a little extra effort. However, what's much more
obvious if you're privy to the raw recordings of each voice-over is the fact
that he suffers from mild dyslexia.

There have been times in the record booth when Ant has struggled to

Nothing like celebrating a job well done, well before the job's actually been done!

string a coherent sentence together due to a certain word combination that his brain simply cannot process. In the early days before he explained the situation to me, I simply put it down to him being severely hung-over, but now that I'm aware of it, with a bit of extra patience we've persevered and got the job done.

Similarly, Dre grew up bouncing between Tonga, Cairns, Papua New Guinea and New Zealand, so this melting pot of influences means that a few of his words have a rather unique inflection. Dre's early days in the booth were also often quite a painful process. While not dyslexic like Ant, as a child Dre had a bit of a stutter, and attended speech and drama classes to help address the issue. After voicing 80 episodes of the show, though, he's now got his systems pretty much nailed.

But getting back to the hāpuku mission, the main reason Ant was there was to help provide some additional comic relief. You could never accuse the show of being too dry (pun very much intended), but I wanted to be sure we had someone aboard to help stoke the fire, to get the team fizzed when the cold deep diving started becoming a bit of a slog.

Ant was the fire starter, the twisted fire starter.

With experience emceeing major events like Rhythm and Vines, and Winterfest, he was confident being in the spotlight, and knew how to put people at ease. Within minutes of the chopper touching down in Supper Cove at the head of Dusky Sound, he'd already cracked his first coldy and had assigned nicknames to half the crew.

The MV *Flightless* making its way towards the entrance to Wet Jacket Arm.

And in regard to crew, as I mentioned earlier, spearing a puka would require deep diving, and the deepest divers in the *South Seas Spearo* team were Dwane Herbert and Julian Hansford, who'd be pairing up in Fiordland again, six months after their bluefin exploits. Also along for her first *South Seas Spearo* mission was the team's newest member, Jordy Bardin, who'd spent a fair amount of time aboard the MV *Flightless* with the Pure Salt team, and, as per usual, on underwater camera duties was everyone's favourite strawberry blond — Sam Wild.

In hindsight, it was a flammable mix even without our Keith Flint Ant thrown in.

Rather than getting stuck straight into the deep diving, we decided to steam our way from Supper Cove up into the marine reserve at the head of Wet Jacket Arm. The Pure Salt team had recently witnessed puka living right up in the shallows there, and while we would be unable to put a spear

into any within this protected zone, it was an amazing opportunity to capture some rare free-swimming footage of the deepwater fish.

We pulled up in Wet Jacket Arm and cast an eye around, and sure enough there they were, a school of hāpuku visible from the surface! Among the puka, a few sevengill sharks swam languidly in the shallows.

I like to equate shark species with dog breeds. As I see it, the great white is equivalent to a rottweiler, the mako is a dobermann, the bull shark's a pitbull, the bronze whaler's a German shepherd, and the sevengiller would be a shar-pei: weird looking and relatively benign, but still able to administer a nasty bite if provoked.

There was something else that was sure to bite — the cold. Mid-winter conditions meant the team needed some very thick rubber to counter the single-digit water temperatures, which got down to just 5 degrees near river mouths and waterfalls due to recent heavy snow. However, one of the

A rather sullen ling, sulking among debris on the sea floor.

joys of the well-appointed charter boat was the spa pool that allowed divers to suit up in comfort.

Once they became attuned to the chilly conditions, the team had an absolute riot swimming with the inquisitive puka, capturing some amazing footage, but it was all a bit like going on a hunting trip to the zoo. So rather than spend any more time diving without a speargun in hand, early the next morning, we made our way out to the Acheron Passage to dive a couple of potential shallow-water puka spots.

While the puka didn't play ball, the day was still an eventful one. There was no shortage of interesting encounters with fish such as ling, gurnard, flounder and giant stargazers, but the undoubted highlight was Jools pioneering the exciting new sport of underwater fishing. After a shaky start, he was able to perfect a method of catching blue cod on rod and reel while submerged in a sunken tree, a few metres below the surface. At one stage, he even hooked a nice-sized cod with a large sevengiller circling a few metres from him.

But the elusive puka remained beyond us. The next morning brought renewed hope, with solid sign on the sounder at around 30 metres depth, but neither Dwane nor Jools laid eyes on any puka over the course of the morning dive.

We kept at it, trying a few spots on our way up towards Shark Cove. At Nine Fathoms Passage, with Dwane diving solo further up the sound, we decided to try to get one up on him. We put a spearshaft through a puka that Brock's old man Trev had just caught on rod and reel, and as Dwane made his way back to the *Flightless*, Julian and Jordy made a song and dance about finally getting the job done. But the wily bugger saw through

it all — repeating a line I've used once before in this book: you can't bullshit a bullshitter.

I take my hat off to the team for sticking at it in such challenging conditions; it was bitterly cold and dark, certainly energy-sapping stuff. As evening approached, and with the sevengillers growing in confidence, the divers eventually called it quits and retreated to marinade in the warmth of the spa, raising their body temperatures while simultaneously raising a glass or two.

Despite failing to achieve the main aim of the trip, we certainly celebrated enthusiastically that evening. As Ant put it: a couple of beers, who cares; a couple of wines, that's fine; a couple of whiskies, let's get frisky.

Without getting into the sordid details, there was Caligula-esque level of debauchery on the back deck that evening. What began with a raucous singalong evolved into plate smashing before 'bubbling over' into nude wrestling. I shudder to think of how feverish the session would have been if we'd have succeeded in spearing a puka!

I was up early the next morning and straight into damage-control mode. I'd been in this position once before aboard the *Flightless*. On that occasion, Tim Barnett and Cam Henderson had really pushed the boat out, polishing off a bottle of whisky into the wee hours and leaving a trail of broken glass in their wake. This was on a par, but after rousing the guilty parties and putting them to work, we soon had the boat looking shipshape once again.

Understandably, Ant had a rather hazy recollection of the events prior, so Séan, the ship's captain, took the opportunity to play a hearty prank on him. While I filmed surreptitiously from the couch, a rather sheepish Ant

Always a good time when this
man is thrown in the mixer!

was called up to the helm, where Séan explained that he needed him to fill out and sign a supposed Maritime New Zealand incident report in light of what went down the previous night.

ANT: Can I genuinely say something? It takes two to tango, and there were four people that were nude, on the deck . . .

We renamed Dusky Sound 'Dusty Sound' for that morning, but consummate professionals Dwane and Jools still suited up for a final attempt at last-minute glory; however, the morning's diving proved fruitless. Despite our failure, I was certain we still had an episode in the can. It would just be a matter of working out how much of it was fit for broadcast!

Ant's two cents

I've lived a pretty neat life, thanks in part to being an inquisitive type of guy, never afraid to shake hands and put my best foot forward at trying to get a smile on someone's ugly mug.
I remember reaching out to Dave around nine years ago when *The Red Stag Timber Hunters Club* started airing. I had just begun hunting, and I wanted to get involved somehow with what Dave was doing. Having worked in the media realm for a few years, I was keen to learn from the best in the biz, something I always push hard for.

Dave has an uncanny knack at entertaining Kiwis through authentic and riveting storytelling. He knows how to hook in an audience and especially has the finger on the pulse when it comes to choosing the best talent to tell any given story. I'll stop blowing smoke up his arse, but Dave and I slowly built up a relationship over the years, and he has presented me with opportunities that many ordinary Kiwi blokes would give their left one (and possibly their right one) for, and I'm bloody thankful.

After lending my pipes to narrate the first series of *South Seas Spearo*, I got the shoulder tap to make my first physical appearance on the show as a 'part-time motivational speaker' for a liveaboard mission into stunning Fiordland. I didn't sleep for a week at the thought of what I was going to experience, teaming up with a heavy-hitting crew of aquatic hunters who were no strangers to stretching their lungs in the salty stuff. I had never met any of the talent myself, except through some ping-pong banter on social media, so I was looking forward to sharing a few tales with the team. The icing on the cake for me, though, was that I would be required to offer absolutely nothing except some marginal chat and some half-baked motivational quotes from Mahatma Gandhi that I twisted and fabricated to sound like my own.

Fiordland is a natural Viagra on the senses. Being dwarfed by such majestic, jaw-dropping surroundings, it's as though every function of the human body becomes heightened. We take it for granted in New Zealand, but we live in the best country in the world.

I had the chance to prove my worth on the second arvo of the trip, donning the neoprene for the first time in close to a decade, although even that task proved troublesome. In my excitement to suit up, I made the rookie error of slipping into my wetsuit backwards, only realising my mistake as I felt the knee pads kissing the back of my calves. But I soon put the embarrassing start behind me and regained a bit of pride by snaffling my first-ever crayfish, with a gallery of support from the rest of the team on the surface. Jeez, I couldn't wipe the smile off my face. All those years standing in the slip cordon while playing cricket had finally paid off, with some of the quickest glove work of mine recorded to date.

Having ticked off a few boxes and feeling like I had contributed to some good telly, Dave, the show's producer, and I start tucking into a bottle of rum called Dead Man's Finger. It has become a bit of a staple on our trips when we are together. A session on the stiff stuff sent us into a delirious state of stupor. Next thing I know, Dave, Sam, Jools, Dwane and I were all naked, straining our larynxes to 80s hip-hop, telling each other how much we loved each other, and even managing to squeeze in a couple of wrestles on the deck which resulted in Sam drawing claret from a cut to his melon. Good thing Jordy was there to make sure things didn't escalate into any further debauchery.

I will purposely leave out some details of this notorious night, but let's just say, what happens on Pure Salt, stays on Pure Salt — and you all have an imagination, so let your minds run wild.

This was my introduction to the team, and you bet your bottom dollar you couldn't write a better script. The next morning, the team and I were all a little sheepish, having had a bit of a talking to from the owners of the boat regarding our frivolity (mainly directed at me for turning the night into a My Big Fat Fiordland Greek Wedding by smashing plates on my head).

I have worked in media for over a decade now, and I still say *South Seas Spearo* is the best thing I have been part of. That is mainly due to the show's authenticity. It's hard to find humans who can be themselves in front of a camera, let alone a bunch of relatively inexperienced presenters that are able to let their outstanding knowledge and humour shine through. It also helps that the big boss Dave has been making quality outdoors TV for well over a decade now. The bloke just gets life on and off the water. Hopefully this little spiel has brown-nosed him enough to get a couple more invites to future trips with the team, because this was certainly one trip that I have already put on USB to take to the grave with me.

Just another million-dollar view, which
are dime a dozen in Fiordland.

Ant and Trev getting a
head of steam up.

18 FAR NORTH BIG SNAPPER

The Fiordland mission left us with one final shoot for the season — wrapping up the Far North big-snapper episode that we'd been chipping away at over the past nine months. I'd filmed a solid sequence with Nat earlier that summer, setting the scene for what we were trying to achieve, but the way the episode was structured meant we really needed a trophy fish to round it all out. The lockdown didn't do us any favours, and poor visibility on our second attempt at the Cavalli Islands made spearing and filming difficult. So, with the season having already begun airing on TV, we mobilised the troops.

Launching *The Orca* from my home ramp in the Bay of Islands, Nat, Dwane, Tim, Jordy, Sam and I set off in search of a 20-pounder to end the season with. The visibility wasn't flash, but beggars can't be choosers, as we needed to get a pin in to something or we risked ending up falling one episode short.

It didn't take long before we had our first chance. Nat knows the Bay of Islands like the back of his hand, or in his case, like the front of his chest, as that's where he has the BOI topographic map tattooed, and the very first spot we focused on provided Jordy with a plum opportunity to nail an absolute tank.

After giving the fresh kina burley a bit of time to soak, she dropped down and peered over a kelpy ledge, spotting a real thumper, but her shot sailed just high, grazing the big snapper and leaving a single massive scale on the spear tip as a memento.

Nat knows a thing or two about big snapper, having once held the New Zealand spearfishing record, and he estimated the missed fish at being close to 30 lbs, so it was an absolute heartbreaker for Jords. Luckily for us, though, later that same morning Nat was able to go one step better, despite almost missing his opportunity thanks to having the safety engaged.

Nat's fish just cracked the magical 20-lb mark, and really took the pressure off, but shooting the big snapper did create a quandary for the show that we would need to address.

During my years on the *ITM Fishing Show*, we'd regularly encourage fishermen to release the big snapper they caught, given that it was believed

these fish were most effective at reproducing. However, the science was not entirely conclusive. There's a different school of thought among some in the commercial sector that perhaps larger snapper actually put less effort into reproduction and more into growth.

Complicating matters further, recent research into fish survivability has shown that even larger snapper suffer from unseen barotrauma following release, so encouraging 'catch and release' may have detrimental side effects, especially when fishers are releasing multiple big fish a day from deep water. Seeing a fish power off after it's released doesn't necessarily mean that it's going to survive, although of course none of this is an issue when spearfishing.

Before making any sweeping assumptions, I wanted to do my homework (me being a zoology graduate and all). However, after reading up online about different studies, I was even more in the dark, as the bulk of the data collected over the years focused on much smaller fish sizes. Of the information pertaining to fish in the 20 lb-plus range, most was anecdotal.

As I see it, there're plenty of reasons why you shouldn't shoot a 20-lb fish, but there're also plenty of reasons why you should:

- It's thought that bigger snapper have the ability to spawn multiple times per year, and produce better quality eggs, but it's also thought that two 10-pound fish produce more eggs than a single 20-pounder. So if bang for buck is your goal, you're better off taking and fully utilising a single big snapper than shooting two smaller fish.

Nat proudly holds aloft the 20 lb snapper that very nearly eluded us.

Jordy's consolation snapper, after missing the big boy earlier in the trip.

- Big snapper are thought to have the ability to prey on kina, reducing their potential for overpopulation and the resultant kina barrens. But big snapper can also eat juvenile pāua, a highly sought-after species which rarely ever reach a legal size in the warm waters of the Far North.
- It takes quite a few years for a snapper to surpass 20 lbs in size, but some 20 lb-plus fish can still be relatively young. Snapper can reportedly reach up to 60 years old, but even at this age, they may only weigh 10 to 12 lbs, as not every snapper has the genetic capability to grow large.
- Big snapper have a reputation of not tasting as good as smaller snapper, but this is mainly down to poor handling of the fish — getting your 20-pounder into an ice slurry and cooled down straight away keeps it in prime eating condition.

We were in a tricky position. I could certainly argue the merits of taking a big snapper but didn't want to undo years of conservation effort by

A dense bait ball hits the surface near Waiwiri Rock.

A humpback feeding on krill, a sight rarely seen in NZ waters.

encouraging viewers to head out and slay the next few 20-pounders they hooked. That being said, no one should have to justify the reasons why they decide to kill a fish. I don't begrudge anyone taking home a 20 lb-plus snapper, so long as they do the big fish justice.

In the end, we chose to simply emphasise to viewers that if you planned to take a fish of this calibre, you needed to look after it properly and make full use of the fish, which in our case included smoking the frame after it was filleted to ensure that nothing went to waste.

As it panned out, when the episode aired there was none of the negative feedback from viewers I had worried about, which came as a surprise. Perhaps I'd made too big a deal of things in my own head. Or perhaps after the failure to secure a hāpuku in the Fiordland episode which aired the week prior, viewers enjoyed seeing the team succeed for a change. Whatever it was, it was great to end the series on a high note, with the final sequence of a breaching humpback whale feeding inside the bay a personal highlight for me. There's a real sense of pride that comes with showing off your own backyard, something I'd been unable to do throughout seven seasons of *The Red Stag Timber Hunters Club*.

While Season 2 of *South Seas Spearo* was again well received, I was equally as proud of the latest *The Red Stag Timber Hunters Club* offering. Feedback from fans was fantastic, and viewership continued to improve year on year. The epic pig-hunting sequence with Tim certainly went down a treat with fans, and I felt extremely proud of the overall calibre of shows we'd manage to create. If I'm being perfectly honest, at the start of the year, we were unsure of how many more episodes we had left in us, but now that the series had run its course, we were itching to crack on with Series 8.

PART FIVE
HIGHS AND LOWS

South Seas Spearo had avoided the dreaded sophomore slump, the term used to describe how a second effort often fails to live up to the high standards of the first, and we had plenty of lofty ideas for future adventures, but we had one major obstacle — we were going broke.

The financial mechanism we relied on to provide funding for the series was hugely dependent on overseas sales, and with the pandemic causing chaos, we struggled to get any cut through into the lucrative European and North American markets. Show quality counts for very little if you're unable to get it in front of the right people, and that was (and still is) our biggest obstacle.

Sure, we had a big new Stabicraft with a custom GFAB trailer, powerful Yamaha outboard and all the latest Garmin electronics, but as we began mapping out Series 3, I realised we needed to tweak the business model. It costs a grand just to fill the tank, let alone all the other costs of production, so we spread the net and brought on a few more paying partners — Beuchat, Just Another Fisherman, Victory Knives, Dirty Steve and Narva.

Around this time, I also received some rather awkward news. We had partnered with a Europe-based distributor that I first met while attending MIPCOM in Cannes. After discussions with a couple of potential German broadcast partners, I received an email from them with some interesting feedback. Turns out that they had serious reservations about the *South Seas Spearo* 'lightning bolt' logo, which they felt too closely resembled the Schutzstaffel emblem, the infamous insignia of the Nazi Secret Service!

Cue a few calls to graphic designers to see if we could come up with a rapid alternative. Thankfully, the oversight was pointed out to us early on in the show's development, and we were able to settle on a new insignia without any horrific white supremacist overtones. It was an important lesson about market research, but at least a logo is easier to change than a name — think about the poor marketing team behind the Mitsubishi Pajero (Spanish for 'wanker') or the Toyota Isis.

SOUTH
SEAS
SPEARO

19 THREE KINGS REDEMPTION

December's always a great time for a mission to the Three Kings — the days are long and if you can catch them out pre-spawn, the kingfish tend to be in their best physical condition. You just need a suitable weather window to be able to make the run there and back without any drama.

It's also a relatively safe bet that a December mission to the Kings would net us an episode to kick off the third season, but in order to mix things up from our previous trip, rather than making it an overnight affair we decided to try to do it all within a single day. This required a pre-dawn start for a remote beach launch all the way at the very tip of Ninety Mile Beach. Long days are not uncommon when we're filming, but this one was going to be right up there in terms of duration.

On diving duties for this trip were Nat, Rochele, Sam, Tim and Kieran, with Kieran being of particular interest given how his previous mission to the Kings had played out.

On that occasion, he'd shot what could quite possibly have been the fish of the trip, but a calf cramp on his ascent meant he ended up losing it, and with a staunch policy in place of one fish per person per trip, that was him done and dusted.

Beach launching can be tricky, especially off the wild west coast, but we managed to get the boat in the drink without incident, and after taking a couple of hefty waves over the bow while punching through the breakers, we were soon en route to Manawatāwhi.

Over the past few years, we've been trying integrate te reo Māori place names into the show as often as possible, for example, Manawatāwhi Three Kings, Rakiura Stewart Island, Tamatea Dusky Sound. The shows are effective platforms to inform viewers on the traditional Māori names of these remarkable locations, although I admit we don't always get the pronunciation 100 per cent bang on. (Ant kind of butchered his delivery of Te One roa-a-Tōhē Ninety Mile Beach in the intro to this episode.)

Our concession to operate on Department of Conservation land also requires us to consult with local iwi before filming taking place, and in this instance, the iwi responsible for Manawatāwhi Three Kings was Ngāti Kurī.

Prepping for an early launch at the tip of Ninety Mile Beach.

We're on good terms with Ngāti Kurī now, but we did have a bit of a scare in the show's infancy, where in the build-up to our first-ever trip to the Kings, a communication breakdown between the DOC representative and Ngāti Kurī led to some frantic petitioning on my behalf to allow the show to go to air!

In that instance, we were able to find a compromise that suited both parties, integrating some key messaging into the episodes around the concept of kaitiakitanga, or guardianship, encouraging visitors to take only what they need and to look after the delicate Far North ecosystem. It was a win-win, giving the episode a bit of extra heart as well as helping educate viewers, but it was a reminder that we needed to have our i's dotted and t's crossed before embarking on future adventures.

The day's diving up at the Kings went to script. There're not a great deal of additional 'behind the scenes' shenanigans that I can regale you with, as things played out pretty much how it all unfolded on camera. Rochele snagged a couple of new New Zealand records for Kermadec kahawai and golden snapper. Nat located an old tank abandoned by a scuba diver who got into trouble on a dive the previous year, and who was thought to have perished before being rescued the following day. Kieran managed to achieve his redemption by landing a top-quality kingi, a fish that we all hoped might crack the 40-kg mark. It was a satisfying day for all, and we made it back to the mainland right on dusk.

The only thing we didn't include in the episode was a final encounter with some nocturnal wildlife on the drive down the beach. We discovered there were a surprising number of possums out foraging around in the sand, but there're now a couple fewer thanks to Kieran's determination to chase them

Kieran achieves his redemption.

down, I believe he even took to the sea in pursuit of one of the pesky pests.

The following morning, we set about getting a weight on each of the four kingfish we had on ice. On past trips, Nat had impressed everyone with his incredibly accurate estimates of big fish, his guesses often falling within a kilogram of the actual weight.

This time, though, we were all taken by surprise by the final figures, which fell well short of our initial estimates.

Nat's fish needed to surpass 31 kg to break the New Zealand pole-spear record, but it was only able to pull the scales down to 27.5 kg. Kieran's big

Kieran's two cents

If you've spent any significant time fishing, diving or hunting, you'll know hard-luck stories are a dime a dozen. I certainly have plenty. For me, they're a motivation that keeps me coming back: the chance to make good on missed opportunities.

Failure is always hard, but it's even harder when you've shared it on TV for the nation to see. Our last trip to the Kings had presented me with a golden opportunity but resulted in an embarrassing failure.

I was never going to turn down a chance at redemption, and with a ten-hour drive north and a massive steam to the Kings, I had plenty of time to reflect on my previous disaster.

As much as there are a lot of laughs in front of the camera, behind the sunglasses, I was feeling the pressure on this trip. But at least we had plenty of time to kill, as tide and current direction are critical for kingfish. If they're not running, you're out of luck.

Thankfully, I was able to spend a good hour stretching the lungs, enjoying the peace and quiet of diving a sheltered anchorage with little current.

Some people have fish sense. It's the ability to instinctively know where to be and when. They're the 5 per cent that catch the 80 per cent. It's instinctive in most of them, built up from a life of experiences and interactions with the marine environment. At the Kings, there's probably no one out there with better fish sense than Nat Davey. His senses were telling us where to head next, but it wasn't quite time for the kingfish hotspot, so we tried our luck diving a deep cave he'd discovered on a previous trip.

We swam hard across the current, until we hit a big back-eddy. From here, we freedived down to the entrance of a giant underwater cave. Our torch beams were swallowed by the blackness beyond. Rare black spotted grouper guarded the zone between daylight and darkness, their white markings often the only thing visible in the shadows.

donk was especially disappointing, at just 33.8 kg despite it being 142 cm long. According to the charts, that length should have put the fish upwards of 40 kg had it been in good condition. Once we began filleting, our suspicions were confirmed.

Sam's was the only fish that hadn't spawned, and at 30 kg it weighed close to what we had estimated. Still, we could hardly be upset, and the spawning fish may have left us with egg on our face, but with Christmas approaching, we had plenty of delicious fish for the holidays and a solid first episode in the can.

Golden snapper, a rare fish for *South Seas Spearo* to shoot in New Zealand because of their preference for deeper water, were living very shallow, and there in large numbers. Nice-sized crayfish walked around in the open, as if they were off to the supermarket.

And then there was the surge. Breathing up on the surface, against the sheer rock walls, the waves would lift you 3 to 4 metres, before sucking back down. On the bottom, a 15-metre dive could become a 19-metre dive despite you being pressed to the rocky sea floor.

It's a cliché, but after this dive, my cup was full. I didn't care if we went home empty-handed on the kingfish front. This dive, the energy, the sights that most will never see. I didn't even pull the trigger. However, that doesn't cut it for a spearfishing show — not by a long way.

By now it was early afternoon, and the current was in full flow. We're not talking about a 'gentle drift down the Avon River, having a cup of tea and scones' kind of current. We're talking about a raging river of water, with vortex-like whirlpools, 2-metre pressure waves, and a change in sea level from one side of the island to the other.

This is the serious part of the day, and what I'd been losing sleep over, the time when I'd seen true monster fish in the past. Now was my chance to rectify my previous failure.

Only, I didn't. Well, not at first anyway. Nat and Rochele barrelled into the water first. The shout went up — 'There's hundreds of kingfish!'

Adrenalin is an awesome thing. It heightens your senses, makes your heart beat faster, makes your reaction times quicker. On land it does lots of good things.

But when you're trying to be calm and slip quietly into the water when people are screaming how many fish there are, it's a nightmare. The fundamental basics, like putting your weight belt on (Sammy) or spitting in your mask (me) get forgotten. All the calmness that spearfishing and freediving require get thrown out the window.

So, while I battled to settle the nerves and fight off the adrenalin, I slipped into the water . . . only to see pretty much nothing.

We drifted, and drifted, and drifted some more. Nothing. No fish.

Not even any bait. The kingi school had seemingly evaporated. However, the upside was that it gave me a chance to reset, to get my breathing sorted, and to become properly relaxed.

The current picked up a little and changed direction slightly. Some bait fish became more edgy. Small kingfish, well for the Kings anyway, appeared. These 15- to 25-kg models would be a decent fish anywhere else in the world, but I wasn't going to pull the trigger on anything 'normal'.

Before too long, I heard the shout go up from Rochele. 'Fish on!' Nat had stuck a shaft in one.

Sammy and I raced over to film and to watch the fight unfold. There's something that stirs the inner caveman (or cavewoman) about fighting a decent fish while you're spearfishing. It's you and the fish. Blood, adrenalin and a little fear mixed in, because we certainly weren't the apex predator in these notoriously sharky waters.

After ten minutes of to and fro, Nat had his fish on the deck, a good start. Dave filmed the necessary pieces to camera, then it was my turn to get on the board.

Before Round 2, I took a few moments to rest and rehydrate, especially important given my predisposition to cramping up late in the day. We continued diving. The visibility had deteriorated a bit but was still in the 15-metre range. Fish, though not many in number, were still passing through. I sat wide of the drop-off, with Sammy and Rochele taking turns filming as I dropped to 12 to 15 metres and waited. I'd drift, and pretend not to be interested in anything,

Rochele's whopper goldie, which set a new New Zealand women's record.

Underwater cameraman Sam getting in on the action.

hoping that the fish's natural curiosity would bring them in. Another dive, nothing to shoot, surface, breathe up, repeat.

The day was starting to drag on. There were some hefty trevally lurking about, screaming out to be shot, but with my triple-rubber homemade rig, I'd purposely armed myself with something I could only use on big fish.

I dropped again. This time Sam and Rochele stayed on the surface.

As I approached my chosen depth, I levelled out. Looking to the deep water for the green and gold torpedoes to come up from under me. They didn't.

I put my head on a swivel, slowly searching from left to right, then from the surface to as far down as I could see, but it looked as though this would be another fruitless dive. Mentally, I prepared to leave, but took a quick glance below my armpit. There was a fish.

Lone fish here at the Kings often means they're big. This guy had a 'presence' too; it's hard to explain, but you just know it when you see it.

I used the slightest of kicks to turn and face the fish head on, staying as relaxed as I could, trying to keep the adrenalin at bay.

Ever so slowly, I raised my hand to hit the record button on the GoPro, listening for the reassuring beep that my head cam was recording. It didn't. I reached up again and pushed the button. Still no beep. Shit.

We have a well-used saying on the show — 'If you didn't get it on camera, it didn't happen'. We're not the kind of show that will re-enact a scene either, and anyway — it's not like I could ask the kingi to politely return to 'first position' and wait for the director to call 'action' again.

Another view of Kieran's big fish, showing off its massive head.

In that moment, I had a choice: bail out on a fish that could put some nightmares to rest, or hope that Sammy and Rochele were watching from above, saw what was happening and hit record . . .

Option B it was.

The fish, despite its size, was displaying curiosity and hesitation. It was heading towards me, face first. My body language was as neutral as it could be. I clearly remember thinking to myself, 'If this fish turns, it's gone.'

Slowly and with as much fluidity as I could, I extended my speargun. I picked out a tiny target on the head of the kingfish — adhering to the adage of 'aim small, miss small'.

I don't remember pulling the trigger, but I do remember watching the 8-mm shaft accelerate through the water, impacting within a thumb's width of where I was aiming. We call it a unicorn shot. Before I'd even turned to the surface, I could hear Sammy shouting through his snorkel. He'd managed to get the camera rolling literally as I'd touched the trigger.

I hit the surface elated.

Sammy and Rochele filmed while I clipped off my float line on a short lead. The kingfish was crippled. There was no blistering run. No tug of war. Though not on the boat, it may as well have been.

After some brief fireworks on the surface, we got the fish aboard. The sheer length of it blew me away. It was significantly longer than any kingfish I'd shot in the past, though, as Dave explained, it had already spawned and lost a lot of its weight.

But in a way, so had I — with that single fish, my one and only for the year, a massive load had been lifted off my shoulders.

20 THE ROCK

After the Three Kings mission and a boisterous AGM in the Far North over the first week of the New Year, we decided our next *Spearo* mission should be to the opposite end of the country, so we set about putting plans in motion to film an adventure that we'd been bouncing around since the very first season of the show.

Known to Southland locals as The Rock, Solander is a remote chain of three volcanic islands off the south-western tip of the New Zealand mainland. It's an intimidating location, rising steeply to 330 metres above sea level, with the islands often shrouded in mist, a bit like the mythical Skull Island from *King Kong*.

The Māori name for Solander is Hautere, which translates as 'swift wind', which is apt considering the prevailing conditions this far off the coast. These forbidding southern waters take no prisoners, and the remoteness and exposure to extreme ocean swells make the islands accessible to only the saltiest of sea dogs.

Being a staunchly proud Southern man, for the past few years Dwane had been going on and on about wanting to launch a mission to Solander, so after chewing our ears off about the potential leviathans that dwell in these untouched waters, we finally relented and began mapping out a mission to the wild south-west.

It wasn't a straightforward planning process. Given the distances involved, we would need a settled weather forecast, but in the days leading up to our filming window, a massive summer storm came sweeping down the east coast of the North Island, causing havoc and sinking boats in northern marinas. On top of that, a series of huge volcanic eruptions in Tonga had rocked the South Pacific, radiating out gigantic shockwaves and explosions that could be heard all the way down in Bluff.

The thought of tectonic activity all the way over in Tonga influencing our spearfishing success at the bottom of New Zealand may sound a little fanciful, but I can recall being out on a lads fishing charter with some good mates in the days following the huge 9.0 Japanese quake of 2011 that led to the Fukushima nuclear disaster, and there were absolutely zero fish around the regular Bay of Islands hotspots. So while it may seem that Tonga's a long way off, the eruptions could still have an effect on fish behaviour all the way down in the Deep South of New Zealand.

We assembled at Dwane's pad in Bluff on the evening before departure. Alongside Dwane, me and underwater cameraman Sam Wild were *South Seas Spearo* regulars with Kieran Andrews and first-timer Storm Lequesne. A Stewart Island local, nineteen-year-old Storm was on board to help motivate us old dogs and keep the excitement levels high!

Rounding out the team was Dave Strudwick, a Wānaka-based owner of a 2500 Ultracab XL in Arctic white, just like our showboat *The Orca*. Dave was a big fan of *South Seas Spearo*, and he had reached out via email offering us the use of his boat if we ever needed it for a Deep South mission, which we eagerly took him up on. He was along for the ride and hoping to learn a few things from experienced skipper Dwane about venturing away on extreme offshore trips.

The excitement levels were certainly high, but after studying the latest weather update in Dwane's lounge, we were disappointed to see that forecasts had deteriorated and we had rather fickle conditions in the days ahead. There was no guarantee that we'd be able to get all the way to Solander, but we decided to roll the dice and put ourselves in the position that if we did get a window, we'd be able to make the most of it.

Given the variables at play, we needed to factor in an additional safety margin, so we made sure we had plenty of spare fuel, lashing multiple jerrycans to the roof of the big Stabi. We launched from Bluff and punched our way across Foveaux Strait, where the strategy was to first dive the productive waters around Stewart Island, before making the run to The Rock if conditions permitted.

Crays for days!

The diving started off with a bang, the team dropping over the side and right into a huge school of trumpeter. A few warehou were then seen on a deep pin, but they eluded us, as did a school of small southern bluefin tuna which had our hearts racing as we pursued them for an hour or two without success.

Over the course of the afternoon, the lads were able to harvest plenty of tasty table fish along with a few nice crays, although Kieran had one moment that he'll want to forget. After a rather deep dive to tangle with a big buck crayfish that was a little more rambunctious than he expected, he required a little assistance back to the surface from Dwane.

The sequence provided a chance to point out the dangers inherent in diving, and how important having a switched-on dive buddy is. Early in his ascent, Kieran reached down to pop his weight belt once he started feeling that he was approaching his 'danger zone'. Dwane could see what was happening from the surface so raced down to lend a hand before things got ugly.

It was nice to be able to show viewers that even the best in the business have their moments. In Kieran's case, his dive was a bit deeper than expected, plus he was forced to ascend with a feisty crayfish disrupting his streamlined shape. It was also nearing the end of the day, a time when shallow-water blackouts more commonly occur due to divers being tired, so all in all, a bullet dodged.

Shortly after Kieran's close call, we had an updated weather forecast come through. While it wasn't ideal, it looked like we would have a window to get out to Solander early the next morning. The plan now was to overnight aboard the boat, which we anchored off Codfish Island, the famous kākāpō sanctuary to the west of Stewart Island. Steaming from Codfish rather than from Bluff or Oban would cut a good 40 minutes off the run, which in heavy seas could make all the difference in terms of fuel. It also saved any risk of the fellas getting a little too exuberant once again at the Oban pub — I for one certainly didn't want a repeat performance of the last visit.

There were no real hijinks on our little sleepover party, the fellas were rinsed after a long day in the drink. With my offsiders catching a few Z's, I found myself sitting on the swim step enjoying a quiet bottle of wine, watching the moon rise over the Ruggedy Range, and listening intently for any distant kākāpō booms emanating from Codfish.

The alarms went off at 4.45 a.m., and after a quick brew to get the motor running, we got straight into prepping for the big steam to Solander. I knew the morning would be a battle for me. After years spent filming on boats, I have managed to identify the various ingredients that go into my personal sea-sickness cocktail — the 'Rusty Cameraman'.

Take one part lack of sleep, add a measure of wind and a splash of rough seas. Shake hard with camera in hand, then strain through exhaust fumes and serve in an enclosed cabin. For an extra strong mix, garnish with a mild hangover.

Nearing little Solander after a long and bumpy steam.

As the sun rose, I was certainly feeling pretty green. I retreated to the back of the boat where I could suffer in silence, but after a couple of hours bashing our way westward in the sloppy seas, the sight of Solander rising dramatically out of the mist in the early-morning sun roused me back to life.

Despite its isolation, Solander has a rather colourful history. A group of Aussie sealers spent a few years marooned on the remote islands way back in the early 1800s. They eventually caught the eye of a passing ship, although the cunning skipper demanded all the seal pelts they'd accumulated over that period as payment for a return to the mainland!

We weren't here for the long haul, though. With the weather expected to deteriorate rapidly by midday, we needed to make the most of the time we had, and then beat a hasty retreat, or we risked being caught with our pants down a long way from the nearest shelter.

While diving commercially in the area in recent years, Dwane and his cohorts have seen plenty of trophy-calibre fish, including some big tuna and possibly a billfish of some kind (although they didn't get a good look at it). There're a number of steep drop-offs, plunging straight to 40 metres, providing great spearing opportunities for the deep-diving Dwane and Storm. It's just one of those wild places where pretty much anything could turn up from out of the blue; we just needed a little luck on our side.

On arrival, we could see dozens of seals swimming and splashing around, so no doubt there would be the odd big shark lurking about as well, adding an extra degree of spookiness to the dive. The water was deep and dark but, overall, a little disappointing. The visibility wasn't as clear as the day prior, but over the course of the morning, the team still managed to spear a few very hefty blue cod, weighing up to 3.5 kg.

Dropping over the side to be greeted by a teeming school of small trumpeter.

Dwane showing off his blue warehou.

Big blue cod are all well and good but spearing them doesn't really make for 'edge of your seat' viewing. We needed to end the trip on something a little more meritorious, but with the clock ticking, we were running short on time to make that happen. The numbers that Dwane and Storm were putting up certainly had a bit of wow factor, though, with both divers regularly hitting 30 metres.

Eventually, their hard work paid off, with a school of cagey blue warehou appearing from out of the gloom. Unlike the previous encounter, this time Dwane was able to pick one off, and he later doubled his tally with a second fish.

Spearfishing for warehou has a few parallels to hunting on land. Dwane, and later Kieran, had to swim up into the current trying to locate the brightly coloured warehou crap which floated about midwater. This spoor had the appearance of someone having spilt a packet of Twisties over the side, and once they had found it and followed it to its source, they would drop down stealthily into the school and put a pin into one. It may sound easy, but it can be anything but.

The warehou provided us with the type of ending that we were after. We had a very hearty bin full of crayfish, pāua, trumpeter and blue cod, so with dark clouds looming on the horizon marking the arrival of the fast-approaching front, it was now time to begin the 100-km steam home.

In the end, we made it back comfortably. Having initially banked on 350 litres for the two days, as we coasted our way into Bluff Harbour, we had a little less than 50 litres left in the tank. But there was one final piece of drama at the boat ramp.

As we went about getting the big boat out of the drink, I noticed a pack of local kids had jumped into the water directly behind us and were having a whale of a time swimming against the river of white water being churned up behind the boat as we tried to power it up onto the trailer. I yelled at them to get the hell out of the way, but they didn't take any notice as they were having a blast. Dwane later told me that's just what the local lads do for kicks, but I reckon they're living on borrowed time. If we had slid back down off the trailer, the props would have quickly minced them into Bluff burley.

Back at Dwane's, we washed the boat and finished filleting our fish, and had just sat down for a beer when we felt the start of a strong sou'west blow coming through, reinforcing the fact that we'd made the right decision to leave when we did. A couple of days later, Dwane steamed past Solander in his big 17-metre steel commercial boat, and it was blowing 25 knots of sou'wester, with huge rollers smashing into the stark rock bluffs — definitely not the place to be caught out. Once bitten, twice shy, as they say.

The aggressive topography of Solander Island.

Dwane's two cents

Solander . . . The Rock . . . everything out here is big! Cod, pāua, crays. You name it, if it's there it'll be big. Not in numbers, but in size.

Once diving out there a few years ago, I dropped below the boat to see what was around and saw a blue cod so gargantuan that it looked almost deformed. I raced up and asked for a speargun and went back down. Sometimes the bigger cod are a bit smarter and will stay right out of range, but after sitting on the bottom for a wee while he made the fatal mistake of being a little too inquisitive, swimming over to check me out, at which point I made him an offer he couldn't refuse.

After spending two days in the hold of the boat with all the kina we'd caught, I weighed him in at 4.06 kg, just over the magic 4-kg mark. I haven't found anything close to that size since, but then I know there're deep rocks that hold larger fish out there.

On another occasion out there, I was swimming out wide just to 'have a look' and as I descended I saw heaps of small schools of bait fish. Thinking to myself, 'This looks fishy, almost tuna-y . . . ' and as I turned my head around, two very large, at least 80-kg tuna glided past in the distance.

Unfortunately, the day we went out filming nothing huge turned up in the limited time we had, but you gotta be in to win, and if you don't go you'll never know! Hopefully we'll get another weather window in the coming years to get back out and roll the dice on another adventure at The Rock.

21 OFF THE DEEP END

At the *South Seas Spearo* AGM earlier in the summer, Ants 'Happy Days' Broadhead pitched a pretty good idea for an episode. It was a rather simple premise: load up *The Orca* with a couple of hundred kilograms of burley, steam towards the horizon for a few hours, then simply drift around way out wide for a couple of days while creating the mother of all burley trails 50 miles off the coast, and film whatever unfolds.

It was a simple but effective premise; who doesn't enjoy the thrill of the unknown? But as the filming window approached, work commitments forced Broady out of the starting line-up. Luckily, Dwane was ready and willing to take his spot, flying up in late February to join Sam, Jordy and me as we set about putting Broady's baby into action.

It wouldn't be all hit and hope, though. Nat had got hold of some GPS co-ordinates from a commercial fisherman who was conducting some experimental deep-water crab fishing in the Far North, dropping pots in around 1000 metres of water. Knowing full well the effect of a floating object in the wide-open ocean, we were eager to check out what might be in hanging out in the vicinity of the surface floats, which had been at sea for well over a week.

So, after loading *The Orca* with 200 kg of frozen pilchards, we set out from stunning Whangaroa Harbour on sunrise, punching our way out towards the distant crab pots.

It was quite a steam, and once at the marks, there was no sign of any floats anywhere on the surface. I was a little disappointed, thinking that perhaps the pots had been pulled in at some point in the previous days. Dwane, however, knew better. As a commercial fisherman, he had a better understanding of how the tides and currents could greatly influence their location, since there was such a huge amount of rope connecting the floats all the way down to the pots on the sea floor.

For example, 1000 metres of rope tied off to pots at a depth of 850 metres would allow the floats to be anywhere within a 1 km radius of the original mark, and while conditions weren't exactly sloppy, there was still enough of a roll to make spotting them a challenge.

To improve his vantage point, Sam climbed on to the roof to scan the horizon and, sure enough, after a bit of a grid search we managed to lay eyes on a pair of large orange windy-buoys bobbing away on the surface.

After an early start and a long steam, the sight of the floats gave the team the boost we needed, but after jumping overboard into the gin-clear waters, we were brought back down to earth. There were just a handful of pilot fish and a school of juvenile kingi lurking around, with no sign of any of the prestigious bluewater species that we were targeting.

We knew there would be more floats around, so we set about finding another set. It was a bit like a game of battleship, taking a stab in the dark at which direction the pots were deployed in. Luckily, we guessed right, as we soon laid eyes on another set of floats off in the distance.

Once again, though, it seemed there was nothing for us to get too worked up about. However, after bobbing around for fifteen minutes, Dwane was just about to call it quits, when suddenly a trio of mahi mahi appeared from out of the blue. Sam swam directly towards them and was perhaps guilty of being a little trigger happy, letting his spear fly at the first available opportunity. While he connected with one of the mahi, the spear quickly pulled free. These fish are renowned for the fierce way in which they fight when hooked or speared, but while we rued the missed chance, we were confident of going one step better on the next attempt.

The third set of floats was found without much trouble, by following in a direct line from the previous two. This time, rather than letting Dawne and Sam jump in first, I put my brand-new Mavic 3 drone into the air to see whether I could spot any mahi mahi from above.

Sure enough, with my bird's-eye view I soon located the floats in frame, and there they were — ten neon-blue fish, looking snake-like apart from their extended pectoral fins and bright yellow tails.

But where he was previously too trigger happy, Sam now seemed a little gun-shy. He was so determined not to make the same mistake as earlier that he turned down a couple of plum opportunities.

Back aboard the boat, neither Jordy nor I could believe what we were seeing on the drone's monitor, and we also couldn't understand why Sam had yet to pull the trigger, as a couple of the fish looked so close that I'm sure he could have reached out and scratched their flanks with the tip of his spear.

Turns out his seeming reluctance to shoot was due to him making the classic mistake — forgetting about the damn safety! It wasn't the first and it wouldn't be the last time the safety switch would cause us headaches this season. But just like Rochele's miss at the Wanganellas which provided Sam the chance to get some gravy underwater footage, Sam's safety snafu allowed me to get some more epic mahi mahi aerials.

The mahi didn't seem to be too worried about things either, happy to stick around while Sam disengaged the safety and waited for another shot. Eventually, with the school packed tightly together, he had his chance, and this time he made it count, twice in fact. After punching through the first fish, the spear still had the energy to pierce a second, although like earlier, that fish managed to fight its way free before Sam could get his hands on it.

But that wasn't the end of the story. As soon as Sam had secured his prize, Dwane took the speargun from him and went in search of the injured fish. It hadn't made it far, and Dwane managed to find it and plug it with minimal fuss. Two prized mahi mahi before lunchtime, that's a mighty good start! It was around the time that the lads were clambering back aboard the boat that I made a decision that saved me a huge amount of grief. Given the calibre of the aerial footage I had captured, I decided to transfer the video files from the drone across to my laptop, always a bit of a niggle to do when out at sea, but it's good practice.

With the files safe and secure, it was now Jordy's turn to add to the tally. The commotion from the earlier fish seemed to have caused the remainder of the school to disperse, as the only fish hanging about the floats was a little triggerfish of some kind.

We thought this was a rather nondescript sequence, but it turns out a sharp-eyed viewer identified the quirky little fellow darting around next to the floats as a spotted oceanic triggerfish, or *Canthidermis maculata*, usually found in tropical and subtropical waters, and our footage confirmed it as the first recorded sighting of one around mainland New Zealand, which is cool in my book.

Anyway, after half an hour drifting about the big blue, there was still no sign of the mahi mahi. So, to stave off the boredom, I decided to put the drone back in the air and see if I could maybe locate the fish myself. I went about the regular routine of pre-flight checks and calibration before releasing the little Mavic 3 into the air from the back of the boat.

Immediately, I could see that something was wrong. The drone began flying in a circular pattern over which I had no control, so I yelled out to Sam and Jordy to keep an eye on it, but before they could locate it in the air,

A rarely seen double —
a mahi mahi and boarfish
speared on the same day.

the drone decided it wished to self-identify as a submarine and flung itself into the ocean, quickly sinking out of sight.

Luckily, I had a second earlier-model drone aboard as a backup, and since I'd recovered the files earlier, it was just a financial hit rather than the emotional gut punch of footage loss (I'd go twelve rounds as a punching bag later in the year, though; more on that to come).

It was rather comical dealing with the warranty folk at DJI, who at one stage asked why we hadn't simply recovered the drone from the water (I explained it's a bit hard in 850 metres). I had Sam's headcam footage of the moment of the crash to back up my claim of calm weather, and the controller analytics eventually proved that the crash was due to an inherent issue in the drone itself rather than any user error, but that was cold comfort at the time.

But no point crying over spilt milk, as we still needed to get Jordy onto a fish. Given we had 200 kg of pilchards defrosting on the deck, Dwane decided to put some to use and try to entice something into the boat, and it had the desired effect. After tossing a handful of fish over, the mahi suddenly reappeared, but they were definitely a lot more cagey than earlier, keeping a safe distance away from Jordy. She had a couple of opportunities, but as is often the case with clear blue water, it's very hard to gauge distance, and that combined with the flighty nature of the fish meant Jordy was unwilling to take a rash shot.

Dwane continued tossing pilchards over the side, where they were happily engulfed by the hungry mahi, welcoming the chance of a free feed, and this provided Jordy with her chance. Rather than pursuing an individual fish, she adopted our Port Fairy bluefin approach, lining up on a slowly sinking pilchard and waiting for a fish to lock in on it. It didn't take long before the tactic paid off, as a large mahi made a beeline for the pilchard that Jordy had her eye on, but rather than chomping down on the mouthful of tasty pilchard, he bit down on a mouthful of cold steel.

Jordy's headshot was spot on, pretty much killing the fish outright, and not wasting any of the delicious meat. From the surface, the clear water provided us with a good view of the action, so we knew the second the shot went off that Jordy had ticked the box. But what I wasn't prepared for was the display of pure jubilation the moment she hit the surface.

It's only natural after having shot so many big fish over the years for the more experienced spearos in the team to become a little jaded and to moderate their celebrations accordingly. For Jordy, though, this was not the case.

Not since the bluefin tuna the year prior had I witnessed such an uninhibited outpouring of emotion. She hit the surface absolutely screaming with unbridled joy and didn't stop! Over the next 20 seconds she barely took a breath. If she'd celebrated any harder, I reckon she would have been at risk of shallow-water blackout! It was awesome to see, her level of stoke was off the charts, and it's easily one of my favourite moments of the season.

Jordy's magic moment,
a split second after
pulling the trigger.

Once back on the boat, we went through the motions with filming, taking photos and getting the fish onto ice, before deciding it was time to press play on the original plan for the trip — creating the mother of all burley trails.

Unfortunately, despite the high expectations, there's not a lot to report about this element of the trip. We needed to have a spearo in the water at all times, given there would be no way to see any approaching fish from the surface, so the threesome of divers took turns in the water breaking up pilchards and watching them slowly sink down into the deep, while *The Orca* drifted along with its large sea anchor deployed.

After eight hours, with nothing other than a solitary devil ray drive-by and the sun beginning to set, we knocked it on the head, but continued to burley from the boat in the hope of attracting a fish or two in overnight.

With darkness upon us, more mahi soon showed up, drawn in by the pilchards and the underwater lights. Sam quickly suited up and went after them, but they weren't having any of it, disappearing as soon as he got in the water. He and Dwane tried again closer to midnight, but once again the fish quickly vanished. Night diving's spooky enough close to the coast, but way the hell out here in close to 1000 metres of water, with piles of pilchards in the water, it was borderline crazy.

After a rather testing night where no one was able to snatch more than a few hours of broken sleep, the morning finally dawned. Sam and I were feeling green, and we added a little of our own brew over the side into the chumline, which although it hadn't brought in any marlin, tuna or sharks, had brought in a few more mahi, which we spied lurking around the back of the boat.

Dwane was eager to make the most of things and add another to the team's tally, so slipped in and quickly got the job done. We then returned to the first set of floats, the spot where Sam had lost the first fish of the trip and were pleasantly surprised to find the very same fish swimming happily among a school, despite the large tear clearly visible in the side of it.

It took him quite some time, but after waiting patiently for the target fish to provide him with a chance, Sam managed to sneak through the school and put a spear into the wounded mahi. Talk about threading the needle — he almost put his spear through the very same hole he left the first time around!

Despite its injury, the fish wasn't short on fight, thrashing about on the surface and tying Sam up in knots, but after a hard, fast tussle, he was able to flick its off switch and secure the fifth mahi of the trip. This also meant that despite having two of his mahi mahi pull off the spear, none were actually lost, a pretty impressive result.

Rather than calling it quits, we decided to stop off at a couple of spots on the way back in to Whangaroa, to help provide a little variety to the bluewater action, and to prove that there was no trickery at play — we were in fact still in New Zealand waters. A quick dive around the Cavallis netted us a few more good fish, before rounding out the diving action with

a great sequence where Dwane bagged himself a highly prized boarfish, one of the most sought-after fish for Kiwi spearos.

The team had battled away for days in a previous episode to secure a boarfish, so to pick one up on a bit of a whim was a welcome bonus. It was also a proud moment for me, as for one of the first times in the history of the show, I'd been the one who selected the spot to dive (although credit where it's due, Nat Davey had shown me the spot earlier in the year during our AGM).

The boarfish wasn't the only bonus. On our way to the ramp, Dwane did a little research and discovered that the current women's record for mahi mahi was just shy of 6 kg. Knowing the fish we had on ice were hefty specimens, we had the weighmaster Laurie meet us at the Whangaroa weigh station, where we were stoked to see Jordy's fish yank the scale down to 8.92 kg, quite an increase on the previous record.

Jordy was over the moon, although there was one downside to her claiming the new national record; someone would have to call Rochele to give her the bad news!

Rewriting records is something that we've been able to do on a number of occasions for *South Seas Spearo*: two striped marlin world records, the slender tuna world record, national records for southern bluefin tuna, bluefin butterfish, Kermadec kahawai, golden snapper, Peruvian mackerel, and now Jordy's mahi mahi — that's quite a list.

However, we've never been able to trouble the record books for *The Red Stag Timber Hunters Club*. Hunting goes back a long, long way, well over 100 years for most of the big game that we target in New Zealand, so breaking into the top ten for any species is a huge accomplishment. But our record drought was to be broken ten days on from our mahi mission, on a trip that those involved in will be able to dine out on for years to come.

Jordy's two cents

Being the new recruit to the team, I'm always eager to jump at any opportunity that arises. And when the other more experienced team members can't make it on a trip, the rookie gets to step up!

This was one of those trips, last minute as per usual, but I was bloody excited for this one. Bluewater spearing is at the top of my list, with so much potential for an array of tropical species making an appearance. I was quite happy to assume my role as skipper and didn't have any expectation of actually shooting something this trip. My froth levels were super high just seeing the mahi mahi in New Zealand waters and watching the boys secure one each. So, when the boys told me to get in the water and shoot one for myself, I was ecstatic . . . which is all caught on camera!

From my time fishing in Rarotonga, mahi mahi quickly became a favourite fish to see and catch, so this was super special. Not only a first mahi mahi for me on the spear but to shoot one in New Zealand waters and then for it to also be a record, it really was a fish of a lifetime. Not to mention the high-quality meat that I was eager to sink my teeth into and share with friends and whānau.

As embarrassed as I am of my uncontrolled display of pure stoke that was aired to the nation, everyone else seemed to love it, saying it was their favourite part of the episode! After all, this is what we live for, and Dave gets to capture and showcase all those raw, real emotions that come along with it.

It's always a bloody good time out there with the crew!

22 THE TROPHY OF A LIFETIME

We'd had a busy summer getting a few *South Seas Spearo* episodes in the can, but as February came to a close, it was time to leave the boat behind and hit the hills for the first *The Red Stag Timber Hunters Club* trip of the year.

To mix things up a touch, rather than another late summer stag mission in the well-trodden hills of Central Otago, we decided to try our luck in a new part of the country that I'd never ventured into before, up into the headwaters of the Rakaia. For the next four days, I would be joining Anto and Yuley in an attempt to track down a trophy Canterbury stag.

After an early-morning chopper drop, we set to work trying to find our prize. However, having had a few months away from the binos, it seemed Anto was a tad rusty. The sound of the machine had yet to finish echoing through the surrounding hills before he spied what he claimed was a chamois buck, living high on a distant face. After getting the spotting scope out, though, he then sheepishly confirmed that it was only a mossy rock.

On the flight in, we'd passed over some good-looking trout rivers, and Anto and Yuley had been talking non-stop all morning about fly-fishing. But after this embarrassing case of mistaken identity, I informed him that any more talk of trout was prohibited for the duration of the trip. The topic of conversation was to remain solely on warm-blooded creatures.

Speaking of warm, as the sun rose over the steep mountains, the temperature soon rose with it. After pitching camp, we followed the lead of the animals in the surrounding hill country — seeking shelter and waiting out the heat of the day. During the long, slow afternoon, we spied a few deer bedded down in the distant tussock tops, but there were no stags living among them.

The evening finally arrived, so we saddled up and headed off upriver, gaining enough elevation to open up a few more viewing options. It was spectacular countryside, some of the prettiest I think I've ever had the pleasure to film, but it took the lads a long time to find any game. With an hour of light left in the day, they eventually spied a couple of very promising-looking stags, one of which had Anto particularly excited.

It's easy to jump the gun and get a little over-enthusiastic at the first

sight of a decent stag, especially at this time of year. It had been over eight months since Anto and I had last laid eyes on a decent rack, but Yuley soon poured cold water on Anto's premature exuberance, pointing out that both animals still needed a couple more years before they'd be takers.

This stretch of the Southern Alps is home to some of New Zealand's strongest bloodlines, so we wanted to convey to viewers the importance of properly evaluating the maturity of all stags in order to hammer home the message that discipline and restraint are needed in order to ensure that these 'close but no cigar' stags are given the time to reach their full potential.

We kept glassing till dark, then made our way back to camp.

The morning followed a similar pattern. We were up early to climb into the same spot to glass, but only picked up a handful of animals, and none worth going after. It was a little disappointing, but we had miles of promising country ahead of us, so we spent the dead hours of the day relocating our base camp further upstream.

Compared to the arduous summer stag missions in previous years, this one was a doddle. We had a nice head wind, a cool stream providing ample water, and only a gradual ascent. We still needed to pay attention to our footing on the loose river rock, but after a couple of hours, we'd made our way to a good-looking spot at the confluence of the main river and a steep side creek. There was no need to press any further, as basing ourselves higher in the valley would risk scenting the head catchment, so we ditched our packs and after a little light landscaping, we had a comfy campsite set up.

But throughout the day, ominous clouds had been gathering, and they now loomed large over our plans. By the time we set off on our evening hunt, a low mist had settled upon the entire valley, reducing visibility to just a hundred metres or so.

You're fighting a losing battle trying to compete against the weather, but rather than writing off the evening, we decided it was still worth a roll of the dice, so we headed off up a side creek hoping to get lucky and perhaps spook a chamois buck. There was certainly a much greater chance of stumbling over an animal up here than there was sitting around back at camp, but in the end, all we did was get ourselves wet.

At times like these, there's little else you can do other than just roll with the punches. Despite the climatic conditions being against us, there was still a feeling of positivity among the team. We could take consolation from the fact that the best terrain still lay untouched ahead of us, and the forecast was for clear weather in the days ahead.

However, rather than the clear dawn we expected, we awoke to another unwelcome helping of the same cold soup that was served up to us the night before. It's not the first time we've been frustrated by bluebird forecasts turning to custard, as these mountainous regions have the uncanny ability to brew their own isolated pockets of bad weather. There was little else to do other than just sit tight and wait for the morning sun to burn through the thick layer of clag that now enveloped the entire catchment.

By 10 a.m., the fog had lifted enough to warrant heading up-valley, so we set off in the hope of getting into a good position as the stags began moving about on evening. Once we'd made our way an hour upriver, we identified a suitable spot to base ourselves, next to a large boulder in the middle of a sloping tussock face, and got to work behind the glass.

Ninety per cent of the time when you're hunting, the animals you pick up through your binos are living above you, especially in the middle of the day. Anto had spent a few minutes glassing the misty hillsides all around us without seeing anything, when he decided to cast an eye down into the valley floor at the very head of the catchment, where the river wound its way around a corner and out of sight.

Sitting there, as plain as day, on an outcrop of rocks was a massive chamois buck, its golden summer coat standing out vividly against the slate-grey boulders.

ANTO: Oh, it's a ripper, mate.
ME: It's a ripper?
ANTO: Don't get too excited but, yip, it's a donk.
ME: Everything's a ripper in Anto's book!

Anto thought it was a world-beater, but I was a little blasé about the cham. Many times in the past, I'd found myself in this exact situation with Sam and Anto, where we were sure a buck was an absolute beauty from a distance, only to find that it was shy of the 10-inch mark that we were hoping for. I didn't want to get caught up in the hype this time around, but I possibly would have if I'd been monitoring the audio between the two hunters as they set about evaluating the buck on the spotter for trophy potential.

It wasn't until much later when I was in the edit suite listening to the raw audio captured by the phoneskope camera that I realised that Sam and Anto were underplaying the situation to me. Upon first seeing the chamois through the spotter, Sam was genuinely shocked by its size, uttering something to the effect of 'Whoa . . . that thing just has to die'.

But I wasn't privy to any of this at the time. So, as Anto and I waved goodbye to Sam and made our way down towards the big buck to get into a shooting position, it's understandable that I was feeling fairly nonchalant about the whole affair. Anto knew full well what was at stake, though. Under usual circumstances, he and I ensure we have a clear plan in place in the lead-up to him taking a shot. But this chamois was anything but normal. I think the significance of the moment led to a lack of dialogue between us, and that combined with me not quite understanding the gravity of the situation almost led to disaster.

We were able to cut the distance easily using the riverbed for cover. We then climbed onto a small rise, where Anto laid eyes on the buck. It was still oblivious to our presence, sitting happily on his large rock, so he worked his way closer, moving towards a grassy rise where he could set up to take a shot.

I'd stayed back 20 metres, waiting for him to get set up. Once he was comfortable and ready to shoot, he gestured for me to sneak forward and pointed out a position where I would be able to film the action. Slow and steady, it was all going well so far. However, Anto overlooked one important fact — I'm a bit of a muppet sometimes.

To stay light and nimble, I'd chosen to leave my binos back up on the hill, and once in my designated filming position, I wasn't able to find the buck in my long lens, which even at its widest setting is still tight.

Anto reiterated that the buck hadn't moved and was still on the large rock just 200 yards from us, but I couldn't make him out. Turns out I was zoomed in on the wrong boulder, and my camera was focused on one about 50 metres in front of where the buck sat.

We couldn't take a shot until I had the buck in frame, so after 30 seconds of trying and failing to locate him, I called Anto back from his shooting position to help guide me onto it.

Meanwhile, Sam was filming everything as it unfolded from his vantage point back up at the large rock. Through the spotting scope, he captured the exact moment that the buck changed from being fully relaxed to on high alert, having either caught sight of our movement or heard some noise. It sat up on its haunches, looking left and right, preparing to bolt, and I think it was at that very moment that I too finally caught sight of it.

ME: Oh f**k, its boosting!

Anto leapt back down into position behind the rifle.

ME: Just take it, take it-take it-take it . . .

Bang! Anto's shot rang out. All I managed to capture was a blurry flash of brown in the distance.

ME: Oh bugger . . . my fault.

There was nothing said for the next five seconds, then a word reiterated four times.

ANTO: F**k, f**k, f**k . . . f**k!
ME: Do you think you got a contact with it?
ANTO: I don't know . . . you've gotta run up the creek with me, Dave.

We grabbed the essentials and started racing upstream in the direction of the buck, not knowing whether it had been wounded or if Anto's shot was a clean miss.

Unfortunately, back up on the hill Sam hadn't witnessed the shot either, as he was trying to reach us on the VHF to alert us to the change in attitude of the buck. It was a total shit show, an absolute circus, and I was the ringmaster responsible.

I spent the mad dash up the creek thinking of ways to apologise to Anto, hoping beyond hope that we'd get to the rock and find blood, but it seemed wishful thinking. Anto had only a couple of seconds between getting back behind the rifle and squeezing off, a very tough ask for even an experienced hunter like him.

But sometimes wishes come true. We arrived at the rock where he'd been sitting and were excited to see splashes of bright red, the kind of vivid, oxygenated blood that comes from a lung or heart shot. We had hope. There were multiple splashes, thick and coagulated, like fresh paint had been spilt on the rocks.

Spurred on by the sight, Anto followed the trail in the direction the buck ran, and having climbed a small rise, he spotted him piled up in the undergrowth, just 10 metres from where he was shot.

Relief flooded through me. Incredibly, in the short amount of time that he had to squeeze the trigger, Anto had pulled off a near-perfect shot, slamming the powerful .300 Mag round into the chamois' front shoulder.

I had thought Jordy's reaction upon surfacing with her mahi mahi on the trip prior was pretty special, but the emotion of this moment was on another level altogether. The fact that for the past ten minutes we'd both believed in our hearts that the trophy was lost only added to the deep satisfaction we felt. It was visible and audible through Anto's face and voice as he delivered the news to Sam, who, despite the crackle of the handheld radio, was clearly equally as stoked.

The only edge of disappointment I felt was the fact that I hadn't managed to make the most of such a plum opportunity. If I'd have taken things a little more seriously, I would have captured an amazing, slow-motion impact shot on the big buck, but I'd squandered my chances, unable to capture even a detailed close-up of the live animal.

In hindsight, the sequence was all the better for the added drama of it all, the intensity in the seconds after the shot rang out, and the genuine emotion and relief when we discovered the buck had gone down. If it had all gone according to plan, we'd have missed all that drama, but that being said, I'm certainly not eager to put myself through it all again for the sake of some additional suspense!

I'll never forget the moment that Anto pulled the buck out from under the overhanging tussock, providing the first real view of the prized horns. It was gigantic. There was a point in the show's past where we considered the chamois to be our absolute bogey animal. For eight long years, we'd been through thick and thin trying to crack the 10-inch mark but had always come up short. But not this time; surely this was our 10-incher.

Surprisingly, it wasn't to be. Our search for a 10-inch buck would have to go on, as after running his measuring tape over the buck, there was a hint of surprise in Anto's voice:

'This thing's 11 inches, it's telling me it's over 11, I'm going to have to remeasure it, this thing's huge, like huge. It's legit way over 11, man!'

Words from the classic mockumentary *This is Spinal Tap* sprang straight to my mind, as out of my mouth came 'This one goes to 11', but I think the obscure reference went over the head of most viewers.

In fact, it went more than 11. Both horns stretched the tape out to 11⅜, with incredibly thick bases to match. Anto could scarcely believe it. Having never had the rub of the green on our chamois hunts, to have things unfold in such dramatic fashion felt like a balancing of the books.

We did the buck justice by spending a bit of time capturing plenty of epic stills, and with the animal caped out and its meat broken down we made our way back to meet up with Sam, who on first sight was just as blown away by the size of the buck as we were. We continued hunting for the evening, but the job had well and truly been done, and with the weather beginning to turn, we made the easy call to punch back towards camp before dark.

I'm a big believer in making sure there's always a tasty drop on hand to toast any major success on the show. We had a couple of nice bottles of rum on board the boat to celebrate Dwane's epic southern bluefin tuna, but usually it means just having a hip flask of nice whisky in my pack. In this instance, I had been carrying a cask of red with me for a moment such as this, made by a winemaker friend from Hawke's Bay under the label Organised Chaos, which I felt was particularly apt considering the way the action unfolded earlier in the day. It was a sweet feeling, having a punchy shiraz to complement our fresh meat dinner, and despite the stunning scenic

Easily the largest
chamois any of us had
ever encountered and
probably ever will . . .

surroundings, that evening all eyes were on our prize, which was looking even more magnificent after Anto had finished the task of head-skinning it.

We managed to get out for one final skirmish the next morning but were only able to locate a couple of small chamois living up in the head of the valley, before it was time for the chopper to collect us at around midday. The main motivation for the mission — finding a monster Canterbury red stag — had been successfully failed, and we couldn't be happier.

A few weeks later, I found myself back down in Queenstown at Anto's place on the evening an official measure was being done, along with Anto's father Eric. Eric had taken plenty of 10 inch-plus chamois over his many years as a hunter, even writing a book on the subject, but even he had never seen a chamois of this calibre.

After a couple of different measures, Anto's buck received an official overall Douglas score of 30.25 (11⅜ length and 3¾ bases), meaning it sits at fifth equal in the New Zealand record books, right near the top of a list where there is well over a century of hunting history. He's not one to ever mention it himself, but it should be pointed out that there's a slight asterisk next to a couple of the trophies above him on that list, with one being a gargantuan 13¼-inch nanny, and one believed to have been hunted using aerial assistance.

It's an achievement that I seriously doubt we'll ever come close to matching on the show. It's one thing to head out and nail yourself a record-book animal, but to have the whole thing unfold on camera was beyond our wildest dreams, although I counted myself bloody lucky that my inattention didn't turn it into an absolute nightmare!

Anto's two cents

While I am fortunate enough to get out into the hills more often than most, I was a more excited than normal about this particular trip. Making the anticipation higher was the fact that this was my first big-game hunting trip for a few months.

Given it was the end of February, mature stags would now have rubbed up their antlers and stripped off their velvet, colouring them while sharpening their points as part of their annual process of getting ready for the roar.

The location we were heading into held the potential for a mixed bag, holding good-quality red stags, chamois and bull tahr. Having options had always proven successful for the show, particularly when we need to be selective about what we harvest.

Changing out the rod and reels for the new Benelli Lupo felt good, and after exiting the helicopter, any worries of civilisation were quicky gone. Like any trip, you begin with aspirations that almost seem like fairy tales, and this trip was no different. I didn't know it at the time, but for me, this trip would end with me living 'happily ever after'.

A 10-inch chamois buck has been on my hit list longer than any other trophy species, starting my journey of hunting them when just a young boy with my father.

Due to a bit of hard luck, it just seemed I would never come across the animal I was searching for. It had been 20-plus years of trying, and I had gone through a few phases of really targeting them. While I had never given up, I was questioning my sanity at times, certainly at the end of each trip after looking over multiple bucks for the umpteenth time but seeing none that met the magical mark.

As described by Dave, when looking for chamois, you are generally always looking up unless in a well-elevated location. However, this time round, the location of the buck was very odd, in the middle of the creek bed, bedded down on a large rock.

While the chamois still had quite a good vantage point overlooking the surrounding terrain, the main creek provided me with an exceptional way to carve off a few hundred metres without being in view at all.

Looking back, the stalk itself was a little more off than normal. I knew the chamois was big, real big, but I needed to focus on my process, and while the chamois was in a great location, I did not want to waste time and have him move off before we could get into a viable shooting position.

After exiting the main creek, I was able to move out onto the edge of the creek and easily find the perfect shooting position lying down at just over 200 yards.

I was confident and calm; now we just had to go through the motions. As described by Dave, he could not see the chamois from his position behind me, but I could see that any movement he made would be obvious to the big buck.

As I moved back to Dave to point out the cham, I couldn't believe it as it jumped to its feet and started to move. My heart sank, but my body leapt into action, seemingly of its own accord.

I had already positioned the rifle on the chamois and was in half-open bolt, so I was able to lie down, close the bolt and squeeze off relatively quickly.

My memory was blurred as to what exactly happened, but upon the shot going off and realising the chamois had disappeared, a wave of frustration hit, resulting in a fair few beeps in the finished edit. I wasn't confident of a clean hit, and with no cameras on the animal to confirm I'd made contact, I'll admit that I was a little panicked at this stage.

Even when an animal is moving, I can usually find enough time to work through a process before squeezing off, but in this instance, due to the chamois only being one good step from going out of view, I just had to let rip, so was not overly confident. I began wishing that I had taken another split second.

Regardless, it was now time for a mad dash to where I had last seen the buck with the hope of him standing up in some bluffs looking down to provide me with a second chance.

The panic ended up being for no reason, with a perfectly placed shot meaning the buck only managed to get a few metres before crumpling into some thick vegetation.

I can vividly remember leaning down and holding onto the horns to pull him out of the scrub. It was like no chamois I had ever encountered. I was able to hold onto the horns, and it seemed like there was another whole set of normal horns emerging from below my trembling hands.

It was such a great feeling to not only achieve my lifetime goal, but to have Sam and Dave with me to share the adventure made it doubly satisfying.

My father made the record books with a monster chamois buck in 1987, and I had the same honour in 2022. I just hope there is still the opportunity for my sons to join us both when the time comes.

23 CHATHAMS AND THE BUTTERFLY EFFECT

For most New Zealanders, the Chatham Islands is the type of place they're lucky to visit just once in their lives. I'd been fortunate enough to spend an action-packed week on the main island, Chatham, during filming for the third season of the show. On the very last night of that memorable mission, I recall a bloke at the pub telling me that for my next visit I needed to skip the big smoke of Waitangi and head down to Pitt Island, as that's where the real action was.

Five years later, and I found myself once more back in the Waitangi pub, this time with Tim Barnett, Dwane Herbert and Sam Wild, on the first evening of a week-long trip which would also encompass a few days on Pitt Island as promised. We'd again be filming for *The Red Stag Timber Hunters Club*, but also trying to nail that elusive hāpuku, or puka, that had eluded us over the past couple of seasons of *South Seas Spearo*.

We would be relying heavily on local knowledge for this undertaking, having the company of some quite colourful characters: Dallon Gregory Hunt, Chase Lanauze, Chase's dad Ruka and Matt Emeny, who was responsible for piloting the Air Chathams' plane on the team's flight over the previous day.

With a big steam to Pitt planned for the following morning, and knowing full well the proclivity for festivity that my Islander hosts are famous for, rather than leaning into a few beers right off the bat I tried to ensure that the team and I had a more subdued first evening. The last thing I wanted was a repeat of the first-night shenanigans from my last trip to the Chathams, which involved waking up dazed and confused in a remote corner of the island as 'little spoon' to a snoring Timmy.

With relatively calm seas, we made the passage across to Pitt Island the next day, being treated to incredible views of the rugged topography of both main islands. Once at Flowerpot Bay, we settled into our digs, and then skidded out on the quad bikes for the first of a few planned hunts, where we would be targeting big boars and the sought-after Pitt Island ram.

We came up short on our first hunt, but it provided a chance to get a feel for the island and its unique topography. Home to fewer than 40 permanent residents, it's a bit more rugged and wild than the much larger

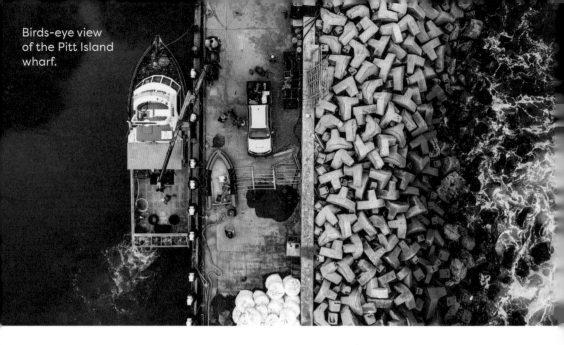

Birds-eye view of the Pitt Island wharf.

Chatham Island, with patches of dense natives interspersed with windswept grasslands and steep cliffs dropping straight down to a wild ocean.

While hunting was important, the main reason we ventured to Pitt was for the spearfishing opportunities, so we were up and about early the next morning for our first day of diving.

Pushing off from the recently refurbished pier, hopes were high that we'd be able to finally nail ourselves one of the elusive puka. Here at the Chathams, the fish inhabit much shallower waters, less than 30 metres in some areas, depths that they were long ago fished out of on the mainland.

On the steam out to the grounds, we spotted the odd reminder along the coast of the island's colourful past as a haven for tobacco and rum smuggling, including small caves carved into sheltered bays and coves. But where Pitt was once notorious for bootlegging, divers need to avoid a different kind of taxman these days, as a healthy population of great white sharks patrol these remote waters. However, Dwane had a trick up his sleeve, quite literally, to help deal with them.

Powerheads, also known as 'smokies', are bullets encased in rubber which can be fitted to the head of a speargun, effectively turning the tip of the spear into an explosive device. Given the protected status of great white sharks, they're a last resort, only to be used in the event of an imminent attack, but having one tucked up the sleeve of your wetsuit helps provide a little piece of mind when diving these famously sharky waters. We've never had to put one to use on the show, and hopefully we never will.

The first day of diving saw the lads succeed in landing a few good-sized kingfish, which in recent years have been appearing in larger numbers around the islands, but unfortunately, there was no sign of any hāpuku. Kingfish are always a welcome addition to the icebox, but these fish were celebrated for a different reason — the Chatham's Kingfish Cup was under way, a winner-takes-all fishing comp where the heaviest fish takes the

Rather menacing looking, The Pyramid stands alone far to the south of Pitt Island.

prize. It was $50 to enter and there were no rules: fish could be landed from anywhere and taken using whatever means. With Air Chathams operating flights between Auckland and Whakatāne, there was even some talk on the island of skidding across to White Island to target a massive mainland fish for the comp!

While we hadn't tasted success in our search for a puka, we were treated to a tasty gourmet lunch while anchored in a sheltered cove off the back of Māngere Island, the last bastion of the endangered black robin. Air Chathams pilot Matt whipped up a delicious kingfish ceviche using the fish shot earlier that morning, along with some fresh ingredients he'd picked up from the mainland the day before — certainly a man of many talents!

Once back on dry land, we reverted to hunting mode. Rather than chasing pigs, though, this time we had our sights set on a prized Pitt Island ram. With no general store on the island, the locals rely on this wild population of sheep to keep their freezers full, and luckily for them, they make for top-quality eating.

While most trophy hunting on Pitt is done with long-range shooting out in the open country, we were keen to try our hand at getting onto a few in the tighter bush, putting our stalking skills to the test. We made our way on quad bikes into the heart of the natives zone in the southern part of the island, eventually spotting what we were after, but some miscommunication between Tim and me meant our first opportunity was lost.

We continued hunting on foot, bumping into another young ram that we chose to let walk, but it was proving hard to spot any sheep in this tight bush. So, we chose to gain a bit of elevation, climbing a small rise that we hoped would open up a good view into the surrounding country, and it immediately paid off.

We spied a few more animals in the distance, including a couple of tasty-looking younger ones feeding their way towards us, and Tim was able to dispatch one with a well-placed head shot, providing us with ample meat for the days ahead.

However, as we stood around working out the best way to get the bikes down to collect the meat, Dwane spied a nice-sized ram with a few sheep nearby, but despite my mad rush, I couldn't get the camera set up in time for Tim to take a shot, and the sheep soon bolted for the cover of the surrounding bush.

We were granted a second chance, though. After dealing to the meat, we saddled back up on the bikes and continued deeper into the natives zone but didn't have to travel far before the sheep that we'd spooked a half hour earlier suddenly reappeared on the track directly in front of us, and bringing up the rear was the nice ram.

Tim floored it, nearly throwing me off the back of the bike. We raced up to the spot where the sheep had crossed and both leapt from the quad, but in the frantic race to get into a shooting position before we lost sight of them, Tim left the machine in neutral and it began rolling its way back down the track!

Luckily, Sam could see what was unfolding and managed to regain control of the errant bike before it gained too much speed.

By this stage, the ram was now over a hundred metres away, following in behind his sheep and close to being lost over the brow of a small hill, but Tim was up to the task, pulling off a good shot that dropped the ram in a heap.

There was more success for the team later in the evening, although it was another near-run thing. After spying a good ram, Sam had to work his way around a patch of natives towards a grassy rise to get into a shooting position. Rather than staying on his shoulder, I decided to try to capture the action from the air with the drone, using the zoom lens so it wouldn't risk spooking the animals.

This was one of my main aims of the trip, to capture a kill shot from the air on the 7x zoom setting, which has the effect of greatly compressing the distance on camera. This enables the viewer to clearly see both the shooter and the target in frame at once. It's a tricky task, relying on the drone being able to film from well back in a straight line between the two targets, but the hillside that Sam was to shoot from provided me with the perfect scenario.

Drones are no good at capturing any sound, so I gave the main camera to Dwane, and tasked him with following in behind Sam to capture the audio from his lapel mic, and then to film his initial reaction following the hopefully successful shot.

As I tracked him from the air, Sam cut the distance and worked his way into position. It was all working out as planned — I had both Sam and the ram in my frame and just needed him to line up and squeeze off, but unfortunately Dwane then came creeping up into the shot.

Rather than staying back and getting the action after the trigger was pulled, Dwane must have thought I wanted him right on Sam's shoulder, filming the entire scene as I normally would. I could see what was going to happen but had no way to communicate to Sam, as the handheld VHF radio was back at the bikes.

It was a bit of a slow-moving car crash. I could see that the sheep the ram was with knew something was up, as it was staring in the direction of the lads on the hill, but I was impotent to do anything about it. Dwane then made a crucial mistake, one that I've no doubt been guilty of many times while filming the show. To improve his angle on the action, he sat up taller in the grass, and immediately the wary sheep bolted, with the ram following close behind.

On a zoom lens, you're forced to work within small tolerances, so in order for me to keep Sam and the ram in frame, I began tracking hard left. Thankfully, Sam was able to reposition himself and squeeze off a shot just as the ram was about to be lost into the native bush, and I managed to capture the big boy going legs up right on the very edge of my frame.

It wasn't the perfectly clean sequence that I had hoped for, but it was another unique slice of action that we now had in the can. We continued hunting till dusk, and had a couple more opportunities on meat animals, but local lads Dallon and Chase were a little wayward with their shooting, probably not helped by the added pressures of filming and an unfamiliar firearm.

The pressure was starting to lift for me, though. We had achieved the first of our three stated goals, but the hardest two still loomed large on our to-do list: bagging ourselves a 200-lb boar, and probably more importantly, slotting a puka on spear — no matter what the size.

For our fourth day in the Chathams, with the seas relatively calm, we decided to commit the entire day to spearfishing. We started by exploring the southern coastline of Pitt, diving a notoriously sharky spot directly out from Glory Bay, where the presence of a dead whale on the beach added a little extra spice to proceedings.

As a quick side note, Glory Bay is named for the 1827 shipwreck of the brig *Glory*, which led to one of the country's most incredible feats of maritime endurance. The crew managed to salvage a lifeboat, and somehow were able to sail it all the way to my home patch of Russell in the Bay of Islands, a herculean journey of 1280 km!

While not on the same scale, we'd need to put in a big effort ourselves if we wanted to taste success. However, the Glory Bay diving proved uneventful, so we punched all the way out to the remote and rather intimidating island of The Pyramid, an old volcanic plug rising up out of the deep in the middle of absolutely nowhere.

If the dead whale on the beach at Glory Bay wasn't enough of an added risk, we went a step further out at The Pyramid — Ruka put the power tools to use to butcher the sheep that was shot the previous day. I noticed that a fair few offcuts ended up over the side, but thankfully not enough to attract any toothy critters.

After a couple of hours, we reluctantly pulled pin. Things certainly weren't exactly going to plan. The Pyramid provided us with some stunning footage, but no trophy fish, and with the day's diving nearing an end, we really needed Tim, Dwane or Chase to pull something out of the bag, but the day was shaping up to be a fizzer.

We tried a couple more spots along the coast but had no luck. En route back towards Flowerpot, the team decided to roll the dice one final time to try to salvage something from their long day in the drink, choosing to dive a small reef just a few minutes from the main wharf.

With the flasher deployed, Dwane dropped down for the umpteenth time that day, and this time a solitary kingfish came in close to investigate, but the fish wasn't any improvement on the preceding day, so he let it be.

I was sitting at the back of the boat, watching the clock and weighing up my options for the remainder of the trip. I wasn't too fazed about the failure to land a fish as we still had a few more days up our sleeve, when a stifled shout came from the fellas in the water. I'd heard that sound before and knew what it signalled — Dwane had spotted something from the surface. I raced to grab my camera which was sitting up in the helm, as I had stowed it earlier given there was nothing much of interest to film, and I told Tim to get down to the back of the boat in case I was right.

Sam hit the surface and confirmed my suspicion. On the ascent from his previous drive, he'd seen a puka come up off the bottom and race in for a look at the flasher which was hanging midwater. Dwane had immediately dropped down in the hope of getting a shot on it before it vanished.

Having travelled miles to all corners of the island, it seems we should have adhered to that adage of 'fish your feet first', as Dwane hit the surface with a scream of delight. He'd pulled off a terrific shot on the puka right as it was beginning to veer off, punching the spear through the back of its head. It was a nice-sized fish too, but at this stage, we really didn't care too much about size! I was just relieved that the job was done.

We'd achieved our main spearfishing goal of getting a pin into a puka, so after celebrating heartily back at base with a huge feed of chops and a few rums, our attention then turned to our final task — bagging ourselves a big old boar.

We awoke to a drizzly morning, but the rain wasn't enough to stop us from getting out with the dogs for a final hunt on Pitt. It was a funny old day this one, a mixture of highs and lows.

After a couple of hours hunting through a mixture of crown fern and farm fringe, the dogs caught wind of a boar and charged off after it into some incredibly thick and uninviting tiger country that we had no appetite for venturing into. The dogs ended up well over a kilometre away, so rather than bush bashing in the wet for hours on end into no-man's land, we looped back around and traced the bush edge, hoping they might break in our direction.

Tim ascends from the wreck holding his rather fortuitous fish.

It seemed luck was on our side. We were all wandering along, shooting the shit and not paying much attention to the Garmin tracking gear, when suddenly a big black shape came barrelling through the wire fenceline just 100 metres in front of us, closely followed by a pair of dogs.

We leapt into action, racing in to grab a hold of the boar's back leg, and shutting it down before it could get away into the thick stuff again. It was a real stroke of luck, although the first thing to grab my eye was the absence of the GoPro 360 on the back of the main dog.

'Bugger it,' I thought. It must have snapped off the harness at some stage. Oh well, 'risk it for the biscuit' and all that. Live by the sword, die by the sword. At least the second dog cam was still operational. As a precaution, I swapped out its onboard memory card just to ensure I had some of the morning's footage secure in case lightning struck twice.

A few of us headed back to collect the bikes, but by the time we'd returned, I was told the dogs had got onto another boar and were bailing it up just inside the bushline. You beauty, another chance for a big boar sequence, and since the second dog cam had a fresh battery and an empty card, there was every chance it was capturing some more epic footage.

The seven of us made our way into the native bush, which was very slow going due to how incredibly dense it was, but on our way towards the bail-up, the pig broke, and the tracking gear soon showed the dogs were again out to nearly a kilometre away. There was no way we could have covered that distance, so we sat tight and hoped for another stroke of luck, but with the earlier boar and the last-minute puka the night before, it seemed that we'd well and truly exhausted our supply.

After possibly realising there were no humans coming to his aid, the camera dog eventually broke away from the bail-up and started making its way back towards us. It was small consolation, but at least we'd be able to work out what calibre of boar it was from the on-board footage. Those hopes were dashed when the dog reappeared with the harness minus the camera for the second time that morning.

Filming pig hunting has always been tough on gear, but losing two cameras in such a short time span was damn frustrating. However, you might be surprised to learn that it's not pig hunting that's been the hardest on my camera gear over the years — I've smashed the most equipment while out chasing birds of all things.

A chukor hunt saw two dog cams hit the dust in the space of an afternoon, and earlier this year, I topped that by crashing two drones in the space of three hours on a Glenorchy duck shoot, putting one into a tree and the other into a lake.

But getting back to the task at hand, as I sulked over another lost camera, Tim debated with the lads about whether there was any point trying to head in deeper to find it. I thought it was worth a punt, but after five minutes we realised it was futile, as it was just too dense, and the tiny black camera could be lying just about anywhere.

It was a blow, but not a fatal one, for at least we had all the main camera action and the drone footage to tell the story, so we traipsed our way back out, loaded the hog onto the bike and headed for home.

The size of the boar surprised us all, weighing over 150 lbs, so that softened the blow a little, and after a hearty feed of Pitt Island chops, by the time evening rolled around I'd put the lost footage behind me and was feeling happy with life. Besides, we still had enough time for a couple more hunts once back on the main island, so the dream of nailing a 200-pounder was still very much alive.

On the steam back to Waitangi the next day, we decided we'd push the no rules element of the Kingfish Cup to the limit. In the end, though, our largest kingi was well and truly the biggest to be weighed in the comp, even without the extra few kg of lead dive weights that we stuffed down its gob.

At this point in the trip, having had a hectic few days of filming and hunting, we felt that we'd earned the right to let off some steam. Anyone lucky enough to spend time on the island knows that the locals don't do things by halves, so after a classic evening on the sauce at Matt the pilot's

The punchline to this pic is that no one is holding anything they were responsible for!

place, we were all feeling fairly dusty.

There was still work to be done. We spent the morning catching up on some odd jobs, breaking down the fish and pork, then decided to head out for a low-key flounder dive at the river mouth of the giant Te Whanga lagoon, which runs over half the length of the main island.

The floundering was a riot. I could locate the flatfish from the air with the drone, and once they had their hand-spearing technique nailed, Dwane, Sam and Tim soon secured plenty of tasty fish.

But on the way back to the trucks, some high-powered hijinks meant I was the one that was left floundering.

Two of the local lads had taken a jet ski across to the river mouth and were having a hell of a laugh by coming in hot and kicking up massive rooster tails of water, drenching the divers in the boat. We were fizzing along in our little two-seater tinny, with me standing in the back, when I saw the jet ski approaching from our left. Just as they were shaping up to give us a hosing, the driver of our boat, Ants, veered hard to the right to avoid the imminent soaking.

I immediately fell victim to the laws of physics, specifically the conservation of momentum principle, and went sailing headfirst over the port side and into the lagoon. While mid-air, I remember thinking that I'd come up needing to tread water, but was quite surprised at how shallow it was, the lagoon being only chest deep in places.

The lads back aboard the boat hadn't noticed they had a man overboard and carried on steaming back across the lagoon, but the boat full of divers behind us saw what had happened and raised the alarm.

Thankfully, I wasn't holding my camera at the time, but I did lose my phone into the drink. This wasn't a major at the time but would have ramifications over the next few days that will be explained soon.

With one final day up our sleeve to make some magic happen, we were up early to make the drive up to Waitangi West for our final pig hunt. This was the same location where we'd filmed a couple of hunts on our previous trip, characterised by wide open expanses known as the 'clears' by the locals. The name belies the thickness of the bracken and fern, which still makes for hard going in places, but nothing like the impenetrable jungle that we encountered on Pitt.

It would prove to be a memorable morning. As the day was still dawning, we headed out on the bikes towards the coast, and it wasn't long before we caught sight of a couple of absolute tanks off in the distance.

Thanks to Ants' experienced pair of dogs and some accurate quad-bike piloting, we were able to nail them both, with the dog cam rolling and even the drone in the air for part of the bail-up. It was exactly the kind of sequence we were after, and I couldn't have been happier.

Even a mishap on the final shot for the morning couldn't burst my bubble. I wanted to fly the drone backwards to get a tracking shot of the bikes with the boars on the back, but I tried to get a little too cute and ended up crashing the drone into a tree, although thankfully it wasn't a fatal collision.

At the time, a final camera incident seemed like an appropriate way to finish the pig-hunting component of the trip, but rather than signifying the end, it foreshadowed the dramas still to come.

The feisty boars both weighed a massive 195 lb, just shy of 'two-tonner' status, but that didn't bother us too much. We'd got the job done and could now reward ourselves with a low-key 'scenic' dive around a couple of shallow-water wrecks in nearby Port Hutt.

Half an hour into the diving and Timmy hit the surface in a frenzy — he'd dropped down to check out the wreck and landed directly on top of a nice-sized puka, plugging it at close range! What a crazy day!

Tim was over the moon, and so was I. Heading to the Chathams was an expensive undertaking, and I had banked on getting a minimum of two episodes from the trip. A little mental mathematics told me we had that and more. It might be a tough ask cramming all the action from the past week into just one *South Seas Spearo* and one *The Red Stag Timber Hunters Club* episode.

But as I was to painfully discover, a simple gust of wind would soon scupper those plans . . .

We're lucky that we took the time to get a couple of good pics of the pigs, given that the bulk of the video footage was subsequently lost.

A smugglers cove on Pitt Island, a perfect place for a bacon butty before suiting up.

Tim's two cents

We had great feedback after the first trip back in the third series, but to be honest, the Chathams is one of those places where it's hard to not have an epic adventure. Shit just happens, so I was quietly confident we could get a banger of a trip in the bag on this return mission.

The wreck in Port Hutt is a spot that's been dived numerous times by mates and me. To my knowledge, no one's seen a puka there, so it was the last thing I was expecting when I dived down and peered in between the rusting beams. After such a hard slog around Pitt, checking numerous well-known puka holes, to end up with a gift like that was unreal.

The Chathams is also one of those places where it's hard to avoid a party — I swear I must have spent half my time working there with a hangover. So to think we were going to avoid at least one good session on this trip would have been naive. Getting away with just one dusty half day was miraculous really in the scheme of things. I'm sure if we weren't such a dedicated bunch of professionals, the wheels would have come off much earlier than they did!

24 WIND, WINGS AND WATER

Most hunters have fallen victim at some point to an unreliable breeze, the unwelcome breath on the back of the neck giving their position away in the heat of the moment, so it's appropriate that this little sob story begins with a strong gust which set in motion a sequence of events that I still agonise over even now.

Earlier on that fateful day, I'd flown from the Chathams to Wellington, where I waved goodbye to Tim, Sam and Dwane and pressed on with my next mission which was kicking off the very next morning — a week-long liveaboard charter into Dusky Sound with ten other keen adventurers from all corners of the country.

But as NZ609 began its final approach into Queenstown airport, the plane's sensors picked up a strong crosswind on the runway ahead. The pilot made the call that conditions were unsafe to land, so we would have to return to our point of departure, all the way back to Wellington. This single decision would result in the loss of some of the best pig-hunting footage I'd ever filmed, and once the dust settled, probably cost me in the vicinity of $15,000.

I could point the finger at the pilot for choosing not to land, but it's me that really has to accept the blame. It was my decision to lean into a few cold ones to celebrate both the big boars and Tim's last-minute puka, rather than remaining disciplined and backing the footage onto *two* independent hard drives. I was to pay the price for my laziness. Having never been victim to a drive failure in the past, I figured I had a few hours up my sleeve between the time I was due to arrive in Queenstown and the time we would be departing for Dusky Sound the following morning.

This Fiordland trip was a major logistical undertaking and would also be the first time my eleven-year-old daughter Ava had joined us on a shoot. There was a hell of a lot to organise, including pre-departure Covid tests and flights from all over the country, a tricky task when your phone is in the bottom of a lagoon. But I had my wife Amber working in the background to keep the train on the tracks, and other than my missing phone, everything seemed well under control.

Anyway, back aboard the plane — the pilot has just made the announcement that we're returning to the capital (to an audible groan from all passengers) and within a few seconds, pretty much everyone on board starts making calls to sort out alternative flight plans. I'm left 90s style with no means of communication, but I was able to borrow the phone of the nice lady beside me to get an SOS out to Amber to start looking into alternative travel plans. Ava was in the air and due to land in an hour's time, so wheels also needed to be set in motion to make sure she was sorted, given that I wouldn't be there to collect her. It was stressful to say the least.

In the end, after getting a connecting flight from Wellington to Auckland, and then the last available seat on the late-night flight into Queenstown, I arrived somewhat flustered and still phoneless, and eager to get some shut-eye before the pre-dawn departure to Te Anau the following morning.

Backing up the Chathams footage to the second drive as I had intended had slipped my mind — I had bigger fish to fry, such as getting the DJI app installed on Dre's phone so I would have a drone to use over the coming week of filming (given I hadn't had time to replace my lost phone which also doubled as a controller). This also led to another expensive mistake, but more on that soon.

We had one final complication hanging over us, one that we were all somewhat powerless to do anything about — the compulsory requirement from Pure Salt that we all pass a pre-departure Covid test. This weighed heavily on me. I'd tested negative a couple of times while on the Chathams, but an incredibly stressful twelve hours the day prior spent bouncing between four planes and four airports had me worried. If ever there was an opportunity for me to pick up the bug from out of the blue then it was now, but only time would tell.

The following morning, the team and I assembled in Te Anau at the local medical centre. We had a wide variety of characters for this mission — Phil and Julie from Hunting & Fishing New Zealand, Dave and Tom from Garmin, *South Seas Spearo* regular Jordy Bardin who was tasked with fishing and diving duties, as well as Jordy's dad Sean and my father-in-law Gerald. However, the bulk of the heavy lifting would be done by Dre and Khan Adam. Khan had featured on a few episodes over past seasons and was now quite comfortable with the unique requirements of filming.

Like me, Khan had been anxious about the pre-departure testing as well, given that a few members of his staff had tested positive earlier in the week. He'd been keeping his distance and working from home, determined not to miss the opportunity to join us on the trip, and I capitalised on this.

As we waited the obligatory fifteen minutes for the test results to process, I asked the nurse if she was game to play a prank on one of the team. Surprisingly, she didn't bat an eyelid, agreeing to tell Khan that he'd tested positive, and holding up a doctored Covid test that I had drawn a second 'positive' line on.

Khan fell for it hook, line and sinker, as did those other members of the team who were unaware of the prank, with everyone taking a step back from the Khan as if he were some kind of infectious plague victim. A smile from the nurse eventually put him out of his misery, though, as it

dawned on him that it was all just a well-orchestrated prank.

Thankfully, the entire team tested negative, so it was game on. For this Pure Salt expedition, our fifth, there was one major difference — the MV *Flightless* had been recently refurbished and upgraded, and now boasted a helicopter landing pad. This opened up all kinds of possibilities for us, allowing us to get up into some of the tops country that would normally require many hours of backbreaking slog to access. It also allowed the machine to remain on the boat as it moved about the fiord, rather than requiring us to be based in close proximity to the designated landing site at Supper Cove.

We flew in with our good mates from Te Anau Helicopter Services, relishing the fact that we didn't have to risk being eaten alive during the usual equipment transfer from shoreline to the boat, but I was about to be bitten by a bug of another kind.

Sitting around the outdoor table which had seen such debauchery on the previous trip, I powered up the drone for the first time and discovered that I hadn't quite completed pairing the device to Dre's phone, and since we were in deepest darkest Fiordland, we had no reception with which to finish the final verification stage of the connection process.

After trying and failing with half a dozen different approaches, it became clear that I only had two options: scratch any plans for aerial filming for the duration of the trip or bite the bullet and fire up the chopper to fly back towards Te Anau in order to get reception.

I chose the latter, but after half an hour of flying, the evening clag that had rolled in meant we were unable to get through any of the alpine passes. We were forced to return to the MV *Flightless* with the issue still unresolved. Imagine the feeling of sitting in a taxi that's stuck in traffic, watching the meter ticking over, but put an extra digit on the end of it —

that's what this flight to nowhere felt like for me. I was effectively tossing 20-dollar notes out the helicopter window every few seconds.

We eventually resolved the issue by making contact with Skipper Sean's partner Maria who was back in Te Anau. She downloaded the drone app on her phone and managed to use my log-in details to confirm the pairing, then donated her device to be used for the duration of the filming. It would be flown in the next day and dropped off to the boat, but during all this drama, unbeknown to me, a far more frustrating and much more expensive situation was unfolding.

At some point in the previous 24 hours of travel, the drive containing the final three days of footage from the Chathams had been damaged, with the drive platter likely taking a heavy knock. The data-recovery experts trying to salvage it explained to me that the knock created a tiny bump on the surface of the platter, which operates a bit like a record player, with the 'needle' being a magnetic reader that was now impacting the platter every time it spun up, making the situation progressively worse.

I didn't realise all this until much later in the year, when I was attempting to finally back up the material onto a second drive (the task that I had intended to do while in Queenstown).

After sending the drive away to the recovery specialists, a couple of months went by with no word, which had me hopeful that progress was being made. I was therefore disconsolate when the call came through confirming my worst fears — the drive was toast. The hurt was compounded by the fact that I was with Tim and Sam at the time, who no doubt were also supremely gutted about the loss.

We'd been stripped of some of the best material from the Chathams: the Kingfish Cup weigh-in, all the main camera and drone aerials of the floundering day, Tim's last-minute puka, but most disappointingly we lost pretty much all of the pig-hunting material that we filmed on Pitt and out at Waitangi West, including both of the big boars.

I only had a handful of files cobbled together from what we'd earlier shared to social media, plus an assorted bunch of dog-cam clips and GoPro files that were able to be salvaged from the broken drive with which to create the end sequences of *South Seas Spearo* and *The Red Stag Timber Hunters Club* episodes.

But there's a silver lining to every cloud. The upshot was that we'd now get to film another pig-hunting mission, but as morning dawned on the boat anchored up in spectacular Sportsmans Cove, I was still oblivious to all these future issues, and eager to simply get up into the hills with Kahn and Dre to try our luck.

It was a truly stunning morning, and after being deposited high up on a grassy knob, which saved us an eight-hour bush bash, the helicopter wasn't even back to the boat before Khan laid eyes on our first stag of the trip. In fact, I think he and I still had our lifejackets on!

My 11-year-old daughter, Ava, was lucky enough to join us for this epic trip and experience Fiordland at its finest — minus the usual sandflies, rain and mud.

We worked our way into a position to get a better view of him. In this part of Fiordland, we weren't expecting to encounter any massive trophies, as there's not enough quality feed available for stags to grow huge racks, and this guy was your typical Fiordland scrubber. But his location on a grassy bench below us presented Khan with a great opportunity to nail him on bow, and with it being early March, he would make for fine eating.

But I blew it. Once again, I could blame the wind, which complicated communication between the three of us, but the reality was that my movement and noise put the stag on alert, and despite Khan being at full draw on him on two occasions, by the time I was ready to give him the green light to let rip, the stag had cottoned on to us and then took off at pace.

It was a missed opportunity, but we'd only been on the ground for half an hour so still had plenty of hunting ahead of us. However, what we didn't have plenty of was gas for the Jetboil cooker. As we set about getting a brew on, Dre realised he'd left two full canisters back aboard the boat, along with the team's toilet paper. I then clicked that I'd also left behind some spare batteries that I needed.

Thankfully, Maria's phone that was being dropped in that morning still needed to be flown up to us so that I could make use of the drone. Dre got on the radio and sheepishly asked the crew to add the additional items into the dropbag. I'm sure that back aboard the boat the team all thought we were real amateurs!

Around mid-morning, the machine touched down to drop off our supplies, and along with the essentials of gas and bog-roll were three huge slabs of delicious chocolate cake and some gourmet BLT sandwiches. It was too embarrassing to document this sequence within the episode, as it showed just how indulgent we'd become in our old age — choppering in from the boat, eating cake in the hills, talk about a gentleman's hunt!

I wasn't complaining though, but Khan soon was. Turns out he'd fallen victim to another prank, this time masterminded by Anna, the chef aboard the *Flightless*. As the three of us sat on the hillside enjoying our tasty lunch, all of a sudden, Kahn started having what looked like a heart attack. Turns out that Anna had loaded up one entire corner of his sandwich with a thick dollop of wasabi.

We had a bit of a laugh at Khan's expense, before it dawned on us that Dre or I could have been the target as well; it was just Khan's bad luck that he grabbed the loaded sammy.

Our bad luck continued throughout the day, with a few more frustrating stuff-ups. In the early evening, we located a suitable meat animal, providing Khan a second chance to feed his bow. But, again, he fell victim to the frustrations of filming.

I wanted to recreate the zoomed-in drone shot that I managed to capture with Sam and the Pitt Island ram. Khan had crept into position and was waiting for the green light from me, but the deer made a run for it as soon as it heard the sound of the drone powering up.

Fortunately, this time we had Dre on the rifle as a backup to ensure we had some meat to bring back to the boat. Unfortunately, the hind that he shot was in such poor condition, with barely any fat on her, that all that was worth taking were the prime back cuts, not enough to feed the twelve hungry mouths aboard the *Flightless*.

We were presented with one more chance at glory, however. With an hour left in the day, the lads spied what looked to be a bloody good stag tucked away on a near-vertical scrub face in the distance. He was a big 10-pointer, totally preoccupied with thrashing the surrounding vegetation, giving it a good old-fashioned workout. A stag of this calibre here in the Fiordland tops would make for a hell of a trophy, so we set about getting into a position to take a shot.

But this time, it was a slightly too leisurely approach from Dre that led to the opportunity being lost. I had the big boy in my sights on the long lens and was waiting for Dre to dial in before sending a collect call his way, but just before he was about to squeeze off, the crafty stag took a step to his left and was lost to view, hidden behind the thick foliage.

We tried to wait him out, but that was it, another missed opportunity. We'd still be able to go looking for him in the morning, so we punched our way back up the hill towards camp, working off a bit of the chocolate cake from earlier in the day.

I did receive one piece of good news that evening. A message came through on the Garmin inReach informing me that my daughter, Ava, had been the day's MVP, snaffling her first-ever crayfish under the expert tutelage of Jordy. I was stoked for her. It can be quite a challenge bagging

your first-ever bug, so hearing that she'd stepped up and nailed one helped make up for the rather disappointing day that we'd had.

I was up first the following morning and went about my normal routine, setting up a couple of timelapse shots to capture the change of light, as it moved from pinpricked starry sky to the deep blue of pre-dawn. As I prepared my morning brew, I noticed something odd in the sky off to our south. At first, I thought it must have been a powerful spotlight being pointed up into the sky from back aboard the *Flightless*, as it seemed to be moving, but as my eyes became better attuned to the darkness I began to pick out shades of purple and green on the horizon. I raced back to the timelapse camera to review a long exposure shot to see whether my suspicions were correct, and yep — standing out vividly in the sky against the foreground tents was the Aurora Australis, aka the Southern Lights.

It was a special moment for us all; we'd never been witness to an aurora like this before, and in hindsight, I think we got a little too excited. Rather than leaving the cameras in position long enough to best capture the phenomenon, we raced about the hillside, repositioning the DSLR and GoPros three or four times over the next half hour, trying different lenses and exposure settings to capture the light as best we could, but with the dawn approaching, the colours began to fade and were eventually lost.

It was a magical way to start the day, but that was to be the highlight on the hill for us. The big stag didn't make a reappearance, and after an uneventful morning, the chopper arrived to collect us around midday. But it certainly hadn't been an uneventful morning for those in the machine.

Along with her first cray, turns out Ava had also experienced her first stag hunt. En route to collect us, chopper pilot Reuben had spied an animal standing brazenly out in the tops. He swung around the hillside out of sight and put the machine down on a flat bench, before he, skipper Sean and Ava jumped out and made their way uphill to gain some elevation on the stag. Reuben was then able to pull off a good shot, dropping the stag and ensuring we had plenty more meat for the days ahead, putting our efforts on the hill to shame!

The next couple of days aboard the boat were just magic. We ditched the hunting boots for jandals, and later that afternoon, managed to land a pair of prized southern bluefin tuna on the rods. We then overnighted at Facile Harbour, the site of New Zealand's first shipwreck way back in 1795, enjoying as much delicious tuna sashimi as we could eat.

The next challenge would be a biggie, trying to put Jordy into a position where she could get a spear into a southern bluefin, something that no woman had every achieved in New Zealand waters. We came incredibly close, with Jordy lining up on a couple of fish, but in both instances, she decided it wasn't worth the risk of taking a long shot and wounding them.

It made for good TV, though, the drone picking up the repeated hits by albacore and bluefin on the hookless teasers we were towing. A third southern was added to the tally, despite the crew trying our best to revive it to allow a release. With the policy aboard being to eat everything that's taken, we had bluefin prepared half a dozen different ways over the remainder of the trip — served raw of course, but also smoked, steaked, marinaded and in kebab form. I doubt I could ever tire of eating fresh tuna sashimi, but to be honest, after two days of nothing but bluefin, it did start to lose its lustre a little.

Having spent the afternoon and evening fishing, diving and gorging ourselves on more gourmet grub, we enjoyed a relaxing night on anchor in Woodhen Cove. Since our focus had been on tuna for the past day and a half, we were starting to run the risk of becoming a fishing show, so for our last full day in Fiordland we chose to spend the morning scoping the numerous slips and faces around Breaksea Sound in the hope of spotting a deer out and about enjoying the morning light.

Despite half a dozen sets of eyes working the glass, we couldn't catch sight of any deer, so decided to give Jords a final crack at a bluefin. We were only just nearing the entrance to Breaksea Sound when we spotted a group of tuna smashing bait on the surface, mere metres from the rocky coastline.

This kicked off a truly insane sequence of action: the aerial footage of big tuna leaping clear of the water among a shower of silvery bait has to be seen to be believed, and it fully justified the cost and trouble we'd gone to earlier in the trip to get the drone situation sorted.

The fish were certainly fired up, and Khan even managed to hook up and fight a couple of them despite having removed the hooks from the poppers he was tossing! But the poor visibility here at the entrance meant that it was too hard for Jordy to get a pin into one, as they were moving fast and were just too crafty.

Looking back on the crazy action that morning, I think we missed a trick here. As I mentioned earlier, I didn't want the episode to devolve into a full-on fishing show, but we could have caught these tuna a dozen different ways: with stick baits and poppers, from stand-up paddleboard and kayak, and I'm damn sure we could have even hooked one from the spa pool on the top deck of the *Flightless* if we had tried — that would have made for amazing footage in anyone's book.

But the trip had one more spectacular moment still to come.

Having packed away the spearfishing gear, we exited Breaksea and steamed a short way north, enjoying the incredibly calm conditions on this normally quite inhospitable stretch of coastline. After another delicious bluefin-based lunch, Dre and I were lazing around the deck, contemplating a quick swim before having to prep for the evening hunt, when Khan's keen eye spied a hind moving about, three-quarters of the way up a steep face.

We weighed up our options. Going after it on land would probably be a waste of time given how steep the face was, and unlike the last time Anto pulled off a shot from the *Flightless* back in our third season, we couldn't run the boat aground into the mud to provide a steady shooting platform.

Khan was confident in his shooting skills, though, and believed it was worth a shot. If he pulled it off, it would surely surpass Anto's 546-yard screamer from the very first Pure Salt mission as the best shot in all eight seasons of the show.

Khan set himself up at the bow of the boat, getting into a comfortable shooting position by propping himself up with a few large beanbags. The seas may have been uncommonly calm, but there was certainly still enough of a rise and fall that it would be an incredibly tough shot.

We had time on our side; there was no need to rush. Khan first had to become familiar with the boat's pattern of movement, as the vision within his scope drifted up past the hind, then down, then up again, and back down. Meanwhile, I had the drone up in the air and was creeping my way closer to the animal on the hill, keeping a close eye on it with the zoom lens while it fed away on the shady face.

A couple of times, the hind was lost from sight to those on the boat as it fed its way around the hill, but the elevation of the drone provided me with a clear view of what was happening, which I conveyed down to the lads. We just needed to wait patiently for it to walk out into the open and present Khan with a broadside shot.

Getting greedy, I slowly drifted in closer, but suddenly the hind became aware of the drone, fixing her stare on the small, buzzing intruder. I thought I'd given the game away, but no — the drone actually helped our cause, as it encouraged the wary hind to run uphill a few metres and into the sun, providing Khan with the perfect side profile he needed.

In the episode, the shot sequence played out quickly, but it was around ten seconds before the wave action plus the rise and fall of the boat had Khan's crosshairs settle on the hind, and the moment it did — he squeezed off.

With a silencer fitted to his rifle, the sound of his shot was lower than the sound made by the dozen spectators on the bow of the boat who had assembled to watch the action. An almighty roar went up immediately after the shot rang out, as we saw the hind shudder and topple over — Khan had hit it square in the shoulder, pretty much perfect placement.

It was an incredible shot, especially with the added filming and spectator pressure. We could scarcely believe it ourselves, but Khan has spent years as a pest-control contractor and had a lot of experience shooting from unstable platforms like helicopters and side by sides. As an experienced bowhunter, he was also quite used to waiting for his bowsight to fall over an animal before releasing an arrow, and this shot involved a similar principle.

But the tough work wasn't over, as Dre and Khan still had to go and get the bloody thing! Even though it had fallen some way down the face, it was still a mighty effort to recover, involving some heart-in-the-mouth moments leaping from the inflatable tender across to the slippery rocks between waves. If they'd got the timing wrong, things could have got ugly, but they were able to clamber up onto the rocks without incident.

The scale of the country was extremely deceptive. Some of the boulders on the shoreline that looked wheelbarrow size were actually as big as cars, and made Khan and Dre appear tiny in comparison.

They then had to make a near-vertical ascent through a haze of hungry mosquitos, before manhandling the hind back down the face, which saw Dre having to clamber down through a thick patch of ongaonga (a stinging tree nettle). Initially, I'd wanted to join the pair on the recovery, but I was now happy to be filming it all on the drone from the comfort of the *Flightless*.

Khan's kill shot was a fantastic way to wrap up what had been a hell of a trip, with plenty of stories that I haven't even gone into with this chapter: Dre's barely legal butterfish, Khan's first freedived cray, a leopard-print g-banger in the spa pool, certainly some great memories that'll stick with me for a long time.

But the memory I'll cherish above all was having my daughter along for the ride, so I thought I'd let her round out this chapter with her own thoughts about the trip.

If you're ever offered the chance to join a Fiordland liveaboard trip, jump at it.

FLIGHTLESS
NELSON

Ava's two cents

One of my favourite things about the Fiordland adventure was helping Anna, the chef on *Flightless*. She taught me how to make some delicious meals using the tuna we caught and the deer that were shot, and for most of the time aboard I enjoyed just watching her from the seats on the side of the kitchen.

I also loved seeing the dolphins; some were almost the size of small cars! Jumping off the top deck of the boat was fun too, although the first time I wasn't so sure, and had to climb back down to hop into the warm spa. A few days later I worked up the courage to jump, and I realised it was not that bad, so I did it again a few more times.

I think the reason I jumped that second time was because the sun was shining and because I was already wet from the most exciting thing that had happened to me on the trip. I joined in with a few others to go diving, and Jordy helped me catch my first crayfish. Even though the water was not that deep, it took me a few tries to get it. Actually, by a few I mean about ten. When I watched the footage with Dad back home, Dad spotted that I was struggling to get down and was kicking quite hard, so I probably didn't have enough weight on, which made it a bit harder as well, but in the end, I caught a crayfish and that is all that mattered to me.

The funny thing was, once Dad came back from hunting up in the hills, he didn't believe me when I said that I had caught the crayfish. He was sure that Jordy had brought it shallower for me to reach, and it took him ages to finally believe me. Hopefully this summer here in the Bay of Islands I can grab another one to prove that it wasn't a fluke!

PART SIX
UPS AND
DOWNS

25 WEST COAST CLOSE COUNTRY MISSION

By the time our next hunt rolled around, we were in the dying days of March, a time when the West Coast waves goodbye to the hot summer sun and begins settling back into its regular rainy rhythm. But this year was a bit different. This year the 'Wet' Coast found itself in the midst of a minor heatwave. There hadn't been any real rain for over a fortnight, and the forecast was for continued hot weather over the days to come. We were hoping we'd have equally hot roaring action to match.

I was back alongside Anto for this trip, our first since he'd taken his monumental Canterbury chamois, but making his *The Red Stag Timber Hunters Club* debut was one of Anto's regular hunting buddies, a hardcase ex-Pom by the name of Alex Ritchie. Over the previous few years, the pair had hunted successfully a handful of times around Central Otago, but it would be Alex's first time hunting the coast, and the first time with a camera thrust in his face.

We were heading into a Haast roar block that we'd been lucky enough to draw in the ballot. It would be my second time up the Waiototo, but a vastly different scenario to the first — on that occasion back in the first season of the show, we were joined by Josh James Kiwi Bushman on a spring meat hunt and were based out of rafts for the duration of the mission. Instead of drifting peacefully down the river, this trip would require a hell of a lot more legwork.

Rather than hunting the block in the most obvious manner by basing ourselves on a wide-open expanse of flats on the river's edge, we wanted to traverse the tops to begin with, making use of the extra elevation to get a feel for what might be living on the valley floor.

We were dropped in by chopper on the very south-western edge of our block. The late-afternoon heat was energy sapping, especially combined with the weight of our heavy packs, but we eventually climbed all the way up onto the crest of a ridge which opened up an amazing view down into our block, 1300 vertical metres below.

We'd be unable to hear any roars this high up, but we were able to locate a few animals kicking about down on the flats, hinds mainly. But at this time of the year, where there were hinds, there would most likely be stags, so we made a mental note of where they were living before heading back to our campsite to rest up for the big day to come.

Working our way back
towards camp after a big
day in the tops.

It was a stunning evening to be up in the tops, and I was in my element, getting scenic pretties and lapses. I was even lucky enough to capture a meteor burning up in the night sky over Jackson Bay in one of the timelapse stills.

The following morning, I was up early to make the most of the clear skies to get some more astro shots, before the three of us continued climbing our way further into the block. It was difficult finding a clear route in the dark, but it was certainly a lot easier on the body climbing in the cool of the morning than the heat of the day.

Along with the cooler temperatures, it's amazing the difference to your mental state a bit of hill fitness makes. By this stage of the year, I'd got a few decent hunts under my belt, so while it still wasn't something to look forward to, I didn't dread the physicality of climbing. I was able to enjoy the view for once, and with the sun rising over the distant hills, it was a spectacular way to start the day.

But you can't mount a pretty view on your wall. You can't smoke a scenic vista in the Traeger. We needed to find some game animals, but it seemed they were in short supply up here in the tops.

However, there were a few birds bouncing around the rocky bluffs. We had noticed signs and traplines on our way in the day before pointing out the work being done by DOC to protect the endangered rock wren, New Zealand's only true alpine bird. These hardy critters are able to survive all year round above the treeline, an incredible feat considering how inhospitable this area can be during the winter months.

I soon spied a couple of birds flitting about in the morning light, so while the lads worked the glass, I stalked in close to get some footage of one, managing to capture a decent slow-motion shot as it jumped from rock to rock.

Unfortunately for me, though, when the episode aired on TV many months later, I discovered that the bird I'd filmed wasn't a native rock wren at all, it was a fairly common skylark! The misidentification was pointed out by plenty of people on our social media pages, and left me with egg on my face, but in my defence, it had also slipped past Anto, Alex and Dre during the review process, so they're equally to blame.

We pressed onwards, dropping down to fill our water bladders and our big 8-litre storage container from a lake in a beautiful hanging basin. 'Alex the Camel' was tasked with being chief water hauler, and he did a hell of a job — I'd say for the first time in years of filming that he was quite likely carrying a heavier pack than I was for a good portion of this trip. It would be critical as well, given that the rocky country that rose ahead of us was parched and dry, with little moisture to be found.

With the sun high in the sky, we plugged away along the main ridgeline, steadily gaining altitude. Once up onto the leading ridge, which opened up a view into the Waiototo and the Arawhata River to our south, we finally started seeing game. Anto spied a young chamois buck tucked away in a shady fold less than 80 metres from us. It wasn't fazed by us in the slightest, and I was able to get some great close-up shots on my long lens.

After 10 minutes, I'd had my fill of footage, so we decided to press on, but not before a rash decision was made that we would all immediately regret.

Anto had asked how far off we thought the chamois was, to which Alex replied, 'I reckon you could lob a rock and hit him.' I thought this would be a grand idea, so encouraged him to do just that, in the hope that I might get an action shot of the chamois bounding away over the steep terrain.

Alex hurled a large rock in the general direction of the young buck. The sound was shockingly loud, ringing out in the hills as it crashed its way down the steep face. Unsurprisingly, the chamois took off, but it wasn't the only animal spooked by the noise. Out of the corner of his eye, Anto spied another chamois pop up among the jumble of rocks and boulders on the ridgeline. This was no juvenile; it had much bigger horns, likely around the 10-inch mark, but with a strong splay.

The sound of the rock had meant it was now on high alert, and very close to bolting off out of sight. We didn't have a lot of time to assess it but made the call that it was a taker, and since Anto had already ticked off a 10 inch-plus buck for the year, Alex had priority on the shot.

It was a bit of a mad scramble to get ready. Alex didn't have his bipod attached, so was rummaging around his pack trying to find it while I had the chamois framed up perfectly on my long lens, ready for the action shot. I needed him to hurry the hell up but didn't want to add to the pressure he was no doubt feeling. The camera adds enough without me barking out orders on top.

The cham was making its way further along the ridgeline, moving from 150 metres out to around 270 metres, and was in danger of being lost behind a large rocky outcrop. Alex would need to act fast or he'd lose his chance. Finally, he found what he was looking for and got himself sorted, lining up on the cham from a prone shooting position on a rock just below me.

Alex's rushed shot wasn't perfect, hitting the cham low and a little further back than ideal, and it quickly bounded around the corner and was lost out of sight.

We were confident it wouldn't go far, and after giving things time to settle down, we started heading in the direction the chamois had run.

It may have been the bullet, or it may have been the fall, but we soon located it piled up near the bottom of a steep scree face. It had come close to sliding 'over the falls', stopping just shy of plunging off the ledge into nothingness. We were stoked, although once we had worked our way carefully down to the animal, our earlier suspicions were confirmed — it wasn't quite the trophy we were hoping for. That's not to say ground shrinkage had struck again, as its horns were well over 10 inches on both sides. It's just that rather than being a buck, it was an extremely old nanny.

That didn't bother Alex as he was rapt, especially since at one stage during the search it seemed like we might well have lost the cham altogether. In the space of a month, we'd nailed the two biggest chamois in the show's history — pretty wild considering our unsuccessful track record up until this year.

The remainder of the day was a real grind. The jagged ridgeline wasn't safe to travel, so we were forced to descend a couple of hundred metres and sidle our way across the sun-baked face. The combination of the oppressive heat of late afternoon and a need to conserve water really sapped morale, but we eventually made it up onto a relatively flat site where we could pitch our tents for the night.

While scouting the area, Anto discovered a mossy soak, hidden out of reach of the sun. There was enough moisture trapped within for him to refill the bladders, which was a godsend and ensured we didn't spend the night parched and suffering from 'wet dreams': fantasising about running rivers and overflowing water bottles.

Our next day in the tops was relatively uneventful. We carried on along the ridgeline, keeping an eye out for any potential routes down to the valley floor, but nothing obvious jumped out. By evening, we'd worked our way to a spot along the ridge that was 500 metres lower in elevation than where we'd ended up the day prior. This meant we were much closer to the bushline, and as a result, we were now able to pick up the sound of stags roaring intermittently throughout the night, which I've found is always a great pick-me-up.

We knew before we left Queenstown that our fourth day on the hill was likely to be one of the more testing days of the trip. Anto had pored over the maps during the planning phase, with a particular focus on how we could get from the tops to the valley floor, but it's hard to get a gauge on country from just the lines of a topographic map. We knew we'd need to see the land in front of us before committing to a route. It was going to be a tough day, but we weren't quite expecting the physical and mental challenge we had in store.

The descent began early, as we aimed to make the shelter of the treeline before the sun was high in the sky. We'd banked on it taking around an hour to work our way safely down the steep face and into the bush, and we made a promising start, following a route that we'd worked out from high on the hillside the previous night.

Things slowed once we hit the monkey scrub, but I was assured by Alex that we'd be through it in half an hour, and that this would be the worst of it over. Alex's claim would be the first of many false assertions over the course of the day.

It became a bit of a theme: we would make solid progress and start believing the worst was behind us, before we would hit another brick wall — impenetrable monkey scrub, a huge boulder blocking our path, a vertical drop-off into oblivion.

We stopped keeping an eye on time when we realised this projected

Alex plots a route down to the river from his rocky perch.

four-hour descent to the valley floor would likely now be a full-day mission, and any hunting was off the table until we were safely down the hillside.

We finally reached the bush edge, where Alex again uttered the fanciful phrase 'we're over the worst of it, lads', but once again he was wrong. We were now at an altitude of 1000 metres, but rather than a simple descent through a tree-lined hillside, the next few hours were some of the most ball-breaking and mentally draining I've had since the long hard slog out of sambar country in Victoria with Dre and Jamie Carle that I discussed at length in the last book.

We needed to find some kind of ridge that we could follow down, to avoid any guts which would be completely impenetrable due to the heavy vegetation. There weren't any game trails that we could follow; it seemed that even the deer didn't want to be up in this crap. We began weaving our way downhill, making slow progress, but it was nice to see that we were slowly chipping away, as the altitude metre on my Garmin watch gradually dropped.

Alex was the first of us to take a tumble. He was at the head of the group, trying to break his way through some thick scrub, when the next thing we heard was an almighty crash — bushes breaking and branches snapping. His voice from way off down the hill confirmed that he was okay but that we should probably choose a different route down.

Over the years of making the show I've been put through the ringer on plenty of tough days. I'm now able to identify the emotional metamorphosis that I go through:

Dave's Stages of a Big Day
Denial: This won't be too bad, we've got this, it can't be as bad as that other trip.
Anger: What the hell? This is insane, we've only gone half a kilometre. WTF!
Bargaining: What if we stop for a break? How about we just pitch camp here?
Depression: This sucks big time. I hate hunting. Stupid bloody trees.
Acceptance: Oh well, just gotta suck it up, we'll get there eventually. What doesn't kill you makes you stronger, etc.

A lot of the movement between stages has to do with fluctuating blood sugar levels, lactate build-up and one more important factor. On this particularly testing day, just like on the Victorian sambar hunt, there was one thing that we were all beginning to crave: water.

It was about now that we all began to run dry. Not only had the coast not seen much rain for the past month, but it was stupidly hot for the end of March, and it had taken a big effort and a lot of energy to get to this point. Dehydration leads to poor decision making, and we were beginning to make some poor choices.

The 600-metre contour became a World War I-esque front line. We launched attack after attack but were repelled by steep bluffs and impassable scrub. Each failed attempt to break the line left us needing to backtrack uphill before veering a hundred metres left to launch another assault.

I was now sliding into the depression stage. It seemed hopeless; we just couldn't crack the bloody 600-metre mark. As I was sulking my way across the face, hoping to stumble over a feasible route down, the ground underneath me suddenly gave way, and off I went.

My momentum was slowed by the heavy vegetation reaching out and snagging my pack, and luckily for me, my fall was broken by a soft patch of moss and bracken, saving me from a potentially messy rescue situation. It certainly took the wind out of me — falling 10 metres vertically down a rugged hillside will do that to you — but it had the effect of immediately lifting my mood. I'd leapfrogged past acceptance and had entered a new stage — relief. It felt like I'd dodged a bullet, coming out totally unscathed when a broken leg or even a broken back could have resulted, given how far I'd fallen.

Anto and Alex yelled out to me from above, worried that I'd knocked myself out or something worse, and seemed surprised by the relaxed tone of my reply. From this point onwards, I was at peace. I was a better person to be around. I started filming more and was taking the challenging situation in my stride. Sure, it still sucked and I was just as thirsty as ever, but at least I wasn't awaiting the arrival of the Westpac rescue helicopter.

With water now really playing on our minds, we decided to head for a creek that the map showed was a couple of hundred metres off to our left and, hopefully, we could follow the edge of it to get down through the dreaded 600-metre mark.

Traversing the hill was a fair bit easier than trying to descend it, and soon we were within sight of the creek. But Anto had some bad news to convey — it was bone dry.

It's certainly rare to find yourself craving water when hunting on the West Coast, but a dry creek in April was almost unheard of. We sat down to evaluate the situation and pull ourselves together. Another claim of 'We're over the worst of it, lads' came from Alex, but by this stage it was more of a punchline than a statement of fact.

The creek did provide us with a route down, though. The lack of water meant the boulders were dry and safe to walk on, and by utilising this 'rocky road' we began to really chip away at the altitude, moving down past the 500-metre mark. As we progressed, the beguiling sound of the Waiototo River in the distance began calling to us. Water, cool, clean water, only an hour away . . . the sound was getting louder and louder . . .

Speaking of sounds, there have been plenty of times throughout the show's history when I seriously regret not filming during a particular moment of action, but it's not always for the vision, sometimes it's the sound that tells a better story — like the time the lads had to deal with my dislocated shoulder, and the visceral noise it made as it 'schlocked' back in made them all jump.

In this case, as I lowered myself off a large boulder, the noise that emanated from me was equally as primal. There, on the edge of the creek bed, protected by an overhanging rock, was a shallow pool of water. The guttural sound that exited my parched lips was almost unintelligible. According to Alex in an article that he later wrote for *Rod&Rifle* magazine:

He was so excited trying to say the word water that it sounded a bit like the squeal of a teenage boy when his voice was breaking.

It was heavenly. We eagerly slaked our thirst before fuelling up with a hot Back Country Cuisine meal, and from this point onwards the mood in the group changed dramatically. We felt like actual hunters once again, and now that we were down in stag country, Anto decided it was time to let out his first roar of the trip. Amazingly, we had an instant reply, from just a couple of hundred metres away down the face.

Unfortunately, despite our best efforts, a sinking wind gave us away, but the encounter put a pep in our step, that's for sure. We bumped another stag once down closer to the river, but by that stage of the day, our tired legs and heavy packs meant we were about as stealthy as a herd of elephants.

But we made it. It was a close-run thing, and we'd each had to overcome a few demons en route, but after eleven gruelling hours we were finally on the valley floor, eager to welcome the warm embrace of sleep.

Between snores, a few more roars were heard throughout the night, but our morning skirmish to the southern edge of our block proved fruitless. Around midday, we saddled back up and pressed on in the direction of the large flats that we'd studied from the ridgeline on our first evening.

Five kilometres later, we arrived at what would be our base for the remaining few days of the trip. Before dropping us into the tops, the chopper had first deposited a cache of gear on the edge of the clearing, including our big M.I.A tent and an assortment of other luxury items. On arrival, we eagerly tucked into some of these treats, rewarding ourselves for the big effort we'd made up to this point. It's a sweet feeling looking up into the distant hills that we'd traversed earlier on in the trip, reassured by the knowledge that there wasn't some giant stag lurking around up there out of our reach.

By the time we'd set up our bulletproof base camp, it was about time to venture out for the evening hunt. Over the next couple of hours, we heard plenty of stags in the surrounding hills, but none seemed game enough to come in and investigate Anto's replies.

As I sat listening to the roars, I did my best to stave off the voracious sandflies by covering up every square inch of exposed skin. The beep of a message coming through from my wife Amber on the inReach filled us in on a couple of major events from the real world — the death of Foo Fighters drummer Taylor Hawkins, and the controversial Will Smith–Chris Rock Oscars slap. It's always an odd feeling getting news from civilisation

Alex's 10-inch nanny that very nearly gave us the slip.

after living in your own little bubble for so long, but it provided us with something new to talk about.

With under an hour of light left in the day, we heard a distant roar coming from a new direction. The stag seemed to be on the flats closer to camp rather than halfway up the hillside, so we decided it was probably our best bet and raced to get into position before the light died.

We arrived on the water's edge to discover that it was roaring from across the opposite side of the river. We had no time to waste, and after locating the stag in the binos, Anto decided it was worth taking. The light by this stage had dropped to the point where things needed to happen very fast, and getting a range on the stag was proving very difficult, thanks to the flatness of the land and multiple layers of riverbed scrub between us and him.

Alex initially conveyed a distance of 230 yards, but this was due to the trees in the foreground obstructing the laser of the rangefinder. Anto's first shot hit the stag, but it was low and a bit far forward, and the stag hobbled off towards the treeline.

What followed was a chaotic sequence, one that I felt was probably best not to portray within the episode for a few reasons, not least for the fact that it made us look bloody amateurish!

Alex's rangefinder kept coming back with what Anto and I felt was a low number. In my experience, with the long lens attached, the animal looked too small in frame for it to be only 230 yards away. Anto found him in his crosshairs again and squeezed off, but again the shot was wayward, as were his next three! The darkness made it impossible to tell if his shots were too high or too low, and at this rate, we were at risk of Anto running out of ammo, but given the stag was already hit we really needed to put him down.

Anto and Alex then re-ranged, using a distant treeline to confirm that the stag was certainly much further off than 230, and in all likelihood, it was beyond 300, possibly now closer to 400.

The footage really doesn't do justice to how dark it was now getting, as by this stage I'd changed across to my ultra-fast 1.5 85 mm prime lens, capable of pulling in more light than the human eye. In this instance, rather than the camera being a hindrance to hunting, thanks to the fast lens I was able to help direct Anto to the movement of the stag on the distant clearing. Thankfully, Anto's sixth and final shot made contact, a little far back, but judging by the puff of air from the point of impact, it was likely through the lungs.

It was a little messier than we had hoped, but we had our first stag down. Now the fun began: getting across the river to recover it!

Along with the M.I.A tent, the chopper had also dropped off three inflatable pack rafts, which we put to good use in crossing the river in the dark. Anto had earlier used his watch to shoot a bearing of where the stag went down, and after following the 'crumb trail', we soon located the big beast piled up on the edge of the treeline.

He wasn't a world beater by any means, but we were happy to have one on the board and made sure to respect the life we'd taken by carting all the meat back to camp. But Alex nearly didn't make it all the way back.

After loading up his pack raft with meat, he set off under head torch to the opposite side of the fast-moving water. But like a one-legged duck, he paddled in a wide arc and ended up running ashore a couple of hundred metres downriver from the point that he'd set off from. It took some convincing from us that he'd stuffed it up — somehow his bearings were so shot that he was convinced he'd made it across to the opposite side.

There wasn't a lot to report on from the next day, as the roaring we'd been hearing had ceased, possibly due to us scenting up the flats. In the middle of the day, Anto decided to kill some time by casting a fly around in a picturesque stream on the edge of the block.

He had one chance on a nice big brown, but his cast wasn't perfect and the fish spooked, which provided me a chance to inject a bit of humour into the episode with some well-timed skinny dipping. It actually took two takes to get the shot that I was after, which had me swim naked all the way through the back of frame as Anto delivered a piece to camera about the spooky trout living in the river. I can assure you that given the water temperature, there was no risk of anything offensive being seen on camera.

Much like the morning, the evening hunt again was a non-event, but we were pleased to hear a few more roars overnight coming from the hills off to our east.

A light clag lay over the flats as we made our way in the dark towards where we figured the roars were coming from. It was tough going, fumbling our way in the pre-dawn through swamps and thick undergrowth. It may not have rained for some time, but there were still pockets of heavy bog that needed to be avoided. After keeping our boots dry for the best part of a week, they were now well and truly sodden, and the stagnant quagmire at the base of the hill we were forced to cross certainly didn't help.

But as the light strengthened, travel became much easier, and the welcome sound of a couple of roaring stags on the hillside kept our spirits high.

We worked our way up the face, trying to pinpoint the location of the stags, but it can be quite difficult to work out exactly where a particular sound is coming from when you're in the bush, so we gained a bit of extra altitude to help discern the direction of the more vocal of the pair.

After half an hour playing a high-stakes game of Marco Polo, we'd moved to within a couple of hundred metres of one of the stags. He was roaring well, returning our calls aggressively, but was reluctant to make the final move and come charging in on us.

Anto decided the best tactic would be for him to stay back and roar, aiming to keep the stag's attention focused on him rather than on Alex and me, as we'd stalk in to try to get a look at him. However, that was easier said than done in this extremely thick tangle of vegetation, but the bush did provide us with plenty of concealment.

The nerves were jangling at this stage, as it's an intense feeling stalking in on a roaring red stag, certainly one of the quintessential experiences in all of hunting. After stealthily working our way towards the stag, being careful not to bump any hinds in the area, Alex caught sight of him, thrashing some foliage around 30 metres ahead of us.

I managed to get a quick shot of his rack through a thick tangle of vegetation, but I didn't have the same angle on the action as Alex did. I worked my way over towards him in the hope of opening up a better view but was still obscured by the dense bush. To Alex's absolute credit, even in the heat of the moment he still had the wherewithal and composure to ask me whether he was able to take the shot, and rather than risk butchering the opportunity by trying to improve my angle, I switched the camera into its slow-motion setting and gave him the green light.

The shot rang out, but all I saw was a shudder of bushes and foliage. Turns out what I thought had been the stag's rump was actually a punga log, bugger it! But Alex was confident that he'd hit the stag and hit him hard.

It's always a nervous time, the period between a shot being fired and locating the animal, even when you're confident of a clean kill. In this case, we could hear the stag as it charged off through the dense bush, so we knew the basic direction to head in order to look for a blood trail. Once Anto caught up with us, we set off in search of our prize, still uncertain whether it was a scrubby 6-point bush stag or something worthy of putting on the wall.

It didn't take long to find the big bruiser, and we were pleasantly surprised to find that he was definitely the latter, a nice West Coast 10-pointer! Just what the doctor ordered, and Alex could hardly have been any more chuffed. I'd enjoyed his quick wit over the previous week, and as he and Anto celebrated his success, he delivered a great off-the-cuff line:

DAVE: 10 inches and 10 points mate, not bad . . .
ALEX: Yeah, two tens. What's that called in basketball a 'double double', innit?

With an extra heavy load of meat and bone to carry out, we decided to forgo the swamp country and take the long route back to the M.I.A. It was a decent old slog for poor Alex, carting two back legs and the rack, but he was happy to shoulder the load.

After recovering from the epic morning, we rolled the dice on a final evening hunt, but we'd done our dash. I was deeply satisfied: we had a genuine hard-yards hunt with three great action sequences in the can, no serious injuries, and — for once — no broken camera equipment!

It's been a long chapter already, but I've got one final story from the trip to recount. Given that my wife's birthday falls on 3 April, it's rare that I ever get the chance to spend it with her in person, as I'm normally out in the hills for the roar.

This year, on the morning of 3 April, I awoke on the floor of the M.I.A (Alex and Anto had the camp stretchers as per the norm) and set about packing up gear for our designated chopper pick-up. I was under strict instructions — I had to make the flight at 2 p.m. from Queenstown, otherwise there would be divorce papers there to meet me at Auckland Airport rather than a smiling wife. Luckily, all went well and I found myself having dinner with Amber and the kids at a swanky gastro bar in the Viaduct, quite a change from the Back Country Cuisine freeze-dried meal and venison heart of the previous night.

And because it was her birthday, rather than heading back home to Kerikeri, I had splashed out so we could all stay a night at the Hilton. I don't think there would have been too many guests arrive in their ritzy foyer with bags smelling quite as funky as mine did, but like the professionals they are, they didn't make a fuss.

I have to say, the room was bloody nice, but to be honest, I think I preferred the view from the 'Waiototo Hilton', which was definitely a 10 out of 10 from me.

The reward for busting our butts earlier on in the trip, a solid West Coast 10-pointer.

True five-star accommodation.

Alex's two cents

I'm sure many people that watch the show think the guys have a great life and it's all fun and games, but it's not always what it looks like.

Dave is fantastic at what he does, but he's not shy about making you do things over and over if he's not happy. This includes taking your pack off and walking a certain way over a rock or round a tree. Before we even started walking at the start of the trip, we spent ten minutes just talking to the camera. But I have to give him full credit. He told me at the start of the week, just be yourself, don't try and think too much about talking to the camera and it'll all be sweet. Anto and I have hunted together for a while now, so at least I wasn't just thrown in the deep end completely. Ultimately, it was an awesome week hunting with a good mate and a bloke with a camera following us, which provided a lasting memento I can look back on in years to come.

26 PROBLEMATIC PUKA

At the end of April, I found myself back in stunning Milford Sound once again. Nine months had passed since our eventful but ultimately unsuccessful attempt to spear a mainland puka in Dusky Sound, so we were back in Fiordland looking to go one step better. We already had the spearing action from the Chathams trip up our sleeve, but we still wanted to achieve the goal that we'd set ourselves the year prior. A puka speared in mainland waters compared to a puka on the Chathams is like a stag taken on public land versus a stag on private: it's got an extra level of prestige.

But in the days leading into the trip, we had a couple of big rusty spanners thrown into our plans. The first was boat related — a mate of Dwane's had a 2500 Ultracab XL that he was willing to let us use for the trip, but it had been experiencing trailer problems and the brakes were only operational on one side, certainly not ideal for towing along the notoriously dangerous Milford Road. As I was ringing around trying to find a replacement vessel, a message came through from Dwane — he'd tested positive for Covid and was now required to self-isolate.

What a shit sandwich. It was looking like we'd have to scrap the shoot, but we had a stroke of luck. A day earlier, Nat and Rochele had met a bloke in Gore by the name of Dave who'd built a boat of his own, and not just any old boat, a gigantic 10-metre beast that he regularly towed all the way to Milford behind his massive Ford F350. It was just under the legal width to require a pilot vehicle, and the whole rig was so big that he needed to lower the radar on the boat's roof to get it through the Homer Tunnel!

Dave was dead keen to help us out with our little adventure, so that solved our boat problem. And with a vessel of this size, we certainly wouldn't be short on space, so to make up for Dwane's enforced absence, I put out an invite to the irrepressible Ant Niterl. Ant managed to shuffle a few work commitments to join us for what would be his second mission in search of the elusive Fiordland puka. Rounding out the team, as per usual, was underwater cameraman Sam Wild.

We had some big plans for this trip. In the days leading up it, footage had been shared on social media taken by some third-period wapiti hunters perched high in the hills overlooking Bligh Sound of massive work-ups of bluefin tuna, smashing the surface into white water as they fed on schools of bait.

We were there primarily for puka, but no spearo worth his salt is going

to turn down the chance at a southern bluefin, especially if we were lucky enough to find them active in the sheltered waters of the sound itself.

However, the tuna were nowhere to be seen, and the puka diving proved to be just as difficult as we envisaged. We took a different approach this time around; rather than diving multiple locations hoping to get lucky on a random fish, we instead loaded up a cray pot with burley and let it sit just up off the bottom, with a few flashing lights attached. Nat would then breathe up on the surface before bombing down on top of it, but the only fish encountered were a few tarakihi, cod and rig, along with a feisty sevengiller which made life at 30-plus metres a little dicey.

The next morning saw the first real excitement of the trip. Given the time of year, we knew we would have a good chance of a deer encounter, so Nat had organised all the necessary permits to hunt the area. The fourth period of the wapiti ballot had just come to an end, so any deer we saw from this point on were fair game.

We'd exited Bligh on the second morning and were on our way south down to Charles Sound, when we spied a stag feeding in the sun out on a seaward face. Its big white rump indicated that it wasn't just any old stag, it was a wapiti bull, but not a whopper. As the fellas discussed the best way to launch an assault from the boat, I managed to get some footage of it on the drone, but it soon made its way further up the hillside and was eventually lost to sight.

Another stag was then spied out on an open slip not far from the first, and this time we decided to have a crack at it. Nat and Sam began suiting up, but the stag must have sensed something strange, as it quickly sought the safety of the surrounding bush.

That half-hour period was probably the day's highlight. We still managed to get some quite entertaining footage, diving Eleanor Island and some beautiful locations along the coast, then on the way back north to our

Where to start?

overnight anchorage at George Sound we had a couple of hits on the tuna lures but were unable to convert them.

Our focus shifted back to puka for the final day of diving, at least, that was the plan to begin with. After warming the lungs up with a quick dive at the entrance to George Sound, we started making our way back to the spot at the head of Bligh that we'd dived earlier, hoping a change of tide might see a few puka lurking around the area. However, en route, Rochele's keen eyes picked up another wapiti bull, standing proud as punch on the top of a rocky promontory, midway up the sound.

We pressed pause on the puka plan to try our luck with more big-game hunting. Rather than having to deal with the crashing waves out on the coast, Nat and Sam, our two 'Gravy Seals', were able to slink quietly into the water and swim silently across to the rocks at the base of the cliff.

Meanwhile, Dave manoeuvred the boat well away from the action, not wanting to spook the bull. I was doing my best to capture events from the air, equally careful to not spook him, but unfortunately, right as our wetsuit-clad hunters began climbing the steep rock face, the bull began sidling off further up the slope into the thick bush. By the time they were up near where he was initially seen, he was long gone.

Time to get back to the task at hand. We returned to our hāpuku hotspot and were pleased to see a bit more sign on the sounder, so hopes were high that we'd finally be able to pull it off. After half a dozen deep drops, though, we were forced to admit defeat. Nat did manage to shoot a consolation snapper — in Sam's words 'task failed successfully' — but no puka were seen. The happy ending we were after would need to wait.

A fortnight later, we found ourselves once again back at the ramp in Milford Sound, but this time in a configuration that more closely resembled our initial puka plan. Dwane had bounced back strongly from his bout of Covid, and we had Dave Strudwick's 2500 Ultracab XL, the same boat we'd used on our trip to Solander.

Having had a bit of time to reflect on tactics, we adopted a different approach for the return mission. Rather than busting the lungs diving deep in search of fish, we'd use technology, so to 'work smart, not hard', we put the cameras to use.

Once we arrived in the head of George Sound, we filled the burley pots with pilchards and bombed them down 40 metres, with GoPros attached. After giving the burley 20 minutes to attract a few fish, we recovered the cameras and reviewed the footage.

It was quite an exciting process, the four of us crowded around the laptop in the cabin of the boat hoping to spy a puka swimming into frame, but after half a dozen drops where only lesser species such as blue cod, kahawai and tarakihi were seen, the process began to lose its appeal and became quite tedious.

With the high-tech approach having failed to deliver any real results, we decided to mix things up and try our luck diving a couple of deeper pins further north, closer to our overnight anchorage in Bligh Sound, but on the way, we ran into an old friend.

The wapiti bull that had proven too cunning for Nat and Sam a fortnight earlier was standing in exactly the same spot on the hillside, almost daring us to come after him. We continued well past the bluff, hoping not to alert him by a change of noise from the boat, and once into position, it was pretty much a repeat of the earlier effort. Sam and Dwane slipped into the water, while I had the drone in the air documenting the action from above.

The lads had taken a VHF radio with them on the previous attempt but had turned it off due to it being too noisy, so we didn't bother giving them one for this effort. And unlike the last time, the stag seemed unaware of the looming danger as the lads removed their fins and began their steep climb.

They gradually closed the gap on the big bull, taking a more direct route straight up the face this time. The mossy rocks would have been slippery enough to traverse in hunting boots, but in their neoprene booties, both wetsuit-clad hunters found themselves sliding about all over the place.

I had a prime view of proceedings from the drone and could quite clearly see the boys slowly making their way up towards the bull on the hillside. It certainly made for intense viewing, and at one stage I found myself screaming at the viewfinder, incredulous that they hadn't seen the big bull, which was just 20 metres from them, but without a VHF we had no way of letting them know just how close they all were to each other. After the mahi mahi safety switch mishap and the Pitt Island ram sequence, this was the third time that I'd found myself yelling at the drone in frustration with Sam and Dwane both in frame.

The vision from the air was deceptive, though, and didn't paint an accurate picture of the situation on the ground. The view from Sam and Dwane's head cameras gave a better idea of just how tall the surrounding vegetation was, so they can be forgiven for not spotting the bull despite his close proximity.

By the time Sam finally became aware, they were within spitting distance, but the bull was one step ahead of the hunters and ran for the cover of some thicker scrub and was eventually lost to view.

At the time, I was disappointed that the guys had butchered such an amazing opportunity, but after reviewing the footage, I think the failure saved us a whole lot of drama. It was clearly a young bull, a few years off its prime, and certainly not the kind of animal you'd take just for its meat. Sure, it would have made for a unique photo, two spearfishermen in 7-mm wetsuits perched on a Fiordland hillside with a wapiti bull, but as I explained earlier, even though we're a spearfishing show, we'd have opened ourselves up to all kinds of criticism from the hunting community.

Dwane and Sam finally got the days diving under way at around 5 p.m., but by this late stage, it was far too dark to make anything out underwater. Finding the fish is one thing, but we still needed to film them, so we called it a day and made plans for another attempt in the morning.

Again, we put the cameras to use to scout a few likely areas (mainly because neither Sam nor Dwane was keen to suit up in the chilly morning conditions) but picked up nothing of interest. Feeling a little deflated, we then headed out to the entrance, quickly spying more animals out on the sunny seaward faces, but the swell out here would have made launching an amphibious assault incredibly difficult. So instead we went wide, hoping lightning might strike twice with a school of bluefin tuna materialising from out of the blue as they did the last time Dwane, Sam and I rolled the dice but, again, nothing.

It looked like Fiordland would be sending us home with our tails between our legs once more, but as we steamed our way north back towards Milford, Dwane spied a splash of red on the hillside — a young deer out feeding in the midday sun.

Redemption time. With the airtight Yeti Panga bag as a flotation device to help keep the rifle dry, Sam and Dwane began swimming their way ashore, having to carefully pick their moments between sets of waves to prevent themselves from being tossed onto the large rocks littering the shoreline.

Once they'd made it through the breakers and along the beach, after a bit of a bush bash, the pair were able to locate the deer again as it fed happily midway up the face, and a well-placed shot from Dwane dropped it on the spot. On their way to collect it, another deer was then spotted, which Dwane was also able to dispatch.

The two deer proved a bit of a challenge to get back to the boat. With the waves now breaking heavily along the coast, Sam and Dwane chose to bind the two carcasses together and tow them out through the worst of the shore break behind their float lines. This would also allow them to maintain a safe distance, as swimming back to the boat among a sea of

A couple of visitors more often seen in the waters of the Far North.

fresh blood in these sharky waters would not be a smart move.

We'd achieved one of the main aims of the trip, with some lightly salted venison now cooling in the kill bag, but had failed on the puka front yet again. However, a little crafty editing meant that I was able to slot the earlier spearfishing material from the Chathams into this sequence to make a cohesive whole. I admit, it was a bit of a cheat, taking a few creative liberties, but for entertainment's sake it made far more sense to piece the stories together this way, especially given the obstacles we had to overcome thanks to the corrupted hard drive.

But before I could even start piecing together the jigsaw puzzle that is the editing process, we first had a mountain to climb.

Roping the deer together to reduce the risk of getting sharked on the way back to the boat.

Sam's two cents

We knew we were setting the bar incredibly high when we set ourselves the task of shooting a mainland hāpuku.

Between the team, we have thousands of underwater hours all over New Zealand, and at most we have only seen a handful of puka in that time. The one and only I have been lucky enough to see was a wee pup that I bumped into off the coast near Wellington Airport, but that swiftly took off back down to the depths. Nat may be the only other team member who had seen one, so it's a real testament to the rarity of these critters of the deep.

But, with the adopted *South Seas Spearo* ethos of 'no risk, no reward' we have given it a bloody good nudge, and through our efforts we have learned a lot about what might work and where our time may be wasted. A couple of moments that have really stood out during our trials have been when we had our first crack on the vessel *Flightless*, where we were diving in the inner sounds near a waterfall pumping out fresh snow melt which sat on top of the salt water, and my Garmin Descent watch read a nice balmy 5 degrees — definitely the coldest water I have been in to date!

We'll no doubt keep chipping away at the task over future seasons, hoping to get lucky with a chance encounter, but as the old cliché goes, it's the journey, not the destination.

27 WINTER BULL TAHR TEAM TRIP

There are often times during the heat of summer when my mind wanders and I find myself longing for the snow and ice of mid-winter. Those hot and sweaty afternoons seem to stretch on interminably, and I've never been one who can sleep during the day — thanks in part to a constant nagging in the back of my brain to make the most of any and all filming opportunities.

Most of the big-game species we target here in New Zealand are crepuscular, meaning they're more active at dawn and dusk, so to give ourselves the best chance at success, we hunters need to become crepuscular ourselves. But that can mean getting by on just five hours of sleep per night, a tough ask given the physicality of most trips.

However, winter's a very different cup of tea, but not necessarily for the better. Many times I've found myself waking up in the darkness of my tent to check my watch, only to find it hadn't even passed midnight. Those long cold nights are certainly difficult, but I'd much rather have too much time to sleep than too little.

It was now early June and summer was a distant memory. I'd been looking forward to a hearty alpine tahr hunt for the whole year, given that we chose not to pursue bulls in Series 7. This wasn't due to a lack of desire; we just decided that we wanted to give those new to hunting tahr the best opportunity. Any bull we took for the show would mean one less potential trophy walking around the hills for the next up-and-coming hunter.

However, after hearing reports of solid tahr numbers in some of the regular hotspots, it became clear that the 'tahrmageddon' control work hadn't knocked numbers down to un-huntable levels. There were still some absolute thumpers coming out of the hills too, so we made plans to head back into the same country where we'd encountered our gigantic chamois in late summer. And to allow us to tell the story of a first-timer, we brought a couple of greenhorns along for the ride.

We decided early in the planning phase that this mission would lend itself to adopting a two-pronged approach. Team A would consist of Anto and Yuley, along with *South Seas Spearo* underwater cameraman Sam Wild who, if the dice rolled his way, would hopefully get an opportunity to take his first bull tahr. Sammy would also have the additional pressure of documenting their hunt on camera as best he could. They would be hunting a side catchment up around 1200 metres, so relatively low, but with good opportunities for chamois or winter stags.

Team B would be big Timmy Barnett, the 'Tongan Tahr' Andre Alipate, me and Marty Verry from Red Stag Timber, who like Sam would also be saddling up for his first tahr trip. We'd be flying into some much higher country on the opposite side of the valley system, well above the snowline. Over the course of a few days, the plan for was both teams to work their way towards a hut on the valley floor at 840 metres, where we would all meet up to share stories and, all things going well, compare trophies.

With the weather looking a little dicey, it was decided that Team A would depart slightly earlier, getting dropped onto the valley floor into their designated area at the precise meeting point of the east and west coast on the evening before Team B's departure. This was a good call, as the following morning greeted us with clag and rain, preventing any chance of an early flight into the mountains as hoped.

Luckily, the weather broke around midday, and the machine skidded us up-valley and dropped us high above the snowline at around 1300 metres. As the chopper returned to base to collect Marty and Tim, Dre and I stood there and took in our surroundings. It was stunning, the type of country that makes you feel totally insignificant but, at the same time, like the king of the world. Wispy fingers of mist hung like feathers over the mountains, and distant glacial lakes reflected a bright blue sky. This was what I'd been longing for all year.

Our first task was to find a suitable campsite. Even though we'd been flown in, we still had quite a climb ahead of us to find a flat-enough plateau to allow us to pitch our four single-man tents. Plugging away uphill under a heavy pack in the thick snow is taxing, but at least you don't end up cooking yourself, the snow offering immediate respite from the heat.

There was one particularly nasty knife-edge section on the ascent that took a bit of extra concentration, and I'm sure it had Marty wondering what the hell he'd signed up for. We don't like doing things by halves on the show, but we'd really thrown him in the deep end for his first true alpine hunt! After a tough old climb, we eventually located a suitable spot to drop packs and make camp on a snowy ledge up at around 1700 metres.

There were plenty of animals spotted from our elevated perch, including a couple of promising-looking bulls, so we were in pole position for our morning hunt. But speaking of pole position; the spot I chose to pitch my tent could have been a little better thought out.

I wanted to camp in a spot that would allow me to film astro timelapses of the surrounding mountains from the comfort of the tent, so pitched it pretty much on the edge of oblivion — upon a snowy ledge that dropped dramatically away a couple of hundred metres. It made for a rather sleepless night, as the wind got up at one stage and I started stressing about

Team B, punching our way
well up above the snowline.

the risk of avalanche, the snowpack cracking and breaking away, or the tent being blown over the drop.

I should have known better and followed in the footsteps of the geo-technical engineer in the team. Dre had used his ice axe to carve out a perfectly flat foundation in the snow, set well back from the edge, and slept like the little pig that built his house out of bricks, while I spent the night worrying about a knock on the door from the big bad wolf.

The freezing temps overnight ensured there was no snow melt, and we awoke to a perfectly still morning, the clear skies helping keep the temps well below zero.

It's a hell of a feeling, sitting high on a snowy ridge and spotting tahr below you for once, rather than the usual scenario where they're only ever seen perched proudly in the craggy tops way above. It was certainly a privilege, and as the sun began to rise, I reflected on what a massive loss to all New Zealanders it would be if we were to ever lose the ability to hunt these charismatic animals.

Over the course of the morning, we spied quite a few animals close by, moving back up into the higher reaches following a night spent feeding in the lower country. They were obviously not too worried about any potential danger from above, and we managed to get some great footage of them as they ploughed through the deep snow.

Marty was eager to make the most of the plum opportunity to plug his first tahr at close range, but the bulls were all in the 11-inch range and still deserved a few more years to reach trophy calibre. Now, more than ever, we hunters need to be selective of the bulls we take, so we were content just to enjoy their company and let them walk.

But back over with Team A, they'd encountered a bull that was well past retirement age!

Having not been privy to how it all unfolded, I can only speak on what I've seen in the episode, but it sounded like Yuley and Anto, having both shot plenty of big bulls in the past, rather generously gave Sam shooting rights on the big bruiser. After waiting him out in some pretty average weather, the pressure of the moment didn't get to Sam, and he managed to drop him with a shot from around 350 metres.

The bull was the first tahr that Sam had ever seen let alone shot, and what a bull it was. It measured an impressive 13⅝ inches, making it the biggest we'd ever taken on the show, but what was even more impressive was its age. After a rudimentary assessment of its growth rings, Yuley estimated it to be around fifteen years of age, although after analysis and scoring at an NZDA event a few months later, the age was increased to seventeen, which is absolutely ancient for a bull tahr.

Another thing interesting to note was the fact that the old fella had successfully been able to elude the aerial culls, as he was actually living within the Northern Exclusion Zone. In recent years, DOC have spent a

Sam Wild modelling his haute couture winter fashion accessory.

huge amount of chopper time trying to eliminate all tahr within these zones, in order to prevent their spread outside of the feral range, but here he was, seeing out his final days in solitude, only to have his twilight cut short by a jumped-up spearfisherman!

Back over in the snow, we were unaware of all the action that had unfolded across the other side of the valley. But before throwing packs on backs to continue climbing, I powered up the inReach to send a message to Anto asking for a little status update. The reply was emphatic, and I'm pleased that I filmed the reaction in real time, as Tim's eyes really lit up on hearing of Sam's success. I love these quite genuine moments on the hill, where the guys can share in each other's success, and for me it was a great relief to know that we had one in the bag for the episode.

News of Sam's success meant that we now climbed with renewed vigour, and it wasn't long before we caught sight of a much better-looking bull, sunning itself on a distant ridge. This guy looked a bit more like what we were after, with Tim and Dre putting it in the 13-plus class.

We descended from our leading ridge onto a beautiful flat patch of knee-deep snow. Having located the bull from the new vantage point, Dre then got himself set up. Time wasn't an issue, and the bull seemed unperturbed. With barely a breath of wind, we were all confident that Team B would soon have a trophy to compete with Sam's monster.

It wasn't to be. It was once again close but no cigar for the Tongan Tahr, as Dre's shot sailed just high, possibly undone by the air pressure at such altitude or the steep downhill angle. It was yet another alpine disaster for Dre, making this the third big bull tahr to slip through his fingers on the show, following near misses at Abel Lake in Season 2 and La Perouse in Season 4.

We were all gutted, both at the lost chance for glory but also for Dre, who had added salt rubbed in the wound by having his miss captured on camera for all to see.

I filmed the usual post-shot talking-head footage, then left Dre to dwell on things himself, but unbeknown to him, I left the camera rolling as I walked away from it, and in the process captured one of my favourite moments from the trip. After running through his process to see if he could identify the cause of the issue, he sat up on his knees, and reflected on the situation.

DRE: I don't know what to say . . . f**k!

There was again some genuine emotion on display. The tahr sure haven't been kind to Dre throughout the show's history, and he'd bowled the old 'Tongan Wrong 'un' once more, but with another couple of days up our sleeve we still had every chance to put things right.

We pressed on, running into a few more tahr, but found nothing to trouble the scorers — just young bulls and a couple of nannies.

Whenever you're hunting in the alpine environment, it's critical to stay abreast of the often-volatile weather, and throughout the day Dre had been keeping tabs on developments using the inReach. We had initially hoped to get three full days up in the snow, but the deteriorating weather forecast cut that plan short, as the little satellite device informed us that it was odds on to really hit the fan by lunchtime the next day.

Having had enough time in the snow, and to get a head start on the long trek to the hut the next day, we decided to drop down into some of the lower fringe country. It made sense, seeing as how the animals we had spied the night prior were doing the very same thing. The tricky descent called for crampons and ice axes, but we made it down unscathed, although Dre did find himself needing to self-arrest at one stage after getting a little complacent near the end of the day.

As we set about pitching our second camp on a small, grassy promontory, the inReach beeped once again. This time we received news that Yuley had delivered the goods, having just earned himself a 10-inch chamois buck! Bloody hell, what a run we were having on the chams!

Again, we were stoked for Team B, but now the pressure on us was really starting to build, we didn't want the embarrassment of ending up back at the hut empty handed. However, rather than bowling over an animal just to save face, we were determined to maintain our high standards.

More tahr were spied the next morning, although by the time we laid eyes on them they were well on their way back up towards their bedding zones. Even a dawdling tahr would outpace our best efforts to close the gap, so we were forced to just watch them climb off into the snow from the traditional tahr hunter's point of view.

We later spied some deer living a few hundred metres below us, including a couple of stags but, again, nothing to write home about. So, with a looming weather front beginning to bare its teeth, we began the big haul down off the hill.

However, half an hour after setting off we were stopped in our tracks. After glassing quickly into some new country, Dre spied an absolute beast of a bull living on a steep face opposite, a bit over a kilometre from us. We certainly had no shot at that distance; we really needed him to make his way closer to provide us with even a sniff of an opportunity, although it was quite tempting to simply drop packs and go after him.

As it turned out, I'm glad we didn't. After a little over an hour of watching and hoping he'd make a move in our direction, the weather took a turn for the worse, with the rain beginning to really hammer down.

We had quite a big scrub bash to get off the hill and down onto the valley floor, but three hours after setting off, we arrived at the hut, a little worse for wear but nothing that a cold beer couldn't fix.

Meanwhile, Team A were being put through the wringer as well. They'd left camp earlier that morning, given they had a few extra kilometres to cover, but rather than a bush bash to hinder their progress, they had the challenge of a raging river to look forward to.

Thankfully, Anto had planned ahead, getting the pilot to drop off an inflatable packraft and lifejacket on their side of the river. They were able to ferry gear and personnel across without any major dramas, and soon enough, they were within sight of the hut, where we had a roaring fire ready to welcome them.

We enthusiastically celebrated the arrival of the three sodden but successful hunters, who by this stage resembled Viking warriors returning home from battle. While we were relieved they had made it without incident, we were eager to lay eyes on the two stunning trophies they were carrying, Sam's caped-out tahr in particular.

It was a memorable moment, made even more so by the fact that Team A lads hadn't had the chance to catch up with Team B before their early departure three days earlier, so this was the first time many of the guys had seen each other for quite a few months.

And Anto hadn't been the only one to plan ahead. Along with the packraft, I'd made certain a few more vital supplies had been dropped off at the hut, which ensured we didn't go thirsty that evening. It was a great way to wrap up the trip, and even though we didn't taste success as a team, we could still bask in the glow of Team A's stunning achievements.

We just had one more box left to tick.

28 MAN, OH MAN, OH MANIOTOTO

As was the case twelve months previously, as the broadcast date for the new season of *The Red Stag Timber Hunters Club* loomed, we found ourselves once again one episode shy of the full complement. We don't like doing things twice on the show, but since it had worked out so well for us the previous season, we decided to retrace our steps and head back to the same epic spot in the Maniototo where the rambunctious Russian boar had taken a shine to Timmy a year earlier.

By this stage, I'd come to terms with having lost the incredible pig-hunting action from the Chathams and was actually quite excited about a return to the Maniototo with Tom and Brett, especially since I now had a rather tidy storyline linking both trips.

The lost Chathams footage tied together quite nicely with a storyline that unfolded in the final days of the first mission a year earlier, as on that outing we had also fallen victim to another camera-related drama.

Following the evening of Tim's close call, we had a young cameraman by the name of Tom join the group for our final two days of hunting. Having a second cameraman would free me up and allow us to better document two hunts at once. It's a luxury that we rarely have on the show given our budget, the flexibility needed, and the overall requirements of hunting. In many cases, an additional person can often limit your options — requiring an extra vehicle, an extra chopper flight, an extra tent site and so on.

Anyway, for the final morning of the shoot, the young cameraman Tom had been tasked with following Anto, Tom and Brett who were hunting from the Polaris side by sides, while I focused on filming with Timmy and Brett's son Clay, with a plan to make our way through the thick snow in search of an alpine boar. Unfortunately, Tim and I had no luck in getting onto the big bruiser we were seeking, but as both parties reassembled around midday, Tim and I were over the moon to see an impressive ginger and black boar hanging off the back of the lads' Polaris.

My stoke turned to sting pretty quickly, when I was informed by the guys that they'd run the dog cam flat by the time the big boar arrived, so I had no dog cam footage; the drone settings were set to manual rather than full auto, so I had no aerial footage; the main cameraman had fallen over in the heat of the moment and accidently stopped recording, so I had no main camera footage.

Hunting's tricky at the best of times, and filming certainly raises the degree of difficulty further, but the missed opportunity to capture some balls-out bailing action with a big boar really stung. The only footage we had was a shaky cellphone shot that Brett managed to get from back on the hill, which showed the young cameraman jumping about like a frog in a sock, right in the midst of the action as Tom wrestled with the big boar.

In his defence, the footage he would have got if he was actually recording would have been spectacular! And in hindsight, the sequence played out quite well within the episode, adding a little splash of humour to proceedings.

But a year had passed since then, and we had a deadline to meet. We were determined to head back and remedy the situation, and while we knew it would be very unlikely that we'd surpass our effort over in the Chathams by bagging two boars just shy of 200 lbs, we were confident that we'd get enough action to create a compelling hour of TV.

But I had a major obstacle to overcome just in getting to the start line.

For a period this year, I wondered whether I might have offended someone high up at Air New Zealand, as my travel plans seemed to be cursed. After the winter bull tahr trip, I'd flown from Christchurch on the early flight to Auckland, hoping to get back to Kerikeri before lunchtime. However, I ended up stranded in Auckland all day, having to collect and recheck my baggage four times as each new flight I was put on was cancelled.

At 8 p.m., the airline finally bit the bullet and put us all on a bus, which arrived in Kerikeri well after midnight. For once I was pleased not to have brought any meat back with me, as it would have been manky by the time I finally arrived home.

A fortnight later, I fell victim to the same cycle, spending another entire day at the airport trying to get from Auckland back to Kerikeri, but thankfully this time the decision to put a bus on was made a bit earlier.

So as I boarded my flight south from Kerikeri, I was a little anxious; these things happen in threes right? The first leg went smoothly, I landed in Auckland and made my way towards the Air New Zealand lounge, past a huge throng of people crowded in the main check-in area. Turns out that Wellington had been experiencing abnormally strong winds, and no flights were getting into or out of the capital. I remember feeling smug, walking past all the frustrated faces waiting impotently in long, snaking queues. I even messaged the pig-hunting team in our group chat, explaining how nice it was to be on the other side of the fence for once, and letting them know I was right on track to be in the Maniototo later that evening.

As they say, pride comes before a fall. Less than five minutes later, a notification came over the intercom in the Koru Lounge. Turns out our flight from Auckland to Queenstown had been cancelled. Just like that, no explanation, no alternative plans, just a 'please collect your bags and make alternative arrangements' from the lady at the counter.

Chewing up the snowy countryside in the warmth of the machines.

The later flights into Queenstown were all sold out, so I was up shit creek. The call centre wait time was approaching three hours, so that was no help. I'd need to join the back of the very same queue that minutes earlier I'd waltzed past wearing a wry smile.

But as wives are prone to do, Amber managed to save the day. I let her know my predicament, and she'd jumped straight online, frantically refreshing the flight booking page like a thirteen-year-old trying to secure tickets to a Taylor Swift concert, and she had somehow managed to snaffle a seat that became available which would get me into Queenstown via Christchurch later that evening. Problem solved! It would mean a much later arrival into the Maniototo, but it was preferable to being stuck in the big smoke for the night.

But once again, my hubris came back to bite. As I was sitting in the Christchurch Koru Lounge awaiting a boarding call, another notification came over the intercom. Due to a 'crewing requirement', our flight to Queenstown had been cancelled. I admit, by this stage I'd lost my patience, and snapped angrily at the young woman running the show in the lounge, saying something to the tune of 'If you're just short a trolley dolly or two then I'll chuck a damn dress on!'

Their hands were tied. Someone had apparently returned a positive test (30 minutes before they were due to board?) and the plane wasn't flying that night. I tossed up the idea of a rental, but in the end made a call to Sam Wild to see if he could come and collect me so I could crash at his place.

I eventually got to Queenstown the next morning, and after a few hours' drive, Anto and I rendezvoused with Tim, Brett and Clay at the entrance to the same property we'd hunted the year earlier. We had lost a morning's hunting, and I had a few more grey hairs, but we still had more than enough time to get the job done.

The afternoon hunt was a little slow, although we managed to nail a few rather comedic sequences. After dispatching a small sow, we relocated higher up into the snowy tops, where the dogs got onto a mob of pigs from above. After some guidance from Tim, I managed to locate and then track them from the air with the drone.

Brett's youngest pup was pursuing a nice black boar, but after reaching a fenceline, the boar spun and gave the pup a bit of a tickle up. It was obviously the first time it had been on the receiving end, so it probably came as a quite a shock. The pup then shadowed the boar at a safe distance for a few metres, before deciding screw this and turning tail for the safety of his mates back at the bike.

The boar continued barrelling on down the fenceline until it reached a gate, but it didn't slow down. Instead, it hit it headfirst at full pace, likely expecting it could barge its way through, but instead it was bounced back hard onto its haunches. Seemingly a little dazed, it took a couple of seconds to straighten itself out before continuing its way along the fenceline towards freedom. The next day we explored another stunning high-country station but didn't have a lot of success, only bagging a small boar and a sow right on dark.

So, we chose to return to where it all began, hunting the property that Tom managed where we'd had success originally. The familiarity paid off, and we got some great sequences, the highlight being Tim's stand-off with a staunch ginger boar. Pigs don't have great eyesight, but this guy seemed to be engaged in a staring contest with Tim, before Pepper arrived and he clicked to the danger of his situation, charging off downhill at pace, and in the process almost steamrolling Tom and Clay who were watching from the valley floor.

We nailed a couple more boars over the next 24 hours, getting some action-packed dog-cam and drone footage, before ending the shoot with what had become the theme of the episode, another equipment-related incident. This time, after climbing high all morning to get into a position above where a good boar had been seen, I took a tumble in the snow and smashed the battery compartment of the main camera, so we were forced to rely on GoPro, dog cam and drone for the final few hours of the trip.

The incredible scenery and camaraderie among the team made up for the lack of main camera action though, and while we didn't run into any big angry boars, overall I was happy with how things had played out. As Anto dropped me off in Queenstown to catch my flight home, I was feeling relaxed and relieved, but it turns out I had one final piece of airport-related mayhem ahead of me.

Rather than flying direct, I once again found myself having to kill time between flights in the Christchurch Koru Lounge, the same place where I'd berated the poor lady in charge a few days earlier. As I departed the lounge to board my flight north, I noticed that she was on duty once again, and I gave her a knowing grin.

I'd only just left the lounge when I heard a loud crash on the escalators up ahead. I assumed that someone in the catering department must have dropped a pile of plates or something, but as I reached the corner where

Tom hoists the big boar
onto his back.

the stairs began, I saw that it was actually an elderly man who had taken a fall, and he was now rolling backwards down the ascending escalator, having become caught in a vicious cycle. I dropped my bags and raced down the stairs, leaping over the side and onto the escalator, where I was able to grab a hold of him and steady the ship.

The poor bugger was covered in blood, with deep wounds to his head and hands from the sharp edges of the escalator steps, and he was clearly very rattled. I yelled out for the Koru lady, who I'm sure probably wondered what my problem was now, but she acted quickly and got a few towels to help stem the flow of blood. The old timer was due to fly to LA later that night, and I never found out if he made it or not, but I doubt it considering the state he was in.

I returned to the lounge to tidy myself up, washing the blood off my clothes and arms, and made my way to the gate just as they began calling for me over the intercom, a bit of residual adrenalin still in my system. The incident certainly put things in perspective for me. Sure, I'd been put through the wringer with various airport sagas over the previous month, but it was nothing compared to the punishment that old mate had been subjected to.

The successful pig hunt meant that we'd wrapped shooting on Series 8 of *The Red Stag Timber Hunters Club*, but for the final shoot of the year, I felt like doing something completely different.

Tim's two cents

It may look all fun and games, but there's a huge amount of blood, sweat, stress and expense that goes into each episode. There are plenty of challenges with filming, so when it comes together, there's a sense of a relief as well as a strong sense of accomplishment.

So to lose our footage after such hard work was incredibly gut-wrenching and deflating. Probably the hardest part for me was the mates, like Ants, Dallon, Chase and others, who had put in such a massive effort to help out. It was gutting that their hard work wasn't rewarded by being able to enjoy the quality footage we'd captured together in a cool episode. I've lost count of the number of cameras and gear that I've lost or broken trying to film with dogs. Not to mention batteries, wrong settings, driver error and dogs slipping away before the camera was switched on. It's a miracle we've got the footage that we have over the years!

To film hunting in general is hard. But to throw in erratic dogs, pigs, remote cameras, scrub and fences means more often than not there will be some degree of stuff-up on any given day of filming. But for all the lost camera gear, the unique angle and perspective you get from the dog cams, which otherwise wouldn't be seen, makes the risk worthwhile.

29 FIJI FUN AND GAMES

As we neared the three-quarter point of 2022, the post-production and delivery schedule for both series was well on track. Things seemed to be going pretty much according to plan, well, as according to plan as it can with our sometimes ramshackle operation. We'd kicked goals on most of our spearo trips, with some seriously action-packed episodes in the can from our missions to the Three Kings, Solander, Fiordland, Raglan, Waihau Bay and the Chathams, covering literally all four corners of New Zealand.

But August was now upon us. *The Red Stag Timber Hunters Club* had already begun airing, and the new season of *South Seas Spearo* was due to kick off the following month, but we still needed to film one more episode to round things out. Complicating matters, a mid-September date with the surgeon's knife loomed for me, and my severely shoddy shoulder was becoming more of a liability by the day.

With the clock ticking, I weighed up our options. Time constraints and the risk of volatile late-winter weather meant that our safest bet would be to up sticks and head over to the islands for our big Season 3 finale, and there aren't too many places higher on the spearo's hit list than the far-flung reaches of outermost Fiji.

Since having our wings clipped by the pandemic, we'd been forced to shoot the previous two years entirely within New Zealand waters, which is by no means a bad thing, but the thought of venturing into the warm, clear waters of the South Pacific had the fellas fighting for a place on the trip.

In the end, it was a simple choice — our two top performers got the nod: 'Dwangerous' Dwane Herbert and Julian 'The Hooligan' Hansford, alongside underwater cameraman Sam Mild, sorry, Wild, and me. Some heavy hitters for sure, but that was far from the full complement.

A few weeks out from departure, Dwane touched base to see whether his young lad Eli would be welcome to join the team, and once I informed him that Eli would be an ideal addition, Jools' protégé (who was also Eli's good mate) Reef also joined the party. The two twelve-year-olds would provide a great chance to showcase the spearfishing opportunities in shallow along the reef fringe, not to mention providing an extra set of hands to help with the rigours of production: opening beers, fetching snacks, applying sunblock — the real glamour jobs.

As things played out, Julian flew to Fiji along with Eli and Reef a week before our departure — which was a bit of a master stroke, as it allowed him time to get the lie of the land and iron out a few logistical issues,

A panga to paradise.

as well as giving the lads a chance to familiarise themselves with the challenges inherent in spearfishing in the tropics.

By the time Sam, Dwane and I dotted down, we had a fairly elaborate plan in place. With a rather stubborn sou'east tradewind forecast to blow over our entire seven-day filming window, we made the call to travel all the way to the remote Kioa Island, tucked between Fiji's northern island of Vanua Levu and the eastern rainforest-laden island of Taveuni. The theory was that Taveuni would act as a windbreak and hopefully provide us with relatively sheltered diving conditions.

After a crack of dawn start, travelling cross country from Nadi to Vanua Levu via plane, truck and eventually panga (long boat), we finally reached our destination. Kioa is home to fewer than 500 people, and we'd be basing ourselves for our time on the island at an old homestead on a remote stretch of palm-fringed beach, just north of Salia, the island's only village. Luckily for us, we'd made good time on the day's travel so had a few hours up our sleeve to get out and wet our beaks.

First in the team's crosshairs was the highly sought-after wahoo, a fish which had proven too much for us on our last tropical sojourn to Vava'u, Tonga, back in the debut season of the show. Wahoo are incredibly fast fish, capable of powerful bursts of speed that can blow gear to pieces, but the lads weren't entering this fight undergunned, bringing long, double-rubber guns, slip tips and heavy-duty floats to ensure they had sufficient stopping power to come out on top this time around.

After quickly locating the offshore fish-attracting device or FAD, the fellas suited up and dropped over the side, to be met immediately by teeming shoals of bait fish and rainbow runners.

The tactic the team chose to try to attract a wahoo was to employ the use of 'throw flashers' — small plastic tubes with reflective coverings that flutter slowly down the water column, and these certainly had an

Our Fijian family waving goodbye on our final morning.

immediate effect — as within five minutes of dropping over the side, a school of mid-sized wahoo came in to investigate.

Having had a rough run in Tonga, Julian didn't waste time in evaluating the fish to seek out the largest in the school; he simply drilled the first that came within reach. Rather surprisingly, the commotion of having a shot fish in their midst did nothing to deter the school, and four more of the prized catch were landed by the fellas before they decided they'd had their fill.

Wahoo aren't a small fish, and there's a lot of great-tasting meat on them, and luckily for us, the local villagers welcomed the delivery of a fresh feed of 'hoo', so we were able to justify taking a few more fish than we'd be capable of eating ourselves. Back at base, we enjoyed a dinner of sashimi and cassava, before relaxing over a few bowls of hard-hitting local kava. But we certainly weren't in any position to kick back and rest on our laurels just yet, and with an early start on the cards, the fellas made their excuses and hit the hay early, long before the guitars came out.

The next morning was an absolute tropical stunner, and after hydrating with a coconut water or two, we punched our way in the pangas out to a reef structure in the Somosomo Strait between Taveuni and Vanua Levu. The tight passage between the two large islands was a pinch point with a huge amount of tidal flow rushing over the reef. As they say, where there's run, there's fun, but over the course of the morning, there's wasn't a hell of a lot for the fellas to get too excited about.

Dwane blew a nice jobfish and ended up bending his shaft in the process (excuse the double entendre). Eli managed to put a pin into a large red bass, but I didn't quite have the heart to tell him that these fish are chock full of the toxin ciguatera and only good for burley. Julian missed a yellowlip emperor, and right as the fellas were about to call it a day, Dwane had a nice walu, aka Spanish mackerel, savaged by a shark.

We returned to Kioa to lick our wounds and plan the afternoon session, which we decided to spend back out at the FAD. Luckily, we were quickly able to put the day's disappointments behind us, as twelve-year-old Eli stepped up and managed to land his first wahoo, a hell of an achievement, especially with the added pressure of having a number of cameras thrust in his face throughout the fight.

With the weather forecast to blow a bit the next day, we could bank on having a decent lie-in the following morning, so we decided to let our hair down and celebrate that evening. On the drinks menu once again was the ubiquitous kava, but also a rather sweet and syrupy coconut wine, made by tapping the sap of young coconut trees and allowing it to ferment. We'd been assured that this miraculous beverage didn't cause any hangover whatsoever due to its purity, and I must say, after a good night's sleep, we all woke up with a spring in our step.

Having rubbed the sand out of our eyes, we were all eager to mix things up a touch, so headed out to hunt some of the monster crabs that we'd heard rumours were living on the opposite side of the island. These big angry bastards certainly didn't disappoint! While the traps only bagged us one crab due to a few tears in the netting, he was an absolute tank, and we looked forward to seeing him again later that evening as a guest of honour at the dinner table. By now, a few days in, we were starting to get into the swing of island time, so were happy to spend the next few hours chilling on the beach and waiting for the winds to die down. Sam used his downtime to hunt successfully for nautilus shells that often wash up on the beach (although I recently discovered that the locals had generously planted the one that he found!), while Jools and Reef took turns on a gnarly rope swing which overhung the shoreline. Dwane and Eli meanwhile prowled the reef edge, picking off a few surgeon fish, mu and other species prized by the locals as table fish, earning us a bit of extra goodwill.

As morning made way to afternoon, we began prepping for the serious work ahead. Having had a tough time of things on the reef in the Somosomo Strait the morning prior, the plan was to now dive it around the change of tide and hope that it brought with it a change in fortune.

After a wet and wild run out to the reef, as hoped, the sloppy sea conditions eased off once we reached the shadow of Taveuni. With an hour or two before the optimum dive time at sunset, the team had plenty of time to stretch the lungs and ensure they were shooting straight before the main event, where the plan was to do battle with the mighty dogtooth tuna, without a shadow of a doubt one of the hardest fighting fish in the sea.

Doggies grow to over 100 kg, but even stopping a 20-kg fish is a tough task given their incredible power and aggression. A few smaller 'puppies' had been seen lurking around the reef fringe earlier in the trip, but nothing worthy of putting a pin through — the fellas were keeping their powder dry in the hopes of something a little more impressive turning up.

Much like the wahoo, the doggies over in Tonga had also taught the team a lesson; we'd landed a few but had our arses handed to us by a couple of larger specimens, so Dwane and Jools were certainly taking the task seriously. Personally, I really needed them to land a decent fish or two in order to round out the episode and end the season on a high note. The wahoo shot early in the trip had made for a solid start, but it's the way in which a show ends that is often how it's measured.

Having waited out the tide, Dwane began diving deep on a likely looking pressure point at the head of the reef. Within a couple of drops, he laid eyes on what we were looking for — a nice-sized doggie cruising along into the current, so he deftly changed his angle of descent and made his way towards it, extending his gun arm once within range, lining up and letting rip.

It was a perfectly placed shot, but disaster struck — as the fish powered off, the shooting line from his reel gun became entangled with the gun's rubbers. The benefit of a reel gun is that it allows you to free yourself from using surface floats and lines, the idea being that you can fight the fish from the surface, using 20 or 30 metres worth of heavy line from the reel which is attached to your spear or slip tip.

But since his line had now locked tight around the speargun itself, Dwane had lost that ability, and since he was using a reel gun, he didn't have a float line attached to a surface float, so was forced to do battle with the hard-fighting fish at a depth of around 20 metres.

Going toe to toe with the doggy in a tug of war to the surface would be a nightmare scenario for most, but luckily for Dwane, fresh legs and fresh lungs meant he was able to get the upper hand over the tuna, and after a bit of effort, he was able to break the surface and recharge with a much-needed breath of air. After a bit of back and forth, he managed to get the upper hand, hauling the fish to the surface and shutting it down with a knife blow to the brain. Jools then added a second slightly smaller doggy to the team's tally, before Dwane mixed things up by slotting a nice-sized walu, highly prized as one of the best eating fish in Fijian waters.

The walu got the last laugh, though. With the sun sinking, just as the team were gearing up for their final few dives, and right as the conditions were at their very best for targeting a big doggy, our Fijian boatman Kiri accidently had his foot badly sliced open by the walu's razor-sharp teeth.

Rather than risk infection, which happens rapidly in the tropics, we pulled pin and punched it back to Kioa to sort the poor guy out, and to be fair — enough blood had been spilt that day anyway. We'd bagged a pair of dogtooth tuna, and with an island celebration planned for our final night, I felt we had a great conclusion to the Kioa-based segment of the episode.

After a monumental feast of wild pork, local root vegetables, monster mudcrab and all manner of fish species, we got stuck into pounding a heap more kava, and I mean quite literally pounding it. Before straining the powder through cloth into water to drink, the dried root needed to be crushed into tiny pieces, in this case by the use of a heavy posthole rammer and a steel dive cylinder that had been cut in half. It's an arduous task, and takes a bit of skill, especially with a litre of coconut wine under your belt! But plenty of hands make light work, and we soon had the job done.

After a great display of traditional dancing from a few of the village boys, the guitars and ukelele were soon out again, accompanying a few Fijian folk songs, with the kava now flowing freely. And after some gentle persuasion from our hosts, we reciprocated with a few traditional songs of our own people — namely, *Country Road*, *Sweet Caroline* and the Sublime classic *What I Got*.

Early the next morning, we reluctantly waved goodbye to our incredible hosts, and relocated to the main island of Viti Levu, where we had another two days up our sleeve to get out and explore the spearfishing options on offer around the Volivoli Peninsula.

The diving here didn't really fire for us, although Jools and Dwane landed some classy fish, including giant trevally, green jobfish and Spanish mackerel. It also provided a chance to showcase the young lads' diving abilities too, as they were able to slot a few good reef fish to add variety to the catch.

With the strong wind and sloppy seas, I was feeling green throughout. We had tied the boat up to a mooring attached to the reef, so were getting pounded constantly throughout the course of both the days we spent out wide. What I initially hoped would be a fun way to round out the trip turned into two days of clock watching for me back aboard the boat, but at least the guys in the water were having a blast.

I admit I was also feeling a little jealous that I couldn't jump in for a spear myself, but you sleep in the bed you make. I could have easily put the camera down and joined the lads in the drink, but I'd have been absolutely livid with myself if a big wahoo or doggy turned up and no one was around to get the necessary footage on the main camera.

I did manage to suit up for the final half hour of diving in closer to the mainland, getting a brief chance to experience the warm, clear tropical waters for myself, and justifying the effort I'd made to bring my dive gear all the way over, even if it was for just six drops.

As it transpired, we had enough material from our time on Kioa for the broadcast episode, so none of the material filmed over the final two days out of Volivoli actually made the cut. Instead, it went into a half-hour online special that's available on YouTube. After eight seasons, I've become adept at knowing approximately when we've reached 50 minutes of *The Red Stag Timber Hunters Club* action, but it's hard to gauge how much material we have for *South Seas Spearo* when the bulk of the action's taking place underwater. It'll no doubt come with time.

We've got some lofty missions to the tropics planned for coming seasons, so rather than trying to squeeze every spare second of filming out of the trip, I'll be sure to factor in a bit more downtime (pun intended) for myself over the coming years.

A hearty haul from the first afternoon out at the FAD.

Eli and the fish of the trip, a hell of an achievement for the young fella!

Jools' two cents

Having had a career as a diver for 20-plus years, which usually involves a large amount of time working in discomfort and in cold water, I'm not shy when it comes time to pitch ideas of where to head for the show, and the tropics are always at the top of my list. Luckily, when I laid out a plan to head to Fiji and hook up with a good mate, Dan Gray, a local Fijian spear fisherman, the team lapped it up.

Fiji is a special place for Dwane and me, having sailed there as teens many years ago with my father. Since then, I've done multiple trips returning to visit the friends we made during the time we spent there surfing and spearing. I relish the chance to spend time with the locals on the remote outskirts of the main islands. Seeing the way these people live and the strong sense of brotherhood they have is something I genuinely respect. They're a very talented, musical and happy people.

Our young fellas have spent enough time over the years seeing us come and go from our adventures, so we felt it was time they joined us for once. The two twelve-year-olds, Reef and Eli, were born just five days apart, and here they were, heading off to Fiji for a two week-long apprenticeship in spearfishing coral reefs — how epic!

Their first week started with time trials, running up and down the airport stairs, holding their breath, training for deep dives, then climbing coconut palms, and papaya trees for the fruit, hunting mud crabs, catching lizards, getting peeled out by big GTs off the beach on their fishing rods, spearing coral trout and surgeon fish, then at the end of every day spending about four hours in Dan's swimming pool. What an introduction to the tropics!

Alongside the highlights featured in the episode, there were also a few lows, which is just all part of the adventure. You have to roll with the punches. We had some massive travel days, young Reef had an ear infection for a period of the trip which ruled him out of diving, we had some gear failure with a few of our guns, and all the usual problems with four types of cameras! The rough weather also limited our diving options, but I'm proud of the way we put all that behind us and made the most what was available, and the fact that we didn't smoke any monster doggies or wahoo isn't the end of the world — it just means the door's open for a return mission in the future.

30 WHAT'S NEXT?

I've been on a roll this morning, having banged out a few good chapters in record time as the words just seemed to flow, but it's just dawned on me that I've completely missed a scheduled video conference with my surgeon to discuss how the shoulder rehab is progressing. It's three months today since I went under the knife, and while I'm still a way off being able to clamber around the hills with a pack and camera in hand, it feels like I might be back in action on *South Seas Spearo* fairly soon.

Speaking of which, as hoped, the third season was just as well received as the previous two. We actually threw a launch party down in Auckland to coincide with Episode 1 hitting screens, the first time we've been able to do so since the pandemic — although I needed to be careful not to get too carried away with my freshly operated-on shoulder. However, there was one other thing I was more anxious about in the run-up to the series start.

The first scheduled episode was our trip to the Three Kings, but in the days leading in, a high-profile Newshub documentary on the *Enchanter* tragedy aired on Three. For those unaware, the *Enchanter* was a commercial charter boat that often operated in the Far North, but in March of 2022, on its return from the Three Kings it had sunk off North Cape in terrible conditions, resulting in the loss of five lives.

On the morning of the tragedy, I had been awoken by a phone call from the Chief of Staff at Newshub asking if it was possible for me to race up to North Cape and capture some footage. I'm what's known in the trade as a stringer, a freelance cameraman, primarily covering stories in the Far North, as living in Kerikeri means I can often be the first cameraman to arrive on the scene.

After they explained what was unfolding, I knew that heading up north would be pointless; I couldn't fly my drone anywhere near where rescue helicopters were operating, and there would be very little to see from the shoreline, plus I really didn't want to inject myself into such an intense environment as it certainly wouldn't help the cause in any way.

Instead, I suggested they reach out to one of the *South Seas Spearo* crew, Nat Davey, whose commercial boat was directly involved in the rescue effort. Later that day, I met up with Nat in Russell to interview him and get his read on the situation. He explained that the weather forecast was so poor earlier in the week that he'd had to call his boats back to the mainland as a precaution. Anyone who's spent time with Nat will know that he doesn't pull his punches, and he wasn't shy about voicing his concerns on camera, but that's understandable given his entire livelihood is dependent on the ocean.

It was an awful tragedy, and I was anxious about how our Kings-based episode might be received in the aftermath of the documentary but, thankfully, it was more a case of me once again overthinking things, as all the feedback we had was extremely positive. Despite the fact we often find ourselves in dangerous scenarios, we've tried really hard within the show to ensure we are never cavalier with safety, and our Kings trip provided a few good examples of that intention. The remaining seven episodes all performed well, the standout for me being the Pitt Island mission, despite the lingering regret of all the material that was lost.

The eighth season of *The Red Stag Timber Hunters Club* also rated highly, and I've gotta say, it was incredibly satisfying to finally let the cat out of the bag and share news of Anto's gigantic chamois buck, which we'd managed to keep a secret right up until the first episode aired.

So that begs the question — where to from here?

We're certainly not short of grandiose plans for shoots over the coming 24 months — including plans to hunt and dive in Tahiti, the Northern Territory & Torres Straits, Saskatchewan, Norway and, most exciting of all, Alaska.

Some of these may never eventuate, but there's one additional international trip I haven't listed that's much more likely to go ahead, although it came about not as a result of extensive planning and research but through my desire to look like 'the big man on campus'. Here's how things unfolded . . .

Following the first day of the annual Sika Show, Dre and I were invited to attend a lavish dinner and fundraiser for Safari Club International at SkyCity Hamilton. We were lucky to have been seated on a pretty interesting table, which included a couple of members of parliament and the two top dogs at the Game Animal Council.

It was an enjoyable night, the beers were cold and the conversations had been free-flowing. Dre had entertained the table by recounting a few stories of his time playing rugby over in Argentina — it seemed that as well as being a paid assassin for *The Red Stag Timber Hunters Club*, he was also a gun for hire on the footy field.

The auction then began. Along with a bunch of hunting-related products like scopes, thermals, boots and packs were some guided hunting trips, but these were not really our cup of tea. However, the second to last item of the night piqued the interest of our table.

AUCTIONEER: Next up, a three-day guided dove hunt for six hunters in Entre Rios, Argentina . . .

At the mention of Argentina, a little noise went up from our table. The auctioneer heard it and looked in my direction.

AUCTIONEER: Aah, Dave from *The Hunters Club*. Don't you think this would make a great episode for your next season? Do you want to start the bidding?

Suddenly, all eyes were on me. I was in a room full of heavy hitters from all corners of the hunting community, so certainly not the time or place to drop nuts. I didn't want to look weak, so I took the bait.

Sure, seven and a half grand . . .

I thought it was a safe first bid, given the valuation on screen said the trip was worth twice that. However, less than 20 seconds later:

AUCTIONEER: Going once, twice, SOLD!

Oh, oh . . . this would make for an interesting conversation with the missus.

In the past, our gamebird and duck-shooting episodes had provided me with great bang for buck, given there are no expensive helicopter flights required or week-long journeys to the back of beyond. This one would be much harder on the pocket!

I jokingly asked the bloke taking the payment if he could attribute it to the SkyCity Casino upstairs, as it would be easier for me to explain it away as a gambling debt. Rubbing further salt in the wounds, I'd left my eftpos cards behind, and had to wear a 3 per cent credit-card fee on top. Youch.

A bit before midnight, I called and left a message on Amber's phone, telling her not to worry but there would be a substantial charge on the Visa, but cell reception must have been poor as my garbled message led to a rather comical miscommunication.

Amber mistakenly believed I'd splashed out $7.5K on actual, physical doves, and was genuinely worried about how and where we would store them all! This played out perfectly for me, as when she eventually clicked to the actual situation, she was more relieved than upset, and I think she's quite looking forward to a trip to Buenos Aires now.

I'll be sure to employ a similar tactic after making any future impulsive decisions, and that's likely to be sooner rather than later given the rogues, rascals and reprobates that I regularly keep as company.

31 CONCLUSION: ENOUGH?

There's a well-worn phrase in TV vernacular: 'jumping the shark'. It was coined in the 70s and was derived from a scene in the fifth season of *Happy Days*, when the leatherjacket-clad Fonzie leapt over a literal shark while he was out waterskiing.

'Jumping the shark' is now used to pinpoint the precise moment when a show that was once incredibly popular reached its peak and began a slippery slide towards mediocrity, which in Fonzie's case, meant relying on a random stunt to generate attention.

Most long-running series fall victim to this phenomenon at some point, but I'd like to think we'll be more aware of it than most, possibly because the moment may well involve an actual shark being jumped.

Seriously, though, it is one of the hardest decisions in life, knowing exactly when to call it quits. The great Muhammad Ali's record of 56 & 5 would look a lot better if he hadn't climbed back into the ring and lost three of his last four fights, which Mike Tyson then replicated a generation later. No matter what, age eventually catches up to you.

While *South Seas Spearo* is still in its infancy and hopefully has many more seasons ahead, having notched up 90 episodes of *The Red Stag Timber Hunters Club*, I'd be lying if I said we had never discussed an exit strategy.

But a meeting this morning helped put things into perspective for me. I caught up for a coffee with my old mate Matt Watson, who was keen to bounce around some ideas he has to commemorate the upcoming twentieth season of the *ITM Fishing Show*.

Twenty seasons, that's an amazing accomplishment. Catching up with Matt brought back memories of a similar powwow we had nearly a decade earlier. On that occasion, he and I sat around a table at a pub in Kerikeri talking turkey about the future of his show, which I think had just finished its tenth season. On that evening, we'd both agreed we had more gas in the tank, there were more stories to tell and more adventures to be had.

With that in mind, I seriously believe we've got a few more solid seasons of *The Red Stag Timber Hunters Club* in us before it's time to hang up our Lowas. But rather than limping to the finish line in five years' time with dodgy knees and bad backs, I want us to go out with a bang. There's still a whole lot more we want to say and do; we're yet to nail the show's first 8-point sika stag for Christ's sake!

I've talked a lot about silver linings throughout this book, the silver lining when Rochele missed her marlin (Sam's epic underwater footage), the silver lining of me spooking Anto's giant chamois (the dramatic sequence that then ensued), the silver lining of Sam and Dwane not seeing the wapiti bull (shielding us from potential criticism). There was even a silver lining to Anto failing to hook a trout on our roar hunt, in that it provided me the opportunity to swim naked on TV for the first time.

Personally, though, this year's biggest silver lining has come about because of my shoulder operation. The enforced break has given me time to reflect on all the amazing adventures that I've been privileged to be a part of, and at a time that I probably most needed reminding.

I'm very lucky to be in a position where I regularly get to challenge myself in the great outdoors, and I'm fortunate to have a platform with which to tell these exciting stories. I hope that my doing so, even in just a tiny way, helps make New Zealand a better place.

I've learned this year that it's easy to get bogged down by focusing on the negatives, so a change of mindset is on the cards for coming seasons; rather than demanding continual improvement, I hope to find satisfaction in the thought that I'm making a difference, however small, to the lives of keen Kiwi hunters, divers and outdoors enthusiasts.

It's hard to know when to quit, but I thought a succinct way to way to wrap things up would be with a little anecdote that caught my eye recently . . .

Sometime during the 70s, a billionaire hedge-fund manager threw an elaborate party in New York. In attendance were two influential American authors, Kurt Vonnegut, author of *Slaughterhouse-Five*, and Joseph Heller, the author of *Catch-22*. At one point in the evening, Vonnegut informed Heller that their host had made more money that day than Heller had earned from his bestselling work over its entire history.

Heller responded, 'That may be, but I have something he will never have — enough.'